Implementing Atlassian Confluence

Strategies, tips, and insights to enhance distributed team collaboration using Confluence

Eren Kalelioğlu

BIRMINGHAM—MUMBAI

Implementing Atlassian Confluence

Group Product Manager: Alok Dhuri
Publishing Product Manager: Kushal Dave
Book Project Manager: Prajakta Naik
Senior Editor: Nisha Cleetus
Technical Editor: Maran Fernandes
Copy Editor: Safis Editing
Proofreader: Safis Editing
Indexer: Hemangini Bari
Production Designer: Jyoti Kadam
Business Development Executive: Puneet Kaur
DevRel Marketing Coordinators: Deepak Kumar and Mayank Singh

First published: September 2023

Production reference: 1220923

Published by
Packt Publishing Ltd.
Grosvenor House 11 St Paul's Square
Birmingham
B3 1RB, UK

ISBN 978-1-80056-042-0

www.packtpub.com

This book is dedicated to my mother and father, who have been an incredible support throughout my life in reaching my dreams. I've always been in awe of my father's deep knowledge of neurosurgery and the magic my mother creates on her canvas. I will forever cherish the joy of being with them.

– Eren Kalelioğlu

Foreword

I've known Eren for many years as one of the most versatile individuals I've ever encountered. Our paths first crossed when he served as the CTO, leading the educational transformation of one of the top private education institutions. This connection was sparked by our shared enthusiasm for Atlassian products. Our collaboration continued even after he founded his start-up, which aids enterprises in creating high-performing teams using collaboration technologies. Eren is highly proficient with Atlassian products and boasts the prestigious **Atlassian Certified Expert** (**ACE**) credential. Additionally, he possesses a keen interest in the future of work.

In this invaluable book, Eren takes you on an enlightening journey, delving into enterprise collaboration and distributed and asynchronous teamwork. He showcases how tools can be pivotal allies when forming high-performing teams in cross-functional, multi-cultural, and multi-regional settings. Distributed work is a vast and multidisciplinary subject. It draws from management sciences, project management, human psychology, and various other domains. This book provides solid, practical examples from all these fields, guiding you in crafting your tool setup.

Eren offers detailed, step-by-step instructions on setting up Confluence, organizing content, collaborating with your team within Confluence, and mastering dynamic content. Through *Implementing Atlassian Confluence*, you will grasp how to construct spaces for software projects, manage products, cater to personal needs, and set up a comprehensive company knowledge base.

The book offers more than just setup and usage guidelines. You will gain insights into the risks, challenges, and solutions associated with scaling Confluence. Consequently, you'll comprehend how Confluence can serve organizations where thousands are engaged in information processing and sharing.

In *Implementing Atlassian Confluence*, professionals from all walks of life – be they developers, software analysts, project managers, senior executives, or CEOs – will discover insights to augment their daily operations and long-term strategies. Prepare to be inspired and chart your transformation journey.

Evren Civelek

Head of Platform&Automation for ECU SW Development

Leader of multi-cultural and multi-regional teams

Mercedes-Benz AG

Contributors

About the author

Eren Kalelioğlu is a collaboration technologies expert residing in Istanbul. With more than 15 years of experience, he's proficient in Confluence and Atlassian Cloud products and holds the prestigious ACE credential. As a former CTO at one of the top private education institutions, he led the educational transformation via technology. Eren's start-up, Ponsatlas, focuses on collaboration technologies and is an Atlassian Solution Partner. He's also a proud father to his daughter, Mavi.

Acknowlegments:

- *Seray Kalelioğlu: For her unwavering support throughout the writing process.*
- *Mavi Kalelioğlu: For infusing energy into my writing journey.*
- *Merve & Müfit Kalelioğlu: For their constant motivation and keen interest in the book's progress.*
- *Evren Civelek: Gratitude for crafting the book's foreword.*
- *Packt Publishing Team: For their collective efforts to bring this book to fruition.*
- *Katarzyna Pawlak: For her meticulous role as Technical Reviewer, ensuring precision.*
- *Utku Aytaç, Kerem Kalelioğlu, Mert Çuhadaroğlu, Irmak Alp & Ponsatlas Team: For supporting the growth of Ponsatlas while I penned this book.*
- *Confidential Ponsatlas Clients: For insights into real-world Confluence challenges.*
- *Atlassian: For their inspiring culture and tools, which have shaped a significant part of my professional journey.*
- *Mina Maraşlıgil: My invaluable companion in writing, ensuring clarity and fluency.*

About the reviewers

Mina Maraşlıgil is an editor and writer with a diverse portfolio of non-fiction and fiction writing. Having experience in different areas of publishing since 2014, Mina worked as a book editor and freelance writer. For the past two years, she's been working at Ponsatlas, an official Atlassian Solution Partner, focusing on teamwork technologies and tech writing to deliver knowledge on how human intellect can thrive with technology.

Katarzyna Pawlak is a co-founder of Appsvio, an Atlassian Marketplace Partner specializing in IT service management apps. As Chief Product Officer, she shapes a vision for their products published on the Atlassian Marketplace. As an active community member since 2017, she has been recognized as an Atlassian Community Leader. Her proudest achievements are numerous Atlassian certifications, earning her the title of Atlassian Certified Expert. Additionally, she holds certifications including Professional Scrum Product Owner and ITIL® Foundation Certificate in IT Service Management. In her spare time, she explores new places through jogging and hiking.

Sajit Nair is an Agile consultant working with technical teams to deliver quality solutions to end customers. Sajit believes in empathy and prefers openness over flawlessness at work. A musician and bike enthusiast by hobby, Sajit takes pride in delivering on his commitments to clients. Currently, Sajit is focused on building capabilities for the Atlassian Marketplace to drive project management strategies and instill shared accountability among team members for project milestones.

Table of Contents

2

Setting Up Confluence 35

3

Creating and Organizing Content 79

Part 2: Building a Real Confluence Site

6

7

8

Setting Up a Knowledge Base   235

9

Setting Up a Personal Space   243

10

Connecting All Teams with Confluence   255

Part 3: Scaling Business

11

Introduction to Scaling Confluence   273

12

Assuring Security and Compliance   287

13

Integrating and Extending Confluence   313

14

Challenges and Solutions   345

15

Preface

In the digital age, the way teams collaborate and communicate has undergone revolutionary changes. The advent of platforms such as Confluence by Atlassian underscores this evolution. At its core, Confluence is a cloud-based platform renowned for its reliability, maturity, and constant evolution. Developed by Atlassian, it offers an avenue for teams, irrespective of their physical location, to collaborate with speed and security from both computers and mobile devices.

Confluence's adaptability is one of its strongest traits. Its flexible nature means it can be tailored to various purposes and scenarios. Today, countless organizations worldwide harness the power of Confluence for diverse functions, including remote work, distributed collaboration, and corporate knowledge management. While Confluence has long established itself as a trusted system, what's notable is Atlassian's commitment to its evolution – with nearly weekly updates and enhancements.

Cultural diversity and multilingualism aren't barriers to Confluence. It's been crafted to resonate with people from different linguistic and cultural backgrounds. Its scalability, from catering to small teams to being the backbone of multi-thousand-employee corporations, is a testament to its versatility.

Implementing Atlassian Confluence is not just another dry, technical manual. Instead, it presents a holistic view, enabling you to grasp both the overarching themes and intricate details of Confluence. Drawing from over a decade of experience, this guide merges theoretical constructs with practical insights.

Beyond mere functionalities, the book ventures into the strategic realm of how Confluence fits into the broader spectrum of remote and distributed work. The aim is to offer you more than just an understanding of features; it's about harnessing Confluence's potential to redefine collaboration and productivity. Peppered with practical tips and hands-on advice, the book serves as a comprehensive guide, crafted to assist every professional looking to leverage Confluence to its maximum potential.

Who this book is for

Implementing Atlassian Confluence is designed for anyone aiming to strengthen the remote collaboration muscles of their company or team using Atlassian's Confluence platform. This book will serve as an invaluable guide for all of the following:

- Company executives and entrepreneurs aiming to drive digital transformation
- Professionals responsible for company transformation and the integration of remote work strategies
- *Heads of remote*, and those actively engaged in *future of work* discussions

- Team leaders, managers, and decision-makers looking for optimized collaborative processes
- Software developers, particularly those working in remote settings
- Any individual keen on mastering Confluence and enhancing their proficiency in this tool

While a basic understanding of Atlassian and Confluence would be beneficial, this book is crafted to be accessible to individuals from diverse backgrounds. Experience in remote or distributed work will provide a contextual foundation but isn't strictly necessary. We expect you to be an adept computer user, meaning that you can readily implement the strategies and tips outlined.

By delving into this guide, you will address the coordination challenges that distributed teams often face. This book offers solutions to reduce cognitive load, elevate productivity, and boost motivation – enhancing the overall distributed work experience. After finishing this book, you will have knowledge akin to having received one-on-one consultancy from an expert. This newfound understanding will empower you to structure and use Confluence more effectively.

Professionals across all fields and sectors can benefit from this guide, with teams engaged in knowledge-intensive sectors such as software development and technology finding it particularly useful.

What this book covers

Chapter 1, Introducing Enterprise Collaboration, offers a comprehensive introduction to Atlassian, Confluence, and the vital principles of enterprise collaboration, with a particular emphasis on remote collaboration. You will gain insights into how Confluence can aid organizations in enhancing their remote collaboration experiences. The foundation laid in this chapter equips you with a robust understanding of Atlassian's values, the challenges of contemporary collaborative environments, and how to harness Confluence's capabilities effectively for distributed teams. By the end of the chapter, you will be well versed in Confluence basics, key modern collaboration terms, and best practices for assembling a team dedicated to Confluence development and maintenance.

Chapter 2, Setting Up Confluence, delves into the foundational steps for successfully launching Confluence. It emphasizes the importance of organization and structured planning, especially given the rapid accumulation of diverse information on the platform. Through introducing key principles such as **information architecture** (**IA**), the chapter provides a roadmap for initiating a Confluence environment that is both user-friendly and efficiently organized. Topics covered include a detailed look into information architecture, guidance on Confluence site planning, steps for installation and configuration, user management techniques, and insights on setting up various types of spaces such as team, project, company, and personal spaces.

Chapter 3, Creating and Organizing Content, delves into the core functionality of Confluence, focusing on creating, managing, and organizing content. After setting up the Confluence environment, it's essential to understand how to maximize the platform's features for effective collaboration. This section provides a thorough exploration of the new Confluence editor, shedding light on the creation and maintenance of dynamic content. By highlighting real-world collaboration examples, you will gain practical insights into content organization. Key topics explored include navigating within Confluence, strategies for content management, and effective methods to systematically organize content.

Chapter 4, Collaborating with Your Team, offers a comprehensive guide to establishing a virtual workspace for a globally distributed team. Recognizing the challenges faced by teams operating across diverse time zones, this section elucidates how Confluence can be harnessed to simulate the collaborative ambiance of a physical office. By walking you through the creation and configuration of a team space, the chapter equips you with the expertise needed to structure collaborative platforms for your teams. The topics covered encompass the foundational steps of preparing a team space, fostering collaboration among team members, overseeing meetings and decisions, and presenting innovative ideas to enrich the team's virtual workspace.

Chapter 5, Mastering Dynamic Contents, dives deep into the realm of dynamic pages in Confluence, highlighting their potential to transform a static knowledge base into a vibrant and interconnected hub of information. Dynamic pages, characterized by their capability to auto-update and interact with other Confluence pages, bring forth the efficiency of organizing and reusing content across the platform. By emphasizing the significance of such pages, this chapter offers step-by-step guidance on converting static pages into dynamic ones. From the rudiments of labeling pages and acquainting oneself with macros to advanced topics such as implementing label-driven macros, exploring page-interactive macros, and harnessing the power of Smart Links, this chapter is a comprehensive guide to fully utilizing dynamic content in Confluence.

Chapter 6, Creating a Space for a Software Project, navigates the intricate landscape of establishing a dedicated Confluence space for managing software projects. Building on the foundational knowledge of dynamic content and macros from previous chapters, this section zeroes in on the unique challenges and demands of remote software development. With Confluence at the helm, teams can overcome these challenges by centralizing project materials, fostering collaboration, and effectively tracking progress. The chapter offers a deep dive into the roles within a software project, presenting strategies to craft a unified project hub that integrates seamlessly with tools such as Jira. Whether you're exploring the in-built software project space template or seeking to optimize it for bespoke requirements, this chapter provides a roadmap. By its conclusion, you will be equipped with the knowledge to leverage Confluence for end-to-end software project management, ensuring that remote teams operate in harmony and projects culminate successfully.

Chapter 7, Creating a Space for Product Management, delves into the realm of product management in a remote setting. This chapter spotlights the pivotal role of Confluence as a beacon for seamless collaboration and organization. Recognizing the multifaceted responsibilities of product management teams, from planning and forecasting to marketing and enhancement, the essence of this chapter is the centrality of a unified platform. With Confluence, teams can weave a tapestry of shared knowledge, ensuring everyone remains in sync despite geographical disparities. This chapter emphasizes Confluence's prowess in fostering active collaboration, providing real-time feedback mechanisms, and serving as the bedrock for product management endeavors. Structuring spaces tailored to specific teams or projects, will unearth the potential of Confluence to transform it into your team's flexible powerhouse. By the chapter's end, a blueprint will emerge on harnessing Confluence as the linchpin for effective, remote product management operations.

Chapter 8, Setting Up a Knowledge Base, unveils the significance of a knowledge base as the epicenter of an organization's vast informational landscape. In today's digital era, especially in remote work settings, a centralized hub of vital operational details, organizational procedures, and domain expertise is indispensable. Using practical examples, such as the onboarding process within an HR department, you will appreciate the knowledge base's power to expedite processes and its role in bridging informational gaps. As we journey through this chapter, the democratizing effect of a well-structured knowledge base emerges, ensuring equal access to crucial information for every team member irrespective of location or role. The chapter underscores the knowledge base's pivotal role in bolstering transparency, promoting continuous learning, and driving unified organizational objectives, particularly in the realm of remote work.

Chapter 9, Setting Up a Personal Space, introduces the concept of personal spaces within Confluence, a beacon for individuals amid the evolving digital workplace. With the lines between office and home blurred, mastering tools such as Confluence's personal spaces is no longer a luxury but a necessity. Such dedicated spaces serve as personal repositories, ensuring efficient management of individual tasks, ideas, and projects. By delving into this chapter, you will grasp the immense potential of these personal realms within Confluence. Beyond merely a digital storage space, they embody transparency, structure, and individualized workflow management. Embark on this journey to unravel the intricacies and potentials of setting up your personal space within the vast digital expanse.

Chapter 10, Connecting All Teams with Confluence, emphasizes the importance of interconnectivity and cohesion when using Confluence within a distributed organization. We'll focus on creating a cohesive environment where every space, be it for software projects, product management, or personal use, seamlessly interacts with one another. Dive in to discover the intricacies of creating a company handbook that speaks to everyone and setting up an HR space that caters to all teams. This chapter aims to provide you with the tools needed to establish a unified, collaborative ecosystem within your organization.

Chapter 11, Introduction to Scaling Confluence, delves into the realm of adapting Confluence to cater to an expanding organization. While the platform's cloud capabilities naturally ease the process, a deep comprehension of the underlying principles remains crucial. We'll explore the intricacies of scaling, discerning both the necessity and the strategy behind it. As we progress, the emphasis will shift from mere expansion to intelligent adaptation, ensuring that as your organization grows, so does its efficiency in collaboration. You'll learn about the hurdles, potential risks, and how to strategically overcome them, ensuring a secure and seamless transition.

Chapter 12, Assuring Security and Compliance, emphasizes the paramount importance of security, especially when operating within Confluence's Cloud environment. Although the Cloud version does simplify some security aspects, it's essential to understand that no system is intrinsically impenetrable. As we navigate this chapter, you'll be equipped with a plethora of security tips and actionable steps, ensuring a robust defense for your Confluence setup. From foundational security concepts to an in-depth analysis of Confluence Cloud's advantages, this segment serves as your comprehensive guide to fortifying your collaborative environment.

Chapter 13, Integrating and Extending Confluence, delves into one of Confluence's most potent features: its adaptability. Confluence isn't just a stand-alone tool but a platform that seamlessly merges with other systems, enhancing its functionality. Whether you're looking to integrate with other tools or add novel features to Confluence, this segment unravels the myriad of possibilities available. From instantaneous integrations to more nuanced setups, this chapter sheds light on how Atlassian has designed Confluence to be a versatile hub ready to fit within any digital landscape. So, even if you don't find the need for extensions or integrations now, understanding their potential can be instrumental for future needs.

Chapter 14, Challenges and Solutions, leans into the more practical side of Confluence adoption, with content drawn from years of first-hand experience with Atlassian products. While Confluence offers a plethora of features and integrations, its acceptance within a company can pose its own set of challenges. This section not only elucidates the potential roadblocks you might face but also provides tangible solutions to help ease the transition. From tackling remote collaboration obstacles to leveraging consultants' expertise, the insights shared here aim to provide a clearer path forward, ensuring the sustainable and effective use of Confluence in your organization.

Chapter 15, What's Next?, delves into the rapidly changing landscape of the digital workspace and its profound implications on collaboration. In today's dynamic world, platforms such as Confluence aren't just tools; they are central to our newfound ways of working, bridging distances, and redefining team interactions. We'll explore not only the challenges this shift presents but also the myriad of opportunities it unlocks. From personal mastery in Confluence and the evolving nuances of remote work to the promising role of artificial intelligence in collaboration, this chapter provides a glimpse into the future. Through expert advice and real-world examples, including insights from partners such as Ponsatlas, we'll sketch a roadmap to help you navigate and thrive in this brave new world of collaborative work.

To get the most out of this book

While this book has been written to cater to various knowledge levels, having a basic understanding of Atlassian products or a familiarity with collaborative software will help you grasp concepts quicker and draw parallels to your experiences.

Ensure that you have access to an updated web browser to make the most of the examples and interactive content in this book. Furthermore, a Premium membership for Confluence Cloud is essential. For those eager to delve into advanced security and integration examples, a subscription to Atlassian's **Access** product is recommended.

The chapters of this book are structured to stand alone, allowing you the flexibility to pick and choose topics most relevant to you. However, for a comprehensive grasp of the subject matter and to derive the maximum benefit, it is recommended to read the book from start to finish. Even if you're already familiar with some sections, you might discover new insights or a fresh perspective.

Theoretical knowledge is best solidified with practical application. As you journey through the chapters, try out the examples and exercises. Should you have questions or need clarifications, compile them and reach out to the author. The more actively engaged you are with the content, the deeper your understanding will become.

Conventions used

There are a number of text conventions used throughout this book.

`Code in text`: Indicates code words in text, database table names, folder names, filenames, file extensions, pathnames, dummy URLs, user input, and Twitter handles. Here is an example: "a standard rule for naming the labels – for example, `my-first-label` or `my-second-label`"

Bold: Indicates a new term, an important word, or words that you see onscreen. For instance, words in menus or dialog boxes appear in bold. Here is an example: "**Select System** info from the **Administration panel**."

> **Tips or important notes**
> Appear like this.

Get in touch

Feedback from our readers is always welcome.

General feedback: If you have questions about any aspect of this book, email us at `customercare@packtpub.com` and mention the book title in the subject of your message.

Errata: Although we have taken every care to ensure the accuracy of our content, mistakes do happen. If you have found a mistake in this book, we would be grateful if you would report this to us. Please visit www.packtpub.com/support/errata and fill in the form.

Piracy: If you come across any illegal copies of our works in any form on the internet, we would be grateful if you would provide us with the location address or website name. Please contact us at copyright@packtpub.com with a link to the material.

If you are interested in becoming an author: If there is a topic that you have expertise in and you are interested in either writing or contributing to a book, please visit authors.packtpub.com.

Share Your Thoughts

Once you've read *Implementing Atlassian Confluence*, we'd love to hear your thoughts! Scan the QR code below to go straight to the Amazon review page for this book and share your feedback.

https://packt.link/r/1800560427

Your review is important to us and the tech community and will help us make sure we're delivering excellent quality content.

Download a free PDF copy of this book

Thanks for purchasing this book!

Do you like to read on the go but are unable to carry your print books everywhere?

Is your eBook purchase not compatible with the device of your choice?

Don't worry, now with every Packt book you get a DRM-free PDF version of that book at no cost.

Read anywhere, any place, on any device. Search, copy, and paste code from your favorite technical books directly into your application.

The perks don't stop there, you can get exclusive access to discounts, newsletters, and great free content in your inbox daily

Follow these simple steps to get the benefits:

1. Scan the QR code or visit the link below

https://packt.link/free-ebook/9781800560420

2. Submit your proof of purchase
3. That's it! We'll send your free PDF and other benefits to your email directly

Part 1: Preparing for Confluence

In this part, you'll learn about the fundamental concepts of enterprise collaboration. Following that, you'll discover how to configure Confluence and effectively manage its content. Lastly, you'll learn how to engage with your team on Confluence and collaborate on dynamic content.

This part contains the following chapters:

- *Chapter 1, Introducing Enterprise Collaboration*
- *Chapter 2, Setting Up Confluence*
- *Chapter 3, Creating and Organizing Content*
- *Chapter 4, Collaborating with Your Team*
- *Chapter 5, Mastering Dynamic Contents*

1
Introducing Enterprise Collaboration

This chapter provides a brief introduction to **Atlassian** and **Confluence**. You will also find an overview of the core concepts of enterprise collaboration and, more specifically, remote collaboration. You'll learn how Confluence supports organizations in simplifying remote collaboration by providing a robust yet flexible platform. We aim to set a solid background before proceeding to the practical sides of this book.

Knowing Atlassian will help you better understand Confluence and get the most out of it. You will learn the company values that guide Atlassian in building, maintaining, and improving all the company's products, including Confluence. This knowledge will help you understand the philosophy of Confluence thoroughly. All these benefits are critical when trying to master your company's primary collaboration tool.

The primary concepts of enterprise collaboration will help you focus on the most critical problems of modern collaboration, where people work from different places within different time zones. These concepts will help you prepare for the complexities you'll have (or you already have) while designing and maintaining a collaboration platform for your company.

Having basic knowledge of Confluence, Atlassian, which produces and develops this product, enterprise collaboration concepts, and corporate cooperation will enable you to get much more effective results with the techniques you will learn in the following sections.

After reading this chapter, you'll come away with the following knowledge:

- The basics of Confluence (and Atlassian, the company behind it)
- The key terms related to modern collaboration
- Which types of teams and companies can benefit from Confluence
- How exactly Confluence can simplify remote collaboration
- How to build a team that will develop your Confluence site and maintain it

Technical requirements

You will need the following software to complete this chapter:

- An up-to-date web browser
- A document processor

Introducing Confluence and Atlassian as a company

Our first goal is to familiarize you with Atlassian, the company that built, maintained, and improved Confluence. Our second goal is to introduce you to Confluence from scratch.

We will divide our tour of Atlassian and Confluence into eight parts:

- Introducing Atlassian
- Introducing Confluence
- Exploring the competitors of Confluence
- Discovering the different hosting options of Confluence – Cloud and Data Center
- Discovering the different Confluence Cloud plans – Free, Standard, Premium, and Enterprise
- Accessing the official documentation of Confluence Cloud
- Accessing the service availability information and reports for Confluence Cloud
- Anticipating and preparing for changes with Atlassian's Cloud Roadmap

Introduction to Atlassian

Knowing the company that produces Confluence can help you increase the efficiency you will get from this product. We have compiled summary information about Atlassian as follows:

- Atlassian was founded in 2002 by Mike Cannon-Brookes and Scott Farquhar. They were inspired by the Greek titan when naming the company.
- Their mission is to help teams around the world unleash their potential.
- Atlassian created Confluence Server in 2003 and Confluence Cloud in 2011.
- Atlassian, which went public in 2015, has recently invested heavily in the cloud, and has powerful tools for teamwork technologies in its product portfolio.

- Atlassian is one of the world's most staunch advocates of open work and distributed working, where information is only hidden if specifically needed. They have published much content based on scientific data on this subject.

Region	Offices
Asia Pacific	• Sydney, Australia (Atlassian's Global Headquarter) • Bengaluru, India • Manila, Philippines • Sydney, Australia (Atlassian's second office in Sydney) • Yokohama, Japan
Europe	• Amsterdam, Netherlands • Ankara, Turkey • Gdańsk, Poland
North America	• San Francisco, United States (Atlassian's US Headquarter) • Austin, United States • Blacksburg, United States • Boston, United States • Mountain View, United States • New York, United States

Table 1.1: Atlassian offices around the world

As shown in the preceding table, the company has offices in different parts of the world. Additionally, Atlassian has allowed employees to work from (almost) anywhere since 2020. Being a 20-year-old company with more than 8,000 team members, Atlassian has more than 260,000 customers worldwide.

Atlassian, which went public in 2015, has recently invested heavily in the cloud, and it has powerful tools for collaboration and productivity in its product portfolio, as shown in *Table 1.2*:

Categories	Products
Plan, Track & Support	• Halp • Jira Align • Jira Product Discovery • Jira Software • Jira Service Management • Jira Work Management • Opsgenie • Statuspage
Collaborate	• Atlas • Confluence • Trello
Code, Build, Ship	• Bamboo • Bitbucket • Compass • Crucible • Fisheye • Sourcetree
Security & Identity	• Atlassian Access • Beacon • Crowd

Table 1.2: Products by Atlassian

As you can see, Atlassian provides different solutions for different collaboration needs. Jira and Confluence are the most popular tools; the number of tools grows continually.

Let's talk about Atlassian's Point A, an innovative program that's more than just a buzzword. Point A is Atlassian's incubator for new ideas, where collaboration with customers and partners takes center stage. By focusing on real-world challenges and iterative design, Point A reflects a bold new direction in product development. It's about building tools that people like you really need.

Why should you care about Point A? Because it's shaping Atlassian's future of collaboration tools. Point A isn't just an abstract concept; it's a tangible path to new solutions that could become vital to your daily work. By following Point A, you're not just watching innovation unfold; you're potentially influencing products that may become integral to your workflow. It's a glimpse into the future of teamwork tools, and it offers you the opportunity to be part of something groundbreaking. So far, Point A has given us some incredible success stories such as Jira Work Management, Jira Product Discovery, Atlas, Compass, Beacon, and Confluence Whiteboards. You can find more information about Point A via this link: https://www.atlassian.com/point-a.

Atlassian values

To understand Atlassian, it's beneficial to understand its values. Atlassian has five core values. These values significantly guide the way Atlassian conducts business, develops products, and builds its brand. The company is constantly evolving and changing; however, these five values remain constant. They are as follows:

- Open company, no bullshit
- Build with heart and balance
- Don't #@!% the customer
- Play, as a team
- Be the change you seek

We highly recommend looking into the Atlassian values here: `https://www.atlassian.com/company/values`.

Introduction to Confluence

Confluence emerged in 2003 and is a system used by teams to store, share, and work as teams. At its core is the ethos of combining knowledge and teamwork. It allows collaboration within a single unit and between different departments in small or large companies (marketing, HR, IT, etc.). Users can combine all company-scale projects and teams.

Texts, references, images, and any content can be stored, shared, and edited simultaneously through Confluence. Because all this happens in the cloud, labor is saved and doesn't require much extra effort. It creates an open, easy-to-use, secure platform that allows teams to brainstorm, interact, discuss, and disseminate knowledge. It helps to carry individual studies to the culture of team spirit and transforms monologue into dialogue. Planning, goal setting, executing, and learning come together in one place in an organized and user friendly manner.

Teams working from the office, remotely, or hybrid benefit from Confluence.

According to Atlassian, Confluence has four essential functions:

- Break down team silos
- Turn conversations into action
- Organize everything in one place
- Build a culture of open teamwork

Exploring the competitors of Confluence

There are several competitors or similar products on the market. We can name a few here:

- SharePoint by Microsoft
- Docs and Drive by Google
- Notion by Notion
- Coda by Coda
- Quip by Salesforce

Discovering the different hosting options of Confluence – Cloud and Data Center

There are two hosting options for Confluence:

- Cloud
- Data Center

Atlassian recommends the Cloud version, but the Data Center option better suits you if you have a business requirement preventing you from hosting your data in the cloud. Many companies want to strictly control who has access to data held in Atlassian products such as Confluence or Jira. These companies often choose Data Center over Cloud. Additionally, data residency on Cloud is limited for some countries, which can be a significant obstacle for companies in regulated industries such as finance or medicine. This limitation can make migration impossible, reinforcing the preference for Data Center solutions.

Although they have a lot in common, they have significant functional differences. The Cloud edition is a **software as a service (SaaS)** solution and offers many benefits. For example, Atlassian takes care of all the technical details to provide an always-on, continuously updated, secure system. On the other hand, you must maintain your infrastructure if you opt for the Data Center edition.

Throughout this book, we recommend and assume that you have the Cloud version.

More information can be found here: `https://www.atlassian.com/migration/assess/compare-cloud-data-center`.

Discovering the different plans of Confluence Cloud – Free, Standard, Premium, and Enterprise

Confluence has four different plans for different needs, namely Free, Standard, Premium, and Enterprise:

- **Free plan**: For small teams who need essential project knowledge management solutions
- **Standard plan**: For growing teams who need more powerful collaboration and knowledge management solutions
- **Premium plan**: For organizations with advanced features for scaling knowledge management and achieving a high level of cooperation
- **Enterprise plan**: For enterprises with global scale, security, and governance

This book recommends and assumes that you have the Premium or the Enterprise plan. These plans have all the features that you will need when you study this book. A brief overview of the essential differences between Confluence Premium and Enterprise follows. Although these two plans are similar, they have some important differences that are summarized in *Table 1.3*:

	Premium	Enterprise
Site Limit	One	Unlimited
Atlassian Analytics	-	Yes
Atlassian Data Lake	-	Yes
Data Connectors	-	Yes
Atlassian Access	Requires Access Subscription	Included
Support Plan	24/7 Premium Support	24/7 Enterprise Support
Guaranteed Uptime SLA	99.9%	99.95%
Centralized Per-User Licensing	-	Yes

Table 1.3: Differences between Confluence Premium and Enterprise

As you can see, the Enterprise plan provides the most advanced features of Confluence and a higher SLA.

You will likely need to consult documentation frequently. Confluence's official documentation (see *Figure 1.1*) is one of the most reliable sources in this case:

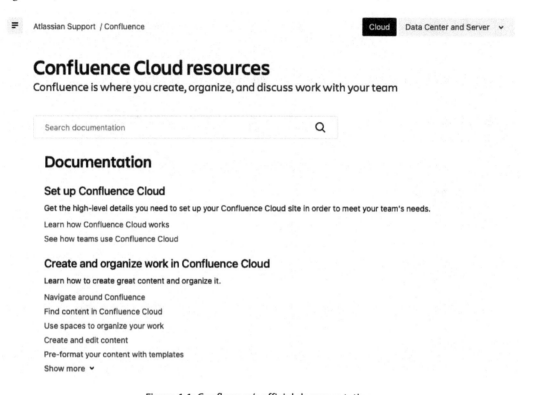

Figure 1.1: Confluence's official documentation

As you can see in this image, in this documentation, you'll have reliable information presented in an efficient way, on topics such as the following:

- How to set up Confluence Cloud
- How to create and organize work
- How to collaborate on content
- And much more…

Atlassian Marketplace

Atlassian Marketplace is a thriving online platform that hosts plugins, apps, and integrations specifically designed for Atlassian products. It's a space where developers can share their creations, and users can find the tools they need to enhance their Atlassian experience.

The importance of Atlassian Marketplace can't be overstated. It enables the customization and extension of Atlassian products, allowing users to tailor them to their specific needs. Whether it's project management, code integration, or workflow enhancement, Atlassian Marketplace offers solutions that can make an Atlassian product an even more powerful part of your toolkit.

Atlassian Marketplace boasts a diverse array of features, including a user friendly interface for browsing and discovering apps, detailed reviews, and support resources. You can find both free and paid solutions, with clear information on pricing and functionality. With robust search and filter options, finding the perfect tool to augment your Atlassian experience is just a few clicks away.

Atlassian Marketplace and Confluence are tightly intertwined. Through Atlassian Marketplace, Confluence users can access a wide variety of add-ons (or plugins) that expand Confluence's capabilities. Whether it's new macros, templates, or integrations with other tools, AM empowers Confluence users to adapt the platform to their specific requirements.

We'll be delving into Atlassian Marketplace in more detail in the later sections of this book. Its rich ecosystem and endless possibilities are worth exploring, and we'll guide you through everything you need to know to make the most of this invaluable resource.

Accessing the service availability information and reports for Confluence Cloud

We expect this critical system on which your team works together to be operational. But unfortunately, no system can be 100% functional. However, in the previous sections, we saw that the service level is 99.9% for Premium licenses and 99.95% for Enterprise licenses. You can find the link to Atlassian's Service Level Agreement in the *Further reading* section at the end of this chapter.

The interruptions are sometimes due to planned maintenance and unforeseen events. When such a situation occurs, our primary expectation is that the problem will be resolved as soon as possible and everything will return to normal. However, our other expectation is to be informed effectively and transparently in this painful process.

This is where Atlassian's status page comes into play. Thanks to this tool, you can instantly monitor the service quality of Confluence and Atlassian's other products. When there is a problem, you are immediately informed first-hand in the most reliable way without having to send a panicked email or make a phone call. Thanks to this, you know that the Atlassian team has already noticed the problem and is working on it, so the team does not become burdened with unnecessary demands and can devote its energy to solving the problem. You can access this tool at `https://confluence.status.atlassian.com`.

The Confluence Cloud status page is pictured in *Figure 1.2*:

Figure 1.2: Confluence Cloud status page

As you can see in the screenshot, this tool has many features. We recommend you learn all these features and try them out a few times. We also recommend you try it when everything is operational without waiting for any interruptions.

With this tool, you can do the following:

- Monitor whether the systems are operational
- Subscribe to instant notifications
- Report a problem you notice to the Atlassian team
- Access the list of past problems

> **Note**
>
> You can stay instantly informed about updates from Atlassian by using the yellow **Subscribe to Updates** button located at the top-right of the screen. You can receive these updates either via email or through a platform such as Slack. We recommend utilizing this service and closely following the updates.

> **Atlassian Statuspage**
>
> This tool works on the status page, another famous product of Atlassian. Here, the status of Confluence and all Atlassian products can be instantly monitored.

We will now provide an example of how Atlassian maintains communication when there is a problem. The following is a screenshot of an issue that occurred on September 29, 2022:

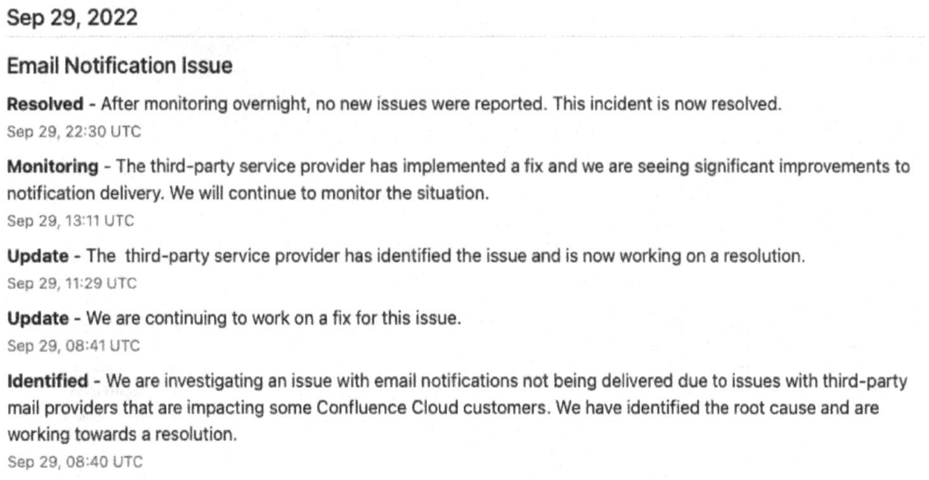

Sep 29, 2022

Email Notification Issue

Resolved - After monitoring overnight, no new issues were reported. This incident is now resolved.
Sep 29, 22:30 UTC

Monitoring - The third-party service provider has implemented a fix and we are seeing significant improvements to notification delivery. We will continue to monitor the situation.
Sep 29, 13:11 UTC

Update - The third-party service provider has identified the issue and is now working on a resolution.
Sep 29, 11:29 UTC

Update - We are continuing to work on a fix for this issue.
Sep 29, 08:41 UTC

Identified - We are investigating an issue with email notifications not being delivered due to issues with third-party mail providers that are impacting some Confluence Cloud customers. We have identified the root cause and are working towards a resolution.
Sep 29, 08:40 UTC

Figure 1.3: Past incident post published on Confluence status page

As can be seen here, the Atlassian team published five papers on this subject during the day. Here you can see the incident management maturity of the Atlassian team.

Anticipating and preparing for changes with Atlassian's Cloud Roadmap

We must always be able to look ahead to maintain a platform on which the whole team will work. Changes we are unprepared for can put us in a difficult position. On the other hand, if we are aware of the upcoming changes, we can make much more sound decisions.

Atlassian is constantly improving Confluence by adding new features, removing some parts, and changing some features.

> **Atlassian Cloud Roadmap**
>
> One of the most reliable and effective ways to learn about the changes that await you is to review the official Cloud Roadmap that Atlassian has published here: `https://www.atlassian.com/roadmap/cloud`.

The Atlassian Cloud Roadmap is shown in *Figure 1.4*:

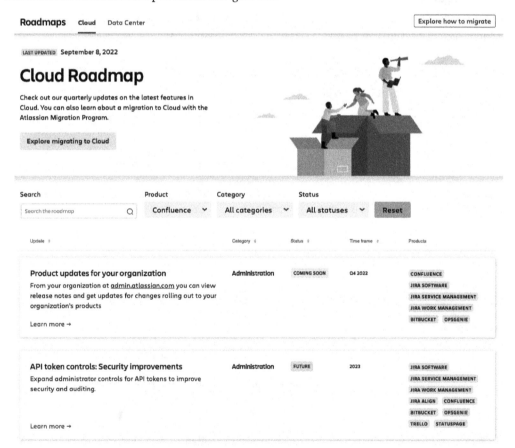

Figure 1.4: Atlassian Cloud Roadmap

As you can see in the previous screenshot, here is the roadmap of all Atlassian products, not just Confluence. You can view the changes that concern Confluence using the **Product** filter near the top of the screen.

Here you can see the following information about the changes:

- The change details
- The timeframe of the change: **Q4 2022, 2023**
- The products affected by the change: **CONFLUENCE, JIRA SOFTWARE, TRELLO**, and so on
- The category of change: **Compliance, Security, Performance & reliability**, and so on
- The status of the change: **RELEASED, COMING SOON, FUTURE**

We recommend that you follow this roadmap, which is updated quarterly. We also recommend that you proactively make the necessary technical and administrative preparations.

Confluence and Jira Software

Confluence and Jira Software are both products from Atlassian, and their tight integration is designed to enhance team collaboration, project management, and workflow tracking within an organization. Here's how the integration between Confluence and Jira Software works, and why it's beneficial.

Unified project management

- **Linking issues and projects**: You can link Jira issues directly within Confluence pages. This allows teams to reference specific tasks, bugs, or stories within their documents and meeting notes.
- **Embedding Jira reports**: You can embed entire Jira projects, dashboards, or filters within Confluence, offering a real-time view of the project's status.

Enhanced collaboration

- **Real-time synchronization**: Changes made in Jira (such as status updates or comments on an issue) are reflected in Confluence and vice versa. This ensures that everyone has the most up-to-date information.
- **Commenting and discussion**: Team members can discuss Jira issues within Confluence, adding context and collaboration around tasks and projects.

Streamlined documentation

- **Creating issues from Confluence**: If a task or requirement is identified within a Confluence document, you can quickly create a Jira issue directly from Confluence without needing to switch between tools.

- **Connecting requirements and development**: You can connect Confluence pages (such as product requirements) with corresponding Jira issues (such as development tasks), allowing seamless tracking from initial idea to development.

Visibility and transparency

- **Shared access**: Team members can view relevant Jira details within Confluence, even if they don't use Jira regularly. This promotes a shared understanding across different roles and departments.
- **Centralized information**: Having Jira data accessible within Confluence means that all project-related information, from requirements to status reports, can be found in one place.

Customization and automation

- **Workflow automation**: You can set up automated workflows that trigger actions between Jira and Confluence, such as updating a Confluence page when a Jira issue is resolved.
- **Custom integration**: Through APIs and various add-ons, organizations can tailor the integration to fit their specific needs and processes.

The tight integration between Confluence and Jira Software supports a more cohesive, efficient, and transparent approach to project management and collaboration. By connecting documentation, discussion, task tracking, and reporting across the two platforms, teams can work more seamlessly and maintain alignment with both high-level objectives and day-to-day tasks. It reduces the fragmentation of tools and information, leading to a more streamlined and productive working environment. We will revisit Confluence's integration with Jira Software in the next chapters.

We have briefly introduced Confluence and Atlassian; this will help you better understand the philosophy of Confluence and get the most out of it. It's now time to meet some fundamental concepts of enterprise collaboration.

Introducing enterprise collaboration concepts

Today, working life practices are seriously questioned. Focused experts are trying to detect and identify problems in the actual ways of working. Based on some of these studies, we would like to review a number of basic concepts frequently mentioned today.

Enterprise collaboration

Enterprise collaboration refers to the ways in which employees within an organization communicate, collaborate, and work together across different levels, departments, and locations using various tools, technologies, and practices. The term can encompass a wide range of activities and processes, supported by collaboration software and platforms designed to facilitate teamwork on a larger scale. What follows is an overview of the key aspects of enterprise collaboration.

Collaboration tools and technologies

Enterprise collaboration often relies on digital platforms, software, and tools that enable seamless communication, document sharing, project management, and more. Examples of collaboration platforms include Microsoft Teams, Slack, and Atlassian products such as Jira and Confluence.

Cross-functional collaboration

Unlike small team collaboration, enterprise collaboration involves coordination and communication across various departments, teams, and potentially different geographic locations. It's about working together on shared goals, projects, or initiatives at the organizational level.

Knowledge sharing

One of the goals of enterprise collaboration is to facilitate the sharing of knowledge and information across the organization. This can lead to better decision-making and innovation by tapping into diverse insights and expertise.

Real-time communication

Enterprise collaboration tools often support real-time communication through instant messaging, video conferencing, and shared workspaces, allowing employees to work together regardless of location.

Integration with existing systems

Successful enterprise collaboration usually requires integration with existing business systems such as CRM, ERP, or document management systems. This helps ensure that collaboration tools align with the broader business processes and objectives.

Security and compliance

In large organizations, collaboration must be managed with attention to security, privacy, and regulatory compliance. This includes managing access controls, data protection, and adherence to various legal and industry standards.

Cultural considerations

Enterprise collaboration isn't just about tools and technologies; it also involves fostering a collaborative culture. Leadership, trust, clear communication, and a shared understanding of goals and values are all vital to making collaboration effective.

Challenges

Implementing effective enterprise collaboration can be complex. Challenges may include resistance to change, difficulties in integrating different tools and systems, ensuring security, and maintaining a consistent collaboration experience across diverse teams and locations.

Measuring success

Metrics and analytics may be used to evaluate the success of collaboration initiatives, including user engagement, efficiency gains, improved innovation, and satisfaction levels among employees.

Benefits of enterprise collaboration

When well implemented, enterprise collaboration can lead to more efficient processes, improved problem-solving, greater innovation, and a more engaged and satisfied workforce.

Enterprise collaboration represents a strategic approach to enabling teamwork and coordination across an organization. It relies on a combination of technology, processes, and a supportive culture to enhance communication and collaboration at all levels of the organization. It can play a vital role in supporting organizational agility, innovation, and overall performance.

Enterprise collaboration is vital in today's complex and rapidly changing business environment for several reasons, and specific circumstances have given rise to the development and adoption of collaboration platforms. The following subsection provides an overview of this.

Why is enterprise collaboration important?

Enterprise collaboration is important for the following reasons:

- **Enhancing communication**: Collaboration facilitates clear and efficient communication across various departments and teams, promoting understanding and alignment
- **Improving efficiency and productivity**: Collaboration tools streamline workflows, reduce duplication of effort, and allow for real-time updates, enhancing overall productivity
- **Fostering innovation**: By connecting diverse teams and individuals, collaboration platforms can spark new ideas and innovations, leveraging different perspectives and expertise
- **Facilitating remote work**: Enterprise collaboration enables employees to work together regardless of location, which is essential for remote or distributed teams
- **Better decision-making**: Shared access to information and insights can lead to more informed and effective decision-making
- **Scalability**: Collaboration platforms can grow with the business, supporting expanding teams, new locations, and evolving projects
- **Enhancing customer service**: Quick and coordinated responses to customer needs or issues can be facilitated through collaborative processes
- **Compliance and security**: Collaboration ensures secure and compliant communication and data sharing across an organization

Circumstances that gave rise to enterprise collaboration platforms

Some of the circumstances that gave rise to enterprise collaboration platforms are as follows:

- **Globalization**: As businesses expand globally, the need to communicate and collaborate across different regions and cultures has increased, necessitating robust collaboration tools.

- **Technological advancements**: The growth of cloud computing, mobile technologies, and broadband internet has enabled the development and widespread use of sophisticated collaboration platforms.

- **Rise of remote work**: With more employees working remotely, especially accentuated by circumstances such as the COVID-19 pandemic, collaboration platforms have become essential for maintaining team cohesion and efficiency.

- **Increasing complexity of business processes**: The growing complexity of projects and interdependencies between different parts of an organization requires more sophisticated tools to manage collaboration effectively.

- **Competitive pressures**: In highly competitive markets, agility, innovation, and customer responsiveness are key. Collaboration platforms support these by enabling quicker, more coordinated action.

- **Regulatory compliance**: The need to manage data and communication in line with various legal and industry standards has also influenced the development of secure collaboration platforms.

- **Consumer expectations**: As consumer expectations for rapid and personalized service have grown, companies have needed ways to collaborate effectively to meet these demands.

In conclusion, enterprise collaboration has become crucial in modern business, driven by globalization, technological advancement, the shift toward remote work, and the growing complexity in business processes. Well-implemented collaboration strategies and platforms can lead to increased innovation, efficiency, agility, and competitiveness, addressing the challenges and opportunities of today's dynamic business landscape.

Remote collaboration

The need for remote collaboration has become increasingly prominent, particularly with the rise of globalization, distributed teams, and the shift toward remote and flexible working arrangements. The following subsection provides a detailed explanation of the need for and benefits of remote collaboration.

Need for remote collaboration

Let's think about why we need remote collaboration:

- **Global workforce**: Companies are increasingly drawing talent from around the world, and remote collaboration allows team members in different geographical locations to work together efficiently.

- **Flexible work arrangements**: Many employees value the ability to work from anywhere, and remote collaboration enables this flexibility without sacrificing productivity.

- **Business continuity**: Unexpected events such as natural disasters or pandemics can disrupt traditional office work. Remote collaboration ensures that work can continue uninterrupted in such scenarios.

- **Access to expertise**: Remote collaboration allows organizations to tap into specialized skills and expertise that might not be available locally.

- **Cost savings**: By allowing employees to work remotely, companies can reduce costs related to office space, utilities, and other overheads.

Benefits of remote collaboration

Remote collaboration offers a lot of benefits:

- **Increased productivity**: With the right tools and practices, remote collaboration can enhance productivity by allowing employees to work in environments that suit them best.

- **Enhanced diversity and inclusion**: Remote collaboration opens up opportunities for individuals who may have been excluded from traditional office roles, such as those with disabilities or caregiving responsibilities.

- **Better work-life balance**: Employees can achieve a more balanced lifestyle by eliminating long commutes and working in a more flexible manner.

- **Access to global talent pool**: Companies can hire the best talent, regardless of location, leading to more diverse and skilled teams.

- **Scalability**: Remote collaboration facilitates business growth and expansion into new markets without the need for substantial physical infrastructure.

- **Real-time collaboration**: Modern collaboration tools enable real-time communication and collaboration, ensuring that team members stay aligned and informed, no matter where they are.

- **Environmental benefits**: Reduced commuting and office usage can lead to a smaller carbon footprint.

- **Robust security**: Secure remote collaboration tools can provide robust protection for sensitive data and information, even when accessed from various locations.

- **Continuous innovation**: By fostering diverse and inclusive teams, remote collaboration can lead to more creative and innovative problem-solving.

Remote collaboration is not merely a trend but a vital aspect of modern business operations. With the strategic use of technology and proper management practices, it can lead to increased productivity, flexibility, diversity, and resilience. By embracing remote collaboration, organizations position themselves to compete effectively in a global marketplace and adapt to the continually evolving business landscape. It is a model that aligns with the needs and expectations of a modern workforce and can drive significant long-term value.

Hybrid working

Hybrid working refers to a working model that combines both remote (off-site) work and in-office (on-site) work. It's a flexible arrangement that allows employees to split their time between working from home (or another remote location) and working from the physical office.

All-remote working

All-remote working refers to a working model where employees work entirely outside of a traditional office environment. Unlike hybrid working that combines both remote and in-office work, all-remote working means that there is no requirement or expectation for employees to be physically present in an office at any time.

Agility

Agility is an iterative approach that focuses on the continuity of new releases and includes customer feedback while managing projects. Teams break the requirements into smaller workpieces sorted by importance, and integrate the plan according to the implementation, which enables the team to respond to changing conditions.

Cross-functional teams

Today, a team specializing in a single function (human resources, software development, finance, etc.) is not enough to handle ambitious projects. On the contrary, we need the cooperation of teams specializing in different fields working for a common purpose. Modern self-sufficient teams and individuals from other specialties are called **cross-functional teams**.

A cross-functional team is a group of people with different functional expertise working toward a common goal. It may include individuals from various departments and levels of an organization, such as finance, marketing, operations, and engineering. The idea is to bring diverse perspectives and skills together to accomplish a specific objective, often related to problem-solving, product development, or process improvement.

Cross-functional teams represent a collaborative approach to tackling complex projects, enabling a more holistic view and drawing on the diverse skills needed to succeed. They can be highly effective but require careful planning, coordination, and leadership to overcome potential challenges related to diversity of thought, priorities, and working styles.

Distributed workforce

A **distributed workforce** refers to a business model where employees work from various geographical locations rather than from a central physical office. The workforce could be spread across different cities, states, countries, or even continents.

Information silo

An **information silo**, or a **data silo**, is a term used in information systems and business to describe a situation where a set of data or information is isolated or segregated from other parts of the organization. This isolation can occur within different departments, teams, or even different systems within an organization.

Information silos can create significant challenges within an organization, inhibiting collaboration, efficiency, and effective decision-making. Addressing this issue often requires a comprehensive approach, including technological, cultural, and organizational changes to foster open communication and collaboration.

Information architecture strategy

Information architecture strategy refers to the planning, organization, and structuring of information within a system or environment, such as a website, application, database, or business process. The goal is to make information easily accessible and understandable, facilitating efficient navigation and meaningful interactions for the users.

An information architecture strategy is a holistic approach to managing information in a way that aligns with both user needs and business goals. It plays a vital role in enhancing **user experience** (**UX**), supporting effective content management, and contributing to the overall success of a digital product or service. It's a multidisciplinary effort that involves collaboration among UX designers, content strategists, developers, and other stakeholders.

Single source of truth

A **single source of truth** (**SSOT**) refers to the practice of structuring information so that there's a singular, authoritative data repository or record for each piece of information. In a business context, it means that everyone in the organization relies on the same data point or definition, reducing inconsistencies and errors across different departments or systems.

A single source of truth serves as the definitive and authoritative reference for a particular set of data. It's a concept widely applied in areas such as data management, software development, content management, and more. It promotes consistency, accuracy, and efficiency, but requires careful planning and execution to be implemented effectively.

Synchronous communication

Synchronous communication refers to a mode of communication where all parties are present and engaged at the same time. This real-time interaction allows for immediate feedback and collaboration, fostering a sense of connection and immediacy.

In essence, synchronous communication is a valuable tool for fostering real-time collaboration and connection, particularly for complex or urgent matters. However, it requires careful planning and consideration of the needs and preferences of all participants. Balancing synchronous communication with asynchronous methods can help create a more flexible and inclusive communication environment, accommodating various work styles, locations, and schedules.

The communication happens in real time. Zoom calls, phone calls, and real-time chat messages are all examples of synchronous collaboration. Synchronous collaboration is the preferred method if you need instantaneous feedback.

Asynchronous communication

Asynchronous communication refers to a mode of communication that does not require all parties involved to be simultaneously present or engaged. Unlike synchronous communication, where everyone must be available at the same time (such as in a live meeting or phone call), asynchronous communication allows people to send and receive messages at their convenience.

Asynchronous communication is an essential aspect of modern work communication, especially as remote and flexible working arrangements become more prevalent. It fosters a more inclusive environment where everyone has the opportunity to contribute, regardless of their location or schedule. However, it requires clear guidelines and expectations to be effective, ensuring that everyone stays engaged and informed.

Communication doesn't happen in real time. You send your messages when you're ready; your colleagues respond when they're ready. For example, you can send a text message, a voice message, or even a video clip of yourself to your colleague. You're not in sync when you're communicating with each other.

Collaboration software

Collaboration software refers to the suite of tools that aid teams in communicating and working together on shared goals and projects, often in real time and across various locations. It can include features such as the following:

- Messaging and chat
- File sharing and collaborative editing
- Video conferencing
- Task management
- Workflow automation

Trends in collaboration software

The landscape of collaboration software is ever-evolving to meet the changing needs of modern workplaces. Some current trends in the industry include the following:

- Rise of hybrid and remote work
- Integration with other tools
- AI and automation
- Focus on security
- User friendly interfaces
- Sustainability considerations

Common use cases for collaboration software

Collaboration software is employed across various scenarios to enhance teamwork, increase efficiency, and streamline operations. Typical use cases for these tools involve the following:

- Project management
- File sharing and document collaboration
- Communication
- Workflow automation
- Knowledge management
- Integration with existing systems

Demand for collaboration software

The need for collaboration software has surged with shifts in work dynamics and technological advancements. Various factors contribute to this growing demand:

- Globalization

- Shift to remote and flexible work

- Complex projects and cross-functional teams

- Compliance and security needs

- Small business growth

Collaboration software plays a pivotal role in modern business, enabling fluid communication and teamwork, irrespective of location or device. As the landscape of work continues to transform, collaboration tools are adapting and innovating to cater to the new norms, facilitating a more connected, agile, and efficient work environment. Whether for global corporations or small start-ups, collaboration software remains central to achieving success in today's interconnected world.

We have covered fundamental concepts of enterprise collaboration that will guide you on your Confluence journey. Now, we will discuss the types of teams that can benefit from Confluence.

Which teams can benefit from Confluence?

You may wonder whether Confluence is the right tool for your team or company. Let's now discuss how Confluence is flexible and can be efficiently used by teams and companies with different backgrounds and needs:

- Your company's focus area does not matter when using Confluence. Any team or company can benefit from Confluence, and the critical point is to have a solid willingness to manage your knowledge for better collaboration. As an Atlassian Solution Partner, we have already helped some very different teams. Some examples of these industries include technology, software development, finance, education, and government.

- Confluence has robust features to adapt to modern teams' different needs. No matter your team type, you can use Confluence as your primary collaboration tool. Some types of teams we have worked with include human resources, finance, sales, marketing, operations management, support teams, project management teams, product management teams, boards of directors, service teams, and many more.

- Your company size does not matter when using Confluence. You can easily use Confluence whether yours is a one-person company or a company of thousands, and you can comfortably go up to 35,000 users within a single Atlassian Cloud site.

- Your company's working practices do not matter when using Confluence. We all work differently, and you may be working entirely from the office, in a hybrid fashion, or entirely remotely. Thanks to Confluence, you can easily manage your knowledge.

- Your information security and privacy needs can vary greatly, but Confluence will adapt. Confluence can be optimized according to your information security and privacy needs. You may apply the principles of transparency to a large extent in the company and want the content to be generally accessible to the entire company. On the other hand, you may be dealing with sensitive content that requires confidentiality due to the nature of your business, and you want only authorized people to see it under certain conditions. Confluence has features to address the needs of these two extremes and all situations in between. In later chapters, we'll look closely at Confluence's security-related features.

- Your cloud adoption preferences do not restrict you from using Confluence. Some companies prefer using cloud products, and others do not. Some companies are not allowed to use cloud products because of their regulations. So, you have two options here: you can use Confluence Cloud or Confluence Data Center. In either case, Confluence will help you master modern collaboration within your company.

- You are always free to use other tools with Confluence. Some teams in your company may already be using SharePoint, Google Docs, Notion, or other systems, and you don't have to quit them. You can use Confluence with these systems.

Proof of concept – how can your company benefit from Confluence?

Confluence is a flexible yet robust environment that can fulfill the most demanding requirements of different teams. It's not just a content creation platform but a solid collaboration environment.

In the previous sections, we mentioned that Confluence could be helpful for different teams. Now, we will see more concretely how Confluence can be used. It is worth remembering that what you can do with Confluence is much more than what is explained here.

There are some features common to all of the following scenarios. Atlassian has placed qualified templates for many different needs within Confluence. You can get effective results in a short time using these templates. In addition to these templates, you can create your own. You can even adapt Confluence according to your needs by using its plugin software.

In the next subsection, we've put together some real-life scenarios that might inspire you. These examples can be beneficial in building your team's collaborative muscles. In this way, it may become necessary for your teams to be in the same environment, but only in some exceptional cases.

Confluence use cases for all types of teams

Confluence offers templates and features that can address some common problems that teams often need, regardless of their types of functions. With Confluence, you can efficiently manage notes, decisions, meetings, to-dos, plans, calendars, and all kinds of content.

Confluence can help you with the following use cases:

- Knowledge management
- Information gathering and sharing
- Announcements
- Meeting notes
- Calendars
- Blogs
- Decisions
- Brainstorming

Introduction to Confluence templates

All teams can get started quickly with Confluence. Templates are one of the essential concepts that can speed up your work. We will look at the templates in more detail later in the book. Now, we're giving you a summary of the templates here to show you how many well-designed, ready-made templates Confluence has for different teams. Meanwhile, a significant portion of the templates found on Confluence has been prepared by Atlassian. However, there are many other companies besides Atlassian that offer templates such as Optimizely, Miro, and Figma.

The numbers of templates available on Confluence as of January 2023 for different kinds of teams are as follows:

Category	Number of Templates
Design	12
Startup	39
Business Strategy	28
Human Resources	17
Marketing and Sales	19
Project Management	32
Product Management	18
Teamwork	45
Productivity	27
Personal	11
Software / IT	19

Table 1.4: Template categories in Confluence

As you can see from the preceding table, there are many templates for different teams on Confluence. You can get a good start on Confluence using these, and later, you can create your own templates.

Templates for sales and marketing teams

Sales and marketing teams are often among the most energetic teams within a company. It's expected that these fast-paced teams have mastery over collaborative work.

On Confluence, there are 19 ready-to-use templates that can accelerate the pace of these teams. Some examples include the following:

- Marketing plan
- Marketing campaign
- Sales account planning

- Marketing blog post
- Email drip campaign

Templates for human resources teams

Human resources teams are at the forefront of the teams that have the most communication with the other teams around them. HR teams must quickly and effectively manage recruitment, adaptation, performance audit, leaving the job, and many other processes, create a large amount of content, and bring together and organize that content. In addition, they can make the rules and procedures that everyone in the company must follow visible to the whole company using Confluence.

There are 17 templates for human resources teams in Confluence, which include the following:

- Employee handbook
- 90-day plan
- Performance improvement plan
- Hiring process
- Career development plan
- Job description
- Job offer letter
- Interview feedback

Templates for project management

Confluence can be very useful for agile project management, especially with Jira. It provides project managers with useful, ready-made templates and reliable features for planning, communicating, working with stakeholders, setting goals, and so on.

There are 32 templates for project management, which include the following:

- Project plan
- Project kickoff
- Stakeholder management
- Risk register
- Daily stand up
- Retrospective

Templates for product management teams

Product management teams are highly specialized in knowledge management. Doing research, collecting requirements, designing, analyzing, interviewing users, making data-based decisions, making roadmaps, holding meetings, and so on, are among product management activities. A large amount of content accumulates while doing these studies. They can use Confluence to keep this content tidy, and they can keep all content in one place that's accessible to both their teams and relevant stakeholders.

There are 18 templates designed for product management teams within Confluence, including the following:

- Product requirements
- Product roadmap
- Product launch
- MVP ideation
- Competitive analysis

Templates for software development and IT teams

Software projects can quickly become highly sophisticated. All the content stakeholders with different needs can be brought together on Confluence. If you start such a project on Confluence, you can create a world-class environment quickly by using ready-made templates. These templates cover essential topics, especially collecting requirements, planning, enabling meetings, and managing decisions. Confluence works in harmony with many different tools used by software developers.

There are 19 templates available for software development and IT teams, including the following:

- DevOps runbook
- DevOps change management
- ITSM change management
- Incident communication
- ITSM runbook

We've discussed how different teams could benefit from Confluence. You can use these use cases to build your company's knowledge management system. Now, it's time to think about your Confluence team that will build, maintain, and develop this system.

Building a Confluence team

We need teams that will prepare, develop, and update our collaboration environment where we can collect and organize our knowledge.

Although we can provide most of this platform's maintenance and development work with automation or Confluence's features, it is people who will do the actual work.

Checking out team building tips

You can benefit from the following tips when building a team that will help you throughout your Confluence journey:

- Every company is unique, whether it's a start-up with 10 people, a small business, or an enterprise with 5,000 people. They all have their own authentic contexts, problems, and needs.
- It may be necessary to set up different teams for different parts of the process (planning, initial setup, and maintenance).
- To keep such a platform alive, we must identify the jobs that need to be done and distribute them to the relevant roles and people.
- We can talk about the fundamental roles in almost every company: site, product, space, and content managers.
- In addition, roles may differ according to the diverse needs of other teams.
- You can build the team iteratively.
- The responsibilities of everyone who will use Confluence must be determined. Everyone should have some duties, but some should have more responsibilities.
- You can make a systematic stakeholder identification.

Identifying roles using RASCI within your team

We recommend that you identify your Confluence team's roles and responsibilities to ensure everything is clear. That's where RASCI comes into play.

RASCI (responsible, accountable, supporter, consultant, informed) is used to identify all the roles and responsibilities within a project. We recommend that you use this technique while adopting Confluence within your company, as it will help clarify the responsibilities of each project team member.

A detailed explanation of RASCI is provided as follows:

- Responsible (R): The person responsible for completing the work. This is an execution role.
- Accountable (A): The person accountable for the work's outcome. This is a management role.
- Supporter (S): People who help those responsible to finish the work.
- Consultant (C): People from whom we'll get help when we're stuck or confused.
- Informed (I): People whom we keep informed throughout the work.

The following is an example of a RASCI table that you can use as a starting point when identifying the roles and responsibilities within your Confluence team:

	Responsible	Accountable	Supporter	Consultant	Informed
Integration with other Saas		1. Management Information Systems manager	1. Confluence administrator 2. Slack administrators 3. Jira administrators 4. Google Workspace administrators	1. Security teams	
Confluence support	1. Support team				
Confluence training			1. People (Human Resources) 2. Contractors 3. Team leaders		
Scaling				1. Atlassian consultants	
Governance				1. Risk management team 2. Atlassian consultants	
Compliance				1. Legal team 2. Atlassian consultants	

Table 1.5: Sample RASCI table

Maintaining your Confluence team

You should maintain your Confluence team and keep it healthy. The following are some tips that can help you when maintaining your team:

- Continuous education on Confluence and content management is a must.

- The use of Confluence can feed the performance evaluation criteria.

- Support from the management and the support team is crucial.

- Tracking, monitoring, and reporting on Confluence teams' performance is vital.

- You must clearly define roles and responsibilities to plan, realize, and maintain a healthy Confluence environment. You can use the previous table as a starting point when determining the roles and responsibilities for this project.

Atlassian University offers numerous, high-quality courses related to Confluence. Some of these courses are free, while others are paid. By studying these courses, you can keep yourself up to date with Confluence. Additionally, you can earn badges and certificates from this platform. We recommend exploring Atlassian University and taking advantage of the valuable resources available there. You can access the Confluence courses on Atlassian University at the following link: `https://university.atlassian.com/student/catalog/list?search=confluence`.

Summary

In the first chapter of this book, you have gained general knowledge about Atlassian, the developer of Confluence. This has provided you with the opportunity to more closely understand Atlassian's thought process, products, and philosophy. Understanding Atlassian and its ecosystem will open the doors to a sound understanding of Confluence. In this chapter, we discussed many important concepts related to teamwork, such as remote, distributed, and asynchronous work. We then began to get to know Confluence and explored the templates available.

We also discussed how teams and companies of different types could benefit from Confluence. Lastly, we introduced insights on building a team that will plan, develop, and maintain an effective collaboration environment using Confluence.

In the next chapter, we will plan a fully working Confluence site and set it up.

Questions

1. Atlassian provides different plans for teams. What are these plans?

2. What's the difference between remote, distributed, and asynchronous work?

3. What is a single source of truth?

4. How can software development teams benefit from Confluence?

5. One of the core values of Atlassian, the company behind Confluence, is open work. Can you explain how Confluence can help companies to build a culture of open teamwork?

Answers

1. Free, Standard, Premium, and Enterprise.

2. Remote working means working from outside your office. A distributed workforce is a team with geographically dispersed members who can work from anywhere. In asynchronous working, the communication doesn't happen in real time. You send your messages when you're ready; your colleagues respond when they're ready. For example, you can send a text message, a voice message, or even a video clip of yourself to your colleague. You're not in sync when you're communicating with each other.

3. You collect all information from across the enterprise and aggregate it into a central repository. This method has a lot of benefits, such as increasing productivity, breaking down information silos, and eliminating duplicate information. This can support decision-makers and strategy-makers.

4. Software teams can use Confluence for technical documentation, project management, testing, meeting notes, decision registers, requirement management, and other purposes.

5. Confluence can help companies to build a culture of open teamwork by organizing, developing, and making visible their knowledge transparently and collaboratively.

Further reading

-   https://www.atlassian.com/point-a

-   https://s28.q4cdn.com/541786762/files/doc_financials/2023/q4/TEAM-Q4-2023-Shareholder-Letter.pdf

-   https://www.atlassian.com/legal/sla

-   https://support.atlassian.com/confluence-cloud/resources/

-   https://www.atlassian.com/software/confluence/pricing

-   https://university.atlassian.com/student/catalog/list?search=confluence

2

Setting Up Confluence

Getting started with Confluence is easy. But things can get derailed very quickly.

The amount and variety of information we collect on Confluence will increase daily, so keeping it organized is essential. To set up a system that people will enjoy using, it is necessary to sit down and plan. While making this plan, it is helpful to benefit from a well-known concept: **information architecture**.

In this chapter, you will first learn fundamental concepts such as information architecture to help you set up the Confluence environment from scratch. The main goal of this chapter is to make an excellent start to your Confluence journey.

In this chapter, we'll cover the following topics:

- Introducing information architecture
- Planning your Confluence site
- Installing and configuring Confluence
- Managing users
- Setting up spaces – team, project, company, and personal

Technical requirements

You will need to have the following software requirements to complete this chapter:

- An up-to-date web browser
- An active subscription to Confluence Cloud Premium

Introducing information architecture

Information architecture is a highly complex concept, and it could easily fill up an entire book on its own. Our aim in this section is to raise awareness about the information architecture concept and to make you think about some basic questions on this subject. If we achieve this goal, we can proceed much more consciously in the following chapters of the book.

Defining the requirements of your knowledge management system

To predetermine the system's features, we want to install and return to them frequently, as this will help us a lot in keeping our focus. The most important requirements are as follows:

- We should be able to record and view information easily
- We should be able to find the information we are looking for easily
- We should be able to quickly reach other concepts related to an idea
- We should be able to view the outline of the information architecture easily
- The system should be easy to use for people from different cultures
- The system should be flexible, allowing us to make changes

At this point, we expect you to do a study. What basic features should the system we design have other than the ones here?

Defining the content types of your knowledge management system

Please list all the content types and information you will manage within your knowledge management system. The following are some examples:

- Document
- Schema
- Meeting note
- Image
- Link
- Video
- Audio
- Spreadsheet

- Presentation
- All kinds of attachments

Some of this content will be added to the Confluence pages; some content will originally be located outside and will be made available by the Confluence environment. For example, we can embed a YouTube video to the Confluence page, but that means that the video gets stored in the Confluence environment. There are three options available when making external content accessible within Confluence:

- Insert into the page
- Give a link
- Embed (practical for YouTube, Miro, etc.)

Thinking about categorizing content

We have to organize all content. This way, we can promptly get the correct information we are looking for. There are multiple methods for classifying data; you can use one or more. The important thing here is to think about categorizing information as early as possible and make certain decisions.

Thinking about the maintenance of your knowledge management system

Accumulating content and knowledge is essential for a robust system, but more is needed. It is necessary to constantly organize all the information and content. It is vital to take care of outdated material, add new information, and adapt the relationship between the content and the information according to the conditions of the phase of the project.

Don't expect these editing jobs to happen by themselves. We suggest you consider how, when, and by whom this will be done.

Now that we've raised awareness about information architecture, we can hopefully move on to the next topic and apply what we've learned here.

Planning your Confluence site

Setting up Confluence is a straightforward task. However, if you do this within a company, you need careful planning. This way, you can foresee your needs, what you can do with this product, the essential decisions, and the risks.

An environment that hosts the knowledge that a large team develops daily can quickly get out of control if not meticulously designed. Content may become inaccurate or outdated, difficult to find and understand, and even cause information security, compliance, and other legal issues. With good planning, you can avoid most of these risks. If you want to gain resistance against all these risks, we recommend you consider the planning process. This way, you can make the right decisions and establish and maintain a collaborative working platform that your teams will enjoy using, while avoiding confusion and lack of motivation among teammates.

Introduction to iterative planning

We live in a time where everything changes rapidly. For this reason, planning even the smallest detail from the beginning is impossible, and it is also not efficient. We advise that you plan as much as needed; nothing less, nothing more. You should be able to adapt your plan according to the changes you'll meet.

How much and when we plan depends on many factors. The company's experience in Confluence, knowledge management, and collaborative solutions are among the most critical factors.

Here are some scenarios where we believe careful planning is almost certainly necessary:

- If you are using Confluence for the first time
- If you haven't used any knowledge management or collaboration solutions before
- If you are migrating from a different collaboration tool to Confluence
- If you are going to make severe changes to the current Confluence environment
- If your company is undergoing extreme changes (e.g., new products or teams)
- If you are merging with another company
- If you are scaling Confluence
- If you are migrating from Confluence Server or Confluence Data Center to Confluence Cloud

Every company's planning ability and habits are unique. If your company structure is appropriate, we have experienced that agile planning can yield outstanding results in this area, which contains many uncertainties. However, you can make very effective plans with other approaches if you prefer.

In principle, we can give the following advice: It would be beneficial to analyze your conditions and plan only as much as necessary. Here, we'd like to also underline that iterative planning will be helpful. You can prepare the near-term in detail and the mid-term roughly.

Putting what we have planned into practice, testing, using, , taking lessons, and planning the next iteration can help you a lot.

Here are our recommendations that we believe will come in handy during the planning phase:

- Identify the people affected by these studies and establish a good planning team.
- Use checklists and sample questions to make systematic and result-oriented planning. You can have these lists created by your team, find them on the internet, or ask your advisors.
- Make your decision register visible to your team.

Using checklists and guiding questions for better planning

We will present some checklists to better prepare you for the planning phase of your Confluence journey.

Checklist no.1 – Tools

Use these questions to clarify your needs before setting up the Atlassian Cloud site and Confluence environment:

	Questions	Your responses
1	Which hosting options best suit you? Cloud or Data Center	
2	Which plan best suits you? Free, Standard, Premium, or Enterprise	
3	On which site will you install Confluence? This may be a new site, or we may create one from scratch. If you build a new site, what will the URL be? A sample URL is myremote.atlassian.net.	
4	How many sites do you need?	
5	Are there any other products you need to integrate with Confluence? Slack, Google Drive, Dropbox	

Figure 2.1 – Checklist no.1

Checklist no.2 – Additional needs

Use the following questions to further clarify your needs:

	Questions	Your responses
1	Do you need to use plugins from the Atlassian marketplace?	
2	Do we need to use Confluence as a hub for other SaaS that we use?	
3	Do you need to scale right now? In the future?	
4	For what purposes will you use Confluence? Collaboration, project management, knowledge base, etc.	
5	Do you have any off-scope requirements? Maybe you have another solution in place, and you won't use some features of Confluence for some of your needs.	

Figure 2.2 – Checklist no.2

Checklist no.3 – People

Use the following questions to think about how you will manage your users and your teams:

	Questions	Your responses
1	How many users will use Confluence?	
2	Who will use Confluence?	
3	Will you onboard all users at the same time?	
4	How will you handle managing users?	
5	Do you need an identity provider?	
6	What kind of teams will you build?	

Figure 2.3 – Checklist no.3

Checklist no.4 – Processes

Use the following questions to plan your project from an information security perspective:

	Questions	Your responses
1	What are the roles and responsibilities during the initiation of your Confluence environment?	
2	What are the roles and responsibilities during the maintenance of your Confluence environment?	
3	How will we handle information security?	
4	How will you integrate Confluence with your Management Information System?	
5	Why do you need a permission management system?	

Figure 2.4 – Checklist no.4

Checklist no.5 – Contents

Use the following questions to gain an idea of the content that will live on your Confluence site:

	Questions	Your responses
1	What type of content will you host? Text, image, video, etc. Do you have any public content or spaces?	
2	How will you organize the content? By teams? By projects? By departments?	
3	What topics will you cover in this system? Projects, products, services, teams, departments...	
4	What is your Information Architecture strategy?	
5	What spaces will be created?	

Figure 2.5 – Checklist no.5

Now that we are done with checklists and ready to move forward, let's discuss how many Confluence spaces you need. It depends on your needs. The following table can give you some inspiration on deciding the number of spaces within your Confluence site:

	Level	Notes
1	Organizational	One space per organization
2	Team	One space per team
3	Project	One space per project
4	Personal	One space per person
5	Product	One space per product

Figure 2.6 – How many Confluence spaces do you need?

As you can see from the previous table, we propose creating one organizational space, one space per team, one space per project, one space per person, and one space per product. Remember that a personal space is automatically created for a new user who is added to Confluence.

Additional tips for more effective planning

As we mentioned, the planning continues after you get the system up and running. We recommend that you constantly plan for the next phase. As a planner, the following tips can help you stay up to date:

- Establish the processes required for regular planning

- Research about Confluence

- Discover working examples of Confluence

- Examine Atlassian's Cloud Roadmap

In this section, we've planned our Confluence site and are now ready to install and configure Confluence.

Installing and configuring Confluence

Our goal here is to create an Atlassian Cloud site, install Confluence on it, and configure Confluence to meet our needs.

Mastering the terminology – sites and products

Before installing Confluence, we present you with two fundamental concepts:

- Product

- Atlassian Cloud site

First, Confluence is an Atlassian product like others such as Jira, Trello, Bitbucket, and so on.

On the other hand, Atlassian Cloud products reside within an Atlassian Cloud site. Your Confluence product must therefore be installed on an Atlassian Cloud site. An Atlassian Cloud site generally hosts multiple products such as Confluence, Jira Software, Jira Service Management, et cetera.

If you already have an Atlassian Cloud product such as Jira, you can easily add Confluence alongside this product in the same Atlassian Cloud site. If you don't have an Atlassian Cloud site, you should create one. Every Atlassian Cloud site has a URL (for example, `myremote.atlassian.net` or `myatlassiancloudsite.atlassian.net`).

The next screenshot shows how to create an Atlassian cloud site and install Confluence on it:

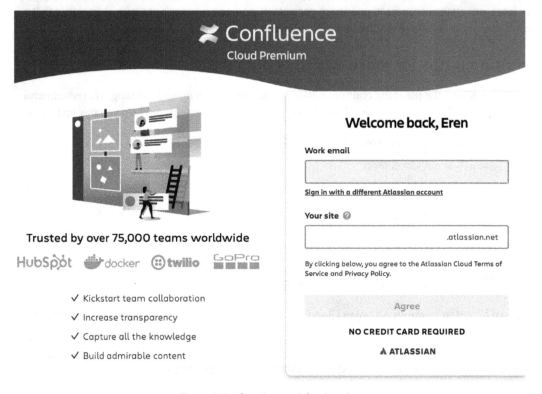

Figure 2.7 – Creating an Atlassian site

As you can see in the previous screenshot, you need only an email address and a name to create a fresh Confluence environment on a new Atlassian Cloud site.

If you do not have an Atlassian Cloud site, you should create one now. First, you need a unique site URL where Confluence will be accessible. When your site is ready, you can install Confluence on it.

Each Atlassian Cloud site has a unique web address. We advise you to be careful when choosing this address. You have the right to change this address three times, and changing it brings risks. Remember that you won't be able to reuse previous URLs.

Installing Confluence

Follow these instructions to install Confluence:

1. Visit `https://www.atlassian.com/software/confluence`.
2. Choose **Start my free 30-day trial**.

Your Confluence installation will start when you click the **Start my free 30-day trial** button shown in the following screenshot. The process is relatively straightforward:

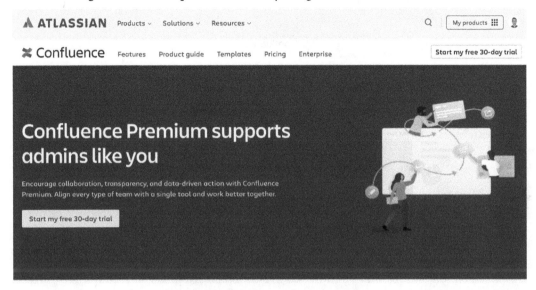

Figure 2.8 – Start my free 30-day trial

The interface shown in the preceding screenshot will guide you on whether to create a site first or install Confluence on an existing site.

Remember that you can try Confluence Premium for free for 30 days.

Comparison between Standard and Premium plans

In terms of the topics discussed in this chapter, there isn't a significant difference between the Standard and Premium plans. However, it's worth noting that the **Copy Space Permissions** feature is exclusive to the Premium plan. Being on the Premium plan enables you to copy permissions from one space to another, which is a handy tool for saving time and avoiding errors.

Upgrading to the Premium plan

You are automatically included in the Free plan when you install Confluence for the first time. We highly recommend the Premium plan to perform the transactions covered in this book. You can easily upgrade Confluence to the Standard or Premium plan using the **Select Standard** or **Select Premium** buttons shown in the following screenshot:

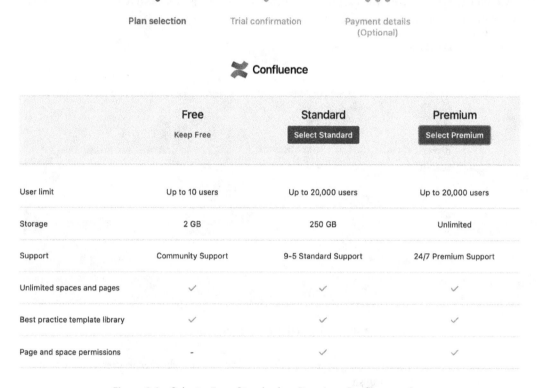

Figure 2.9 – Select a Free, Standard, or Premium Confluence plan

As you can see in the previous screenshot, there are three plans available: Free, Standard, and Premium. By default, you take the Free plan when you install Confluence for the first time, but you can always select the Standard or Premium plan later.

> **Note**
>
> With Standard and Premium plans, you can try the product for a certain period; however, you should fill out your credit card information as soon as possible so that the service is not interrupted.
>
> You cannot switch to the Enterprise plan here; you must contact Atlassian for that.

Understanding the different types of administrators

In this section, we want to provide you with a summary of the different administrative roles associated with Atlassian Confluence Cloud.

In Atlassian Confluence Cloud, there are four different types of administrators, each with their own set of permissions and capabilities:

- **Site administrators**: They have the highest level of permissions and can manage global settings across all Atlassian products in the cloud instance (e.g., Jira, Confluence, etc.). They can manage users and groups, billing and subscriptions, and other site-wide settings.

- **Confluence administrators**: They have administrative rights specifically for Confluence. They can manage spaces, global permissions, and configure Confluence settings, but they don't have access to site-wide settings or other Atlassian products.

- **Space administrators**: They have administrative rights for a specific Confluence space. They can manage pages, permissions, and settings for that space only.

- **Organization administrators**: They can manage Atlassian accounts, security settings, and domain verification for the entire organization, but they don't have administrative rights in Confluence or any other Atlassian products unless explicitly granted.

Remember that Confluence Cloud has different permission settings compared to Confluence Server and Data Center, so make sure to check the Atlassian documentation for the latest information as it might change over time.

Managing technical and billing contacts

We recommend that you specify **Technical Contacts** and **Billing Contacts** carefully. You can add more than one person to either category, and both categories must have a primary contact.

Technical contacts are the people who will seek support directly from Atlassian. The primary technical contact's address information (including VAT) will appear on your invoices.

Billing contacts are the people who will have access to billing-related sections. Here, you can add people who will be able to see the invoice history.

You can update both contacts via the **Manage Contacts** button accessible at: `https://my.atlassian.com/`

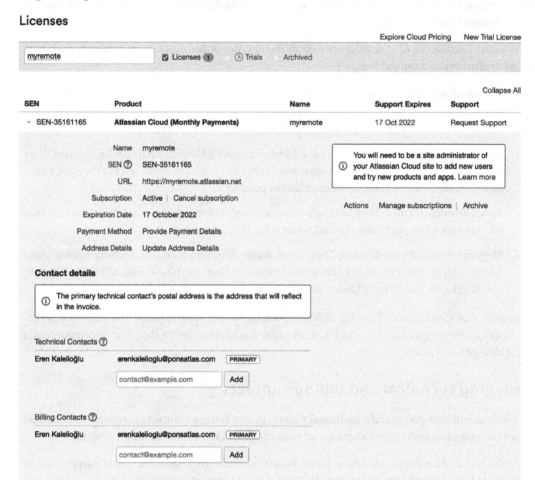

Figure 2.10 – Managing technical and billing contacts

As you can see in the previous image, it is easy to manage the technical and billing contacts for your Atlassian Cloud site. Once you set up the site contact details, their names and email addresses will be visible in the **Billing details** section that you can see in the next screenshot:

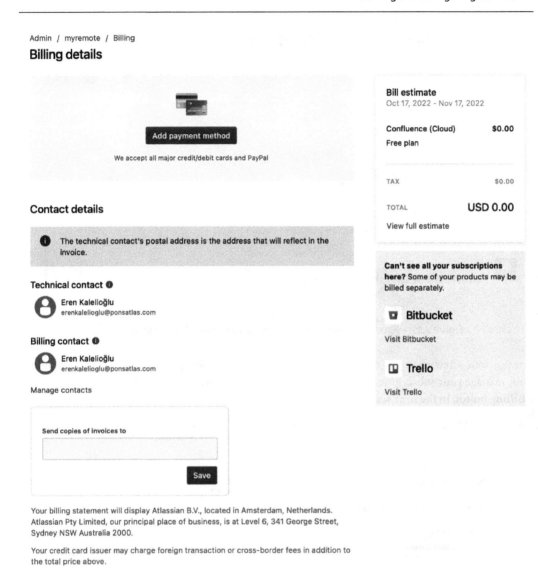

Figure 2.11 – Modifying billing details

As you can see in the previous screenshot, you can send copies of invoices to another address such as that of the accounting department. Here, you can also add a payment method for your monthly or annual subscription.

To access the **Billing** screen, follow these steps:

1. Click on the gear-shaped button in the top-right corner of the screen.

2. In the **Settings** menu, click on the **Billing** button in the **Atlassian Admin** tab.

The **Settings** menu is depicted in the following screenshot:

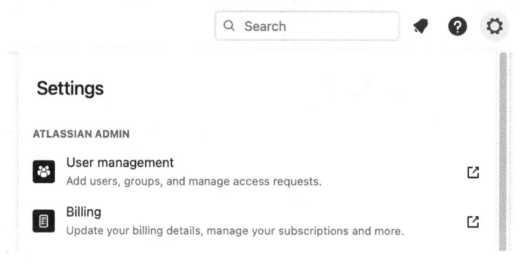

Figure 2.12 – Accessing billing operations through the Atlassian settings

In the previous screenshot, you can see what you can do in the **Billing** section: update your billing details, manage your subscriptions, and more. You can see the interface that opens when you press the **Billing** button in the next screenshot:

Products and apps	Plan	Users	Next price estimate ⓘ	Billing cycle	Next bill date	Actions
Jira Service Management myremote.atlassian.net	Standard	1 / 3		Annual	Jan 17, 2024	Manage
Gliffy Diagrams for Confluence Cloud myremote.atlassian.net		1 / 10		Annual	Jan 17, 2024	Manage
Easy Integrations for Jira Cloud myremote.atlassian.net		1 / 10		Annual	Jan 17, 2024	Manage
Jira Software myremote.atlassian.net	Standard	1 / 10		Annual	Jan 17, 2024	Manage
Jira Work Management myremote.atlassian.net	Standard	0 / 10		Annual	Jan 17, 2024	Manage
Confluence myremote.atlassian.net	Premium	1 / 10		Annual	Jan 17, 2024	Manage

Figure 2.13 – Billing preview

You can see the list of Atlassian applications and plugins installed on your Atlassian site in the interface shown in the previous screenshot. Here, you can access the billing details interface by clicking on the **Manage** button in the Confluence row.

Configuring basic security settings

Atlassian provides an essential part of the security of the system. However, it would be a mistake to assume that the responsibility lies entirely with Atlassian. You can find more detailed information on sharing responsibility later in the book.

When starting Confluence, it is helpful to go through some basic security settings immediately and configure them according to your needs. At Atlassian, there is a security trail from the general to the specific. We will go on this path too. Here, we will configure the general settings that concern the whole system; we'll look at more detailed, pinpointed security settings later in the book.

Configuring the default permissions

Spaces are frequently used concepts in the Confluence ecosystem. All content on Confluence is located within a space. For this reason, we attach great importance to the security of the spaces.

The default settings determine the access settings with which a new space created on Confluence will be activated. After you create a space, you don't want this space to stand up with inappropriate access settings. Although you can change these settings after you create the space, this has many disadvantages in practice. For example, during a busy period, you can forget to adjust the security settings. For this reason, unauthorized people may access the space or take some erroneous actions. If you are deleting, modifying, or exporting content, manually updating these settings will be a waste of time. During this process, users may experience access problems. That's why we set the default settings once, and then we usually never touch them. You can review the **Default Space Permissions** interface in the next screenshot:

Space Permissions

Default Space Permissions   ✎ Edit Permissions

These are the default permissions that will be assigned to groups when someone adds a new space.

	All		Pages			Blog		Comments		Attachments		Restrictions	Mail	Space	
	View	Delete Own [?]	Add	Archive	Delete	Add	Delete	Add	Delete	Add	Delete	Add/Delete	Delete	Export	Admin
confluence-admins-myremote	✓	✓	✓	✗	✓	✓	✓	✓	✓	✓	✓	✓	✓	✓	✓
confluence-users-myremote	✓	✓	✓	✗	✓	✓	✓	✓	✓	✓	✓	✓	✓	✓	✗
site-admins	✓	✓	✓	✗	✓	✓	✓	✓	✓	✓	✓	✓	✓	✓	✓

Figure 2.14 – Viewing default space permissions

In the previous screenshot, you can see the permissions that will be automatically granted to user groups when a new space is created.

The default settings will depend entirely on company policy. Some companies want a new space to be visible to everyone when it is created, while others wish for the new space not to be seen by everyone and for authorizations to be given individually. These companies have strict security policies. Others may be in the middle. Default settings are not just about view permissions; they include settings for deletion, modification, exporting, and so on.

If you want to make changes to the default space permissions, you should click on the **Edit Permissions** button located at the top-right of the screen. In the next screenshot, you can see the interface where you can set the default space permissions:

Space Permissions

Default Space Permissions

These are the default permissions that will be assigned to groups when someone adds a new space.

		All		Pages			Blog		Comments		Attachments		Restrictions	Mail	Space	
		View	Delete Own [?]	Add	Archive	Delete	Add	Delete	Add	Delete	Add	Delete	Add/Delete	Delete	Export	Admin
confluence-admins-myremote	Select All	☑	☑	☑		☑	☑	☑	☑	☑	☑	☑	☑	☑	☑	☑
confluence-users-myremote	Select All	☑	☑	☑		☑	☑	☑	☑	☑	☑	☑	☑	☑	☑	
site-admins	Select All	☑	☑	☑		☑	☑	☑	☑	☑	☑	☑	☑	☑	☑	☑

Grant browse permission to [   ] [Q] [Add]

[Save] Cancel

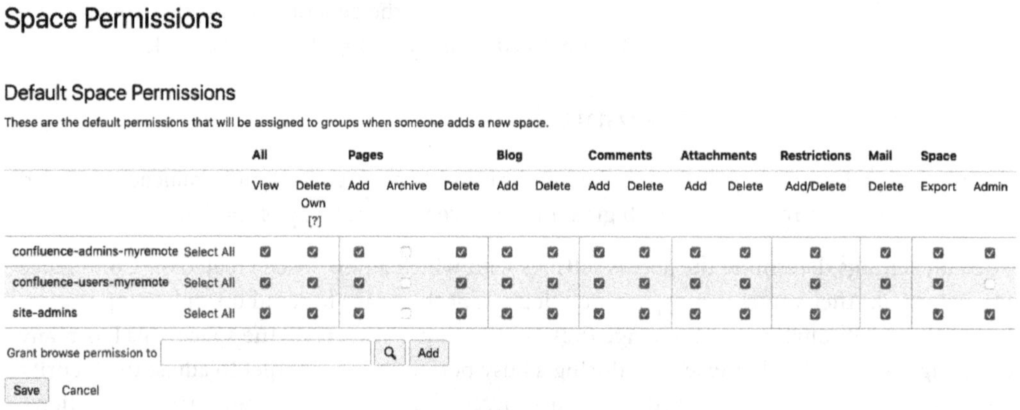

Figure 2.15 – Configuring default space permissions

In the previous screenshot, you can see the permissions you can grant to user groups. This interface is almost identical to the interface where you set space permissions. The only difference is that the settings you make here affect not just a single space, but all spaces that will be created in the future. It is worth noting that the changes you make here do not affect spaces that were created previously.

At this point, we would like to give you an important reminder. Detailed page and space permissions are only available in the Standard and Premium plans. If you cannot adjust these settings, you are probably not on the Premium plan yet. Please make sure that you are on the Premium plan.

The space permissions are explained in the following table:

Content type	Permission	Description
All	View	Users can view all content
	Delete Own	Users can only delete the contents the created
Pages	Add	Users can add new pages
	Archive	Users can archive any page
	Delete	Users can delete any page
Blog	Add	Users can add new blog contents
	Delete	Users can delete any blog content
Comments	Add	Users can add new comments
	Delete	Users can delete any comment
Attachments	Add	Users can add new attachments
	Delete	Users can delete any attachment
Restrictions	Add/Delete	Users can edit page restrictions on all contents
Mail	Delete	This is a legacy permission. Please ignore it.
Space	Export	Users can export all the contents
	Admin	Users can administer the space

Table 2.16 – Definitions of space permissions

We are setting up Confluence for the very first time. Currently, our user management groups still need to be finalized. For this reason, it would be beneficial to come back here once you're done with all user management groups.

One of the most critical questions is: Will anyone with access to Confluence be able to access every created space? The answer is no. You can define granular restrictions on Confluence. Let's learn how to manage them.

Configuring global permissions

To access global permissions, follow these steps:

1. Click on the **Settings** button at the top-right of the screen.
2. In the left menu, click on the **Global permissions** button under the **Security** heading.

You can see the **Global permissions** interface in the next screenshot:

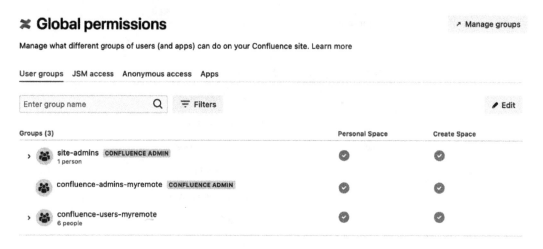

Figure 2.17 – Viewing global permissions

In a moment, we will edit the global permissions that are visible in the previous image. There are four tabs at the top of this interface:

- User groups
- Jira Service Management access
- Anonymous access
- Apps

The first tab contains the global permissions for the user management groups. Global permissions can't be assigned to individual users, only to the group.

You can decide who can create a personal space or a company space. Personal and company spaces are for very different purposes. According to your company policies, you can easily set the global permissions for creating spaces in Confluence. One of the most common scenarios is where everybody can create a personal space, but only some people can generate company spaces. This limitation generally prevents creating spaces unless there is a significant need.

Please be aware that when someone creates a new space, they automatically become an admin for that space.

If you are using Jira Service Management to serve internal or external customers, you can add a helpful knowledge base feature to your system using Confluence. Your customers can access the content prepared from the Jira Service Management interface. As you might expect, these contents are kept on Confluence.

This section on global permissions is precisely about this feature. You provide your customers with access to content on Confluence, even if they do not have Confluence licenses.

The **Global permissions** interface for JSM is depicted in the following screenshot:

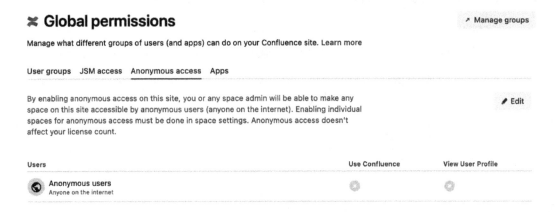

Figure 2.18 – Viewing global permissions for Jira Service Management

You can make some of your Confluence spaces open to everyone. In this way, people who do not have a Confluence license can access your content. In this type of global permission, you can allow spaces to be made open to the world. We recommend that the company policy is determined and implemented immediately.

The **Global permissions** interface for anonymous access is depicted in the following screenshot:

✖ Global permissions

↗ Manage groups

Manage what different groups of users (and apps) can do on your Confluence site. Learn more

User groups   JSM access   Anonymous access   Apps

By enabling anonymous access on this site, you or any space admin will be able to make any space on this site accessible by anonymous users (anyone on the internet). Enabling individual spaces for anonymous access must be done in space settings. Anonymous access doesn't affect your license count.

✎ Edit

Users	Use Confluence	View User Profile
🌐 Anonymous users Anyone on the internet	☼	☼

Figure 2.19 – Viewing global permissions for anonymous access

The last setting of this section is related to applications. Many applications run on Confluence. Some of them are Confluence's applications. Also, there may be applications that you have installed. You can set the permissions of these applications here:

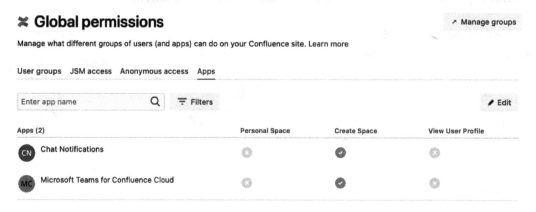

Figure 2.20 – Viewing global permissions for apps

In the previous screenshot, you can see that two applications, **Chat Notifications** and **Microsoft Teams for Confluence Cloud**, have the **Create Space** permission.

Discovering security configuration

Confluence provides an interface to configure the settings for user management, site security, and user privacy. To access the **Edit Security Configuration** interface, follow these steps:

1. Click on the **Settings** button at the top-right of the screen.

2. On the left-side menu, click on the **Security Configuration** button under the **Security** heading.

You may not choose to change the default values of the security settings in this section. However, we recommend that you go through all the settings:

Edit Security Configuration

Security and Privacy   ✎ Edit

Settings for user management, site security and user privacy.

External user management

Disable Confluence's internal user management (for example if you've delegated user management to Jira). More about User Management

✓ Append wildcards to user and group searches

✓ Hide External Links From Search Engines

This helps discourage spammers from posting malicious links by preventing search engines to follow the site. More about External Links

Anonymous Access to Remote API

Enabling this will allow 'anonymous' to access Confluence remotely.

Custom Stylesheets for Spaces

Maximum RSS Items	**200**
	Limit the maximum number of items an RSS Feed can request.
RSS timeout	**60**
	The time in seconds allowed to create each RSS Feed. Any items rendered within the timeout will still be returned.
Page timeout	**120**
	The time in seconds allowed to render the content of each wiki Page. Pages taking longer to render will display a timeout error to the user. The default is 120 seconds.
CAPTCHA on login	✓ Enable
	(After 3 failed login attempts)
Secure administrator sessions	☐ Enable
	Requires Confluence Administrator login to access administration functions. More about Secure Administrator Sessions
Attachment Download Security Policy	**Default: Automatically display attachments inline or prompt to download, based on attachment type and browser settings. This is secure in most environments.**

XSRF Protection   ✎ Edit

Some third-party or deprecated Confluence themes will not work with the new Confluence XSRF protection. You may disable XSRF protection to support old themes at the cost of reducing security. If you turn off any of these settings, your Confluence site is open to XSRF attacks. That means that an attacker could fool any Confluence user into submitting data by simply clicking a link.

✓ Adding Comments

This removes the automatic xsrf check when adding comments. Turn this option off only if you want to use an older theme that does not support this feature.

Figure 2.21 – Editing security configuration

You can review the settings under the **Security and Privacy** heading as seen in the previous screenshot. To change these settings, you should click the **Edit** button in the top-right. We will examine the security settings in more detail in the security-related chapter of our book. However, we still want to explain some of the settings here:

- **Maximum RSS items**: You can limit the maximum number of items an RSS feed can request.

- **RSS timeout**: This is the time in seconds that is allowed to create each RSS feed. Any items rendered within the timeout will still be returned.

- **Page timeout**: You can set the time in seconds that is allowed to render the content of each wiki page. Pages taking longer to render will display a timeout error to the user. The default is 120 seconds.

- **CAPTCHA on login**: You can set the maximum number of failed login attempts before enabling CAPTCHA.

- **Hide external links from search engines**: You can prevent spammers from posting malicious links by preventing search engines from following the site.

- **Anonymous access to remote API**: You can disable anonymous users from accessing Confluence remotely.

Accessing the General Configuration section

It's time to discover the configuration options available within Confluence. These configurations may not be needed at the beginning of your Confluence journey, but you will surely need to come back here to adapt Confluence to your company's needs.

Formatting and international settings

You can modify formatting and international settings by accessing the following:

Settings > Configuration > General Configuration > Formatting and International Settings

You can customize the time and date formatting on your Confluence site:

Formatting and International Settings   Edit

You can change the default language for the Confluence interface on the language configuration page These options relate to the time and date formatting on the site. Unless you are sure of what you are doing, we recommend that you leave these as they are.

> ⓘ   Temporarily, currently only sysadmin can change indexing language and reindex all documents. Contact Atlassian Support if you need help.

Indexing Language	**English**
Encoding	**UTF-8**
Time Format	**h:mm a**
Date Time Format	**MMM dd, yyyy HH:mm**
Date Format	**MMM dd, yyyy**
Long Number Format	**###############**
Decimal Number Format	**###############.##########**

Figure 2.22 – Viewing formatting and international settings

As you can see in the previous screenshot, you can easily edit formatting and international settings for your Confluence environment. Please be careful when modifying these settings, because they will affect every user on your Confluence site.

Configuring attachment settings

You can configure the attachment settings by accessing the following:

Settings > Configuration > General Configuration > Attachment Settings

The **Attachment Settings** interface is displayed as follows:

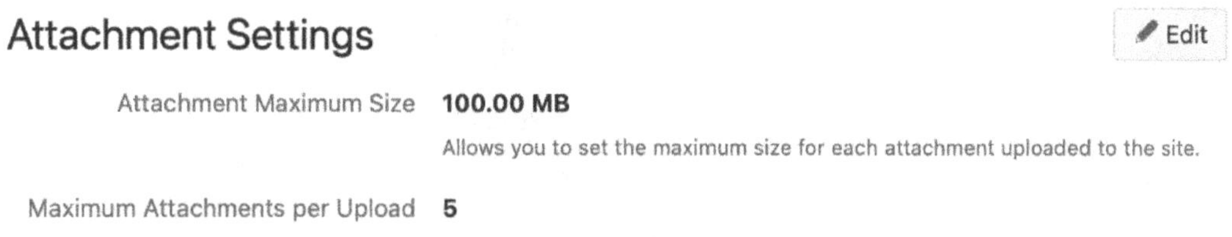

Attachment Settings

        ✏ Edit

Attachment Maximum Size   **100.00 MB**

Allows you to set the maximum size for each attachment uploaded to the site.

Maximum Attachments per Upload   **5**

Figure 2.23 – Attachment settings

As you can see in the previous screenshot, Confluence gives you the ability to set the maximum size for each attachment uploaded to the site and the maximum number of attachments per upload.

Setting the default language

You can set the default language for your Confluence site by accessing the following:

Settings > Configuration > Language

The **Language** interface is displayed as follows:

Language Configuration

Set the default language for this Confluence instance.

Global Default Language

Installed Languages

čeština (Česko)
dansk (Danmark)
Deutsch (Deutschland)
eesti (Eesti)
English (UK)
English (US)
español (España)
français (France)
íslenska (Ísland)
italiano (Italia)
magyar (Magyarország)
Nederlands (Nederland)
norsk (Norge)
polski (Polska)
português (Brasil)
română (România)
slovenčina (Slovensko)
suomi (Suomi)
svenska (Sverige)
Türkçe (Türkiye)
русский (Россия)
中文 (台灣)
中文 (中国)
日本語 (日本)
한국어 (대한민국)

Edit

Figure 2.24 – Language configuration

Modifying the site logo and the favicon

You can change your Confluence site logo and title by accessing the following:

Settings > Look and Feel > Site Logo and Favicon.

The interface is displayed as follows:

Site Logo

You can change your site logo and title here.

Site title	Our company
Site logo	Choose File no file selected
	The height of the logo image will be constrained to a maximum of 48 px.
Options	○ Show logo only
	◉ Show logo and title
	Save

Figure 2.25 – Setting site title and logo

In the interface shown in the previous screenshot, if you enter a name for your site (for example, your company's name) and press the **Save** button, your company's name will always be visible on your site to all users. The title is helpful if you regularly work on different Confluence sites. The site title will be displayed as follows:

Figure 2.26 – Site title

In the previous screenshot, you can see that **Our company** is located immediately to the right of the **Confluence** button in the menu at the top of the screen. If you have access to multiple Confluence sites, this phrase will help you identify at a glance which Confluence site you are working on.

Discovering further configurations

You can access the **Further Configuration** interface by accessing the following:

Settings > Configuration > Further Configuration

There are some other settings in this section that we'll go over. You might need to change their default settings only.

By default, Confluence emails a copy of notifications to users. It's up to you to turn it off. Some companies may want to turn off email notifications for security reasons. Companies that only receive notifications through Slack may also want to turn this option off. A similar restriction can be made for push notifications sent to mobile applications.

Sometimes, you may also want to avoid likes or reactions on any content (page, comment, etc.) on Confluence. In this case, you can disable this feature.

The following screenshot displays the **Further Configuration** interface:

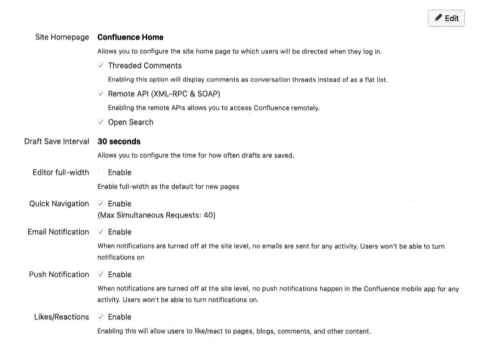

Figure 2.27 – Further configuration

We have installed Confluence and configured its basic settings. Now, it's time to discuss managing users.

Managing users

In this section, we will share the main principles of user management; then, we will immediately move on to practical applications.

Users will be among the most dynamic components of this system. The reasons for this are as follows:

- New users arrive
- Users leave
- Some users' teams and roles change
- User needs change
- Company rules change

The system we will establish must be capable of responding to all this dynamism. In addition to this feature, the system we will install should allow the following:

- We should be able to easily make and maintain authorization according to teams, groups, and individuals. We should be able to ensure data security and privacy easily.
- When designing user management, it is always necessary to foresee. Of course, the current structure of the team is fundamental. However, when anticipating the changes the team may undergo and expectations from Confluence, we must design a sustainable user management system. Otherwise, we may hesitate making the slightest change in the system.
- With any access problem, we should be able to trace it easily and get to the root cause of the problem quickly.
- We should be able to distribute user management to different types of administrators. We should leave as little work as possible to the primary manager of Confluence, especially the site and organization managers.

We will now include users in the system. At this point, users may be in one of the following three categories:

- People who have never had an Atlassian account before
- People who have used an Atlassian product before and have an Atlassian ID
- People with a managed Atlassian ID

We will focus on the first two types of users here. Managed accounts with an identity provider service will be explained in detail later.

Here, we will invite users to Confluence:

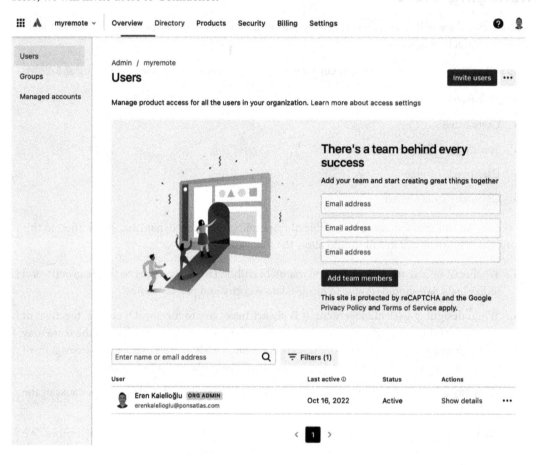

Figure 2.28 – Accessing the list of users

The following screenshot shows how you can easily invite users:

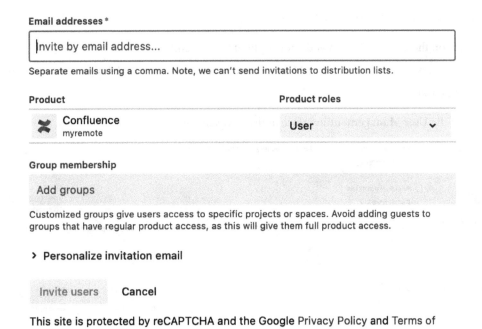

Invite people to myremote

Invite teammates to collaborate and use products in your organization. We'll ask new users to enter their personal details when they sign up.

Email addresses *

Invite by email address...

Separate emails using a comma. Note, we can't send invitations to distribution lists.

Product   Product roles

Confluence   User   ⌄
myremote

Group membership

Add groups

Customized groups give users access to specific projects or spaces. Avoid adding guests to groups that have regular product access, as this will give them full product access.

> Personalize invitation email

Invite users   Cancel

This site is protected by reCAPTCHA and the Google Privacy Policy and Terms of Service apply.

Figure 2.29 – Inviting users to Confluence

To invite users to the system, you must complete the following fields:

- **Email addresses**: Enter the email addresses of the users you invite. This field is required.

- **Product**: You determine what type of user this group will have and in which product. For example, in the previous screenshot, this group has a Confluence license and only user (not admin) rights.

- **Group memberships**: You can assign a group when inviting the user. This field is not required and can be filled in later.

- **Personalize invitation email**: You can customize the invitation email that will be sent to the user.

Managing user groups

To manage user groups, follow the subsequent steps:

1. Click on the **Settings** button at the top-right of the screen.

2. In the left menu, click on the **User Management** button under the **Site Administration** heading.

3. Click **Groups**.

You can see the **User Management** interface in the next screenshot:

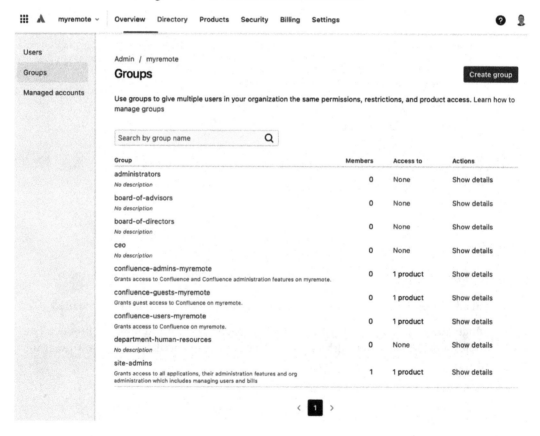

Figure 2.30 – Managing user groups

You can view the list of all groups as shown in the screenshot. You can also see the number of people in each group, the number of products the group has access to, and other details.

When determining user group names, a naming standard is necessary. Otherwise, you may not find what you are looking for and managing user groups can become tricky.

To edit a group's name, follow the subsequent steps:

1. Click **Show details** to the right of a group name.

2. Click the **...** button at the top-right of the screen.

3. Enter the group's new name.

4. Click **Save Changes**.

The **Edit group name** dialog is shown in the following screenshot:

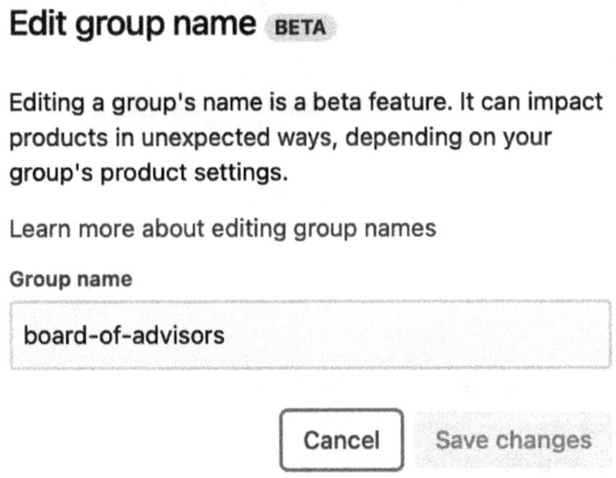

Edit group name BETA

Editing a group's name is a beta feature. It can impact products in unexpected ways, depending on your group's product settings.

Learn more about editing group names

Group name

board-of-advisors

Cancel   Save changes

Figure 2.31 – Edit group name

As you can see in the preceding screenshot, editing a group's name is a beta feature. It can impact products in unexpected ways, depending on your group's product settings.

The **Create group** interface will be displayed as follows:

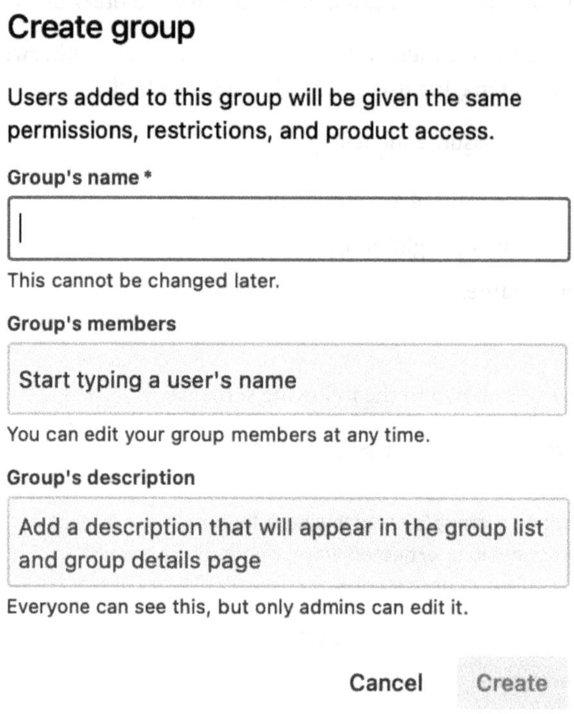

Create group

Users added to this group will be given the same permissions, restrictions, and product access.

Group's name *

This cannot be changed later.

Group's members

Start typing a user's name

You can edit your group members at any time.

Group's description

Add a description that will appear in the group list and group details page

Everyone can see this, but only admins can edit it.

Cancel   Create

Figure 2.32 – Creating a user group

When creating a new group, you can enter three pieces of information:

- **Group's name**: Specify the name of the group.

- **Group's members**: If you wish, specify the group members when creating the group. You can also do this later.

- **Group's description**: We recommend you write the group's purpose in this field. We recommend that you do so carefully and without leaving it blank. This way, you can manage user groups more easily.

Setting up spaces – team, project, company, and personal

In this section, we will increase our knowledge about Confluence spaces. Then, without going into too much detail, we will learn how to create four different kinds of spaces with specific purposes. The following sections will cover the details of configuring settings and creating content.

What spaces should you create?

Any content you create or bring together on Confluence must be in a space. You will have many spaces that serve different purposes according to your company's needs.

As a result of your studies in information architecture, you can have a prominent list of spaces. In some cases (especially if yours is a small company), there may not be enough content to accommodate domains early in the process; however, it is helpful to foresee and open these spaces at the beginning of the process.

What is the life cycle of a domain?

During the work of information architecture, it becomes clear in which cases you need to open a new space. You can create a new space when a new project starts, a new team is formed, or a new employee joins the company. Also, new spaces are created, when necessary, in line with the rules of your company, and the number of active spaces on Confluence increases.

Once a need is met, it is necessary to close the related space. Otherwise, Confluence can turn into a chaotic environment in a short time. Here are a few examples:

- You can close a personal space when an employee leaves your company
- You can close a project space when the related project is completed
- You can close a team space when the connected team is dismissed

So, what does it mean to close a space? It usually happens in one of three different ways:

- The space is frozen. In other words, no changes are allowed to be made to the content of the space. In this way, people who want can access the content in the space, but they cannot make any changes in it.
- The space can be archived, so the content of the space is not lost, but is accessible when necessary. It is also hidden from most users. In this way, Confluence can be kept more organized.
- The space can be deleted completely.

Although the spaces we will create will serve very different purposes, they have many standard features because they are all typical Confluence spaces, and all use the same infrastructure.

In this section, you will repeat the same operations several times to create the spaces. This way, you will have your company's first spaces and gain practice in the process.

The spaces we will create are as follows:

- Team space
- Project space
- Company space
- Personal space

In this section, we will create the spaces and configure the basic settings. We will leave the details until later in the book.

We create all spaces in much the same way. For this reason, we will explain how to create a space once. We expect you to then apply what you learn here as you create the other three spaces.

Follow the **Spaces** > **Create a space** path from the menu at the top of the screen to create a new space:

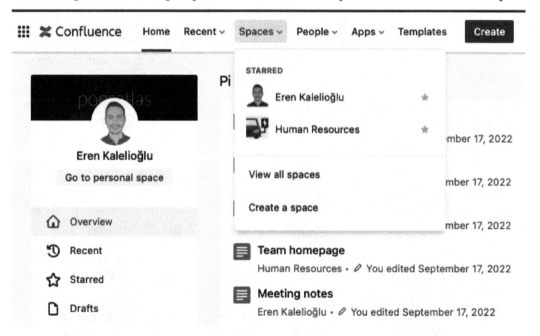

Figure 2.33 – Discovering the Spaces menu item

As seen in the preceding figure, you can easily access the basic operations related to the spaces from the top menu.

First, we want to create a team space. Therefore, select a space template to get started quickly. This interface is shown in the next screenshot:

Figure 2.34 – Creating a new space

In the preceding screenshot, you can see Confluence's **Create a new space** interface. There are more than ten different space templates here. You can choose the one you want, or you can opt for a blank space template. Remember that these are just the starting points to save you time. You can customize your space according to your preferences.

To continue adding details to your space, first select your template and then click **Next**. You will have to add some details, as shown in the next screenshot:

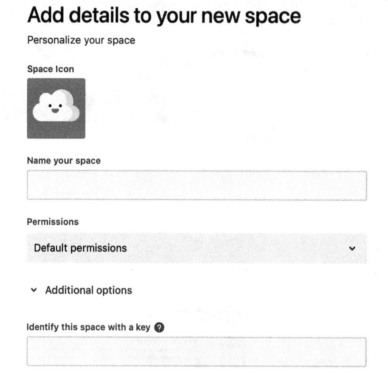

Figure 2.35 – Adding details to your new space

As shown in the preceding screenshot, there are four fields that need your input:

- **Space icon**: You can choose an icon from a library or upload an image.

- **Name your space**: We recommend giving a name that is easy to understand and according to a specific rule. This way, you can easily distinguish all space names from each other and ensure consistency.

- **Permissions**: Here, you can define the visibility of the space.

- **Identify this space with a key**: We recommend entering a unique character string that conforms to a specific standard. For example, you may prefer to use the TeamAlpha or TeamBeta format so that it is immediately recognizable as a team space.

Note that the space's key cannot be changed once the space is created. This key will appear on the space's URL as a unique identifier.

If you decide to customize your space key, remember that the following applies to each one:

- It must be unique

- It can contain any alphanumeric characters (a-z, 0-9)

- It can be up to 255 characters long

Let's examine the space permissions, as shown in the next screenshot:

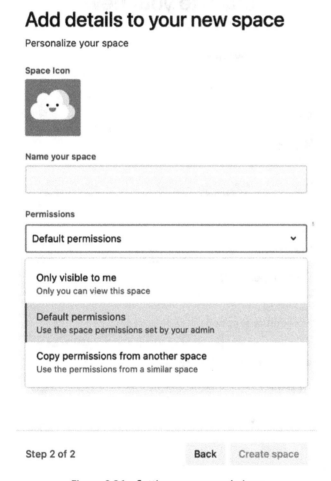

Figure 2.36 – Setting space permissions

As shown in the preceding screenshot, there are three choices for the **Permissions** field:

- **Only visible to me:** You can usually choose this setting in personal spaces. Only you can see this space.

- **Default permissions**: You can use the default space permissions we set up in the previous sections of this chapter.

- **Copy permissions from another space**: You can use permissions from another space here. For example, this setting can save you much time if you are creating all your team spaces one after the other. You can configure the privileges of the first team space as you wish; you can then clone these settings when creating the subsequent team spaces.

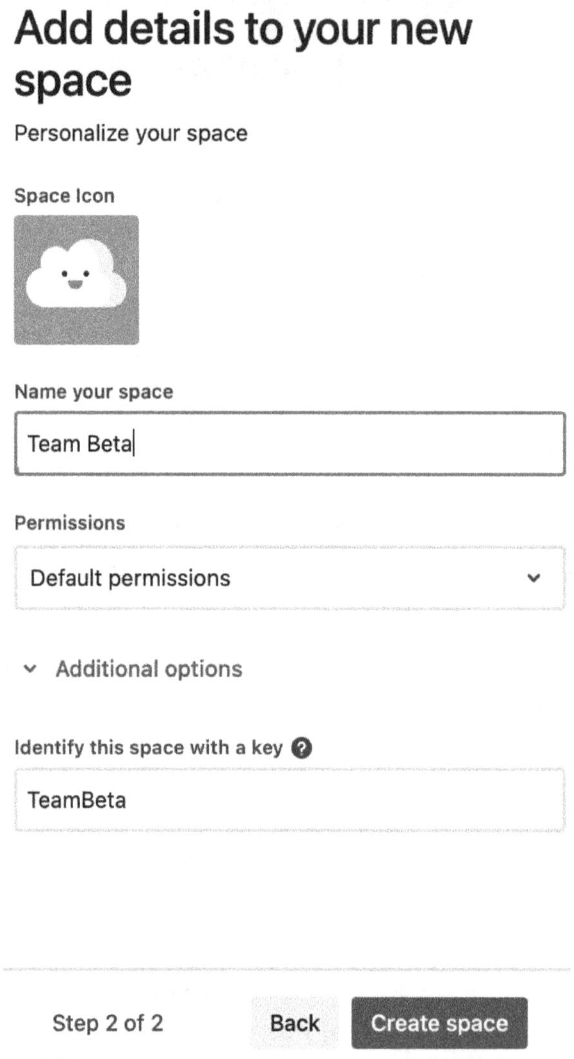

Add details to your new space

Personalize your space

Space Icon

Name your space

Team Beta

Permissions

Default permissions   ⌄

⌄   Additional options

Identify this space with a key ❓

TeamBeta

Step 2 of 2   Back   Create space

Figure 2.37 – Configuring the parameters of the space to be created

As you can see, we've filled in the basic information about the team space we will create using the preceding suggestions.

We will review the space settings in detail in the following sections. However, we want to proceed here with setting the space category. We will assign categories according to the space types we have created.

We recommend that you assign a category to each space you create. The categories are listed in the following table:

Space scope	Category
Company wide	company
Team	personal
Project	project
Personal	personal

Table 2.38 – Space categories

In the preceding table, you can see the category names you can use for spaces that serve different purposes.

Go to **Space Settings** > **Manage Space** > **Space details** to define the space category, as shown in the next screenshot:

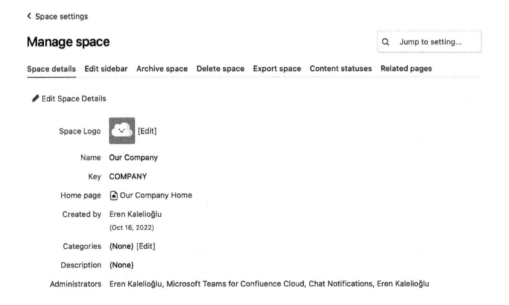

Figure 2.39 – Managing a space

As you can see in the preceding image, this space does not currently have any category assigned. Therefore, press the **Edit** button in the **Categories** section to assign a category to this space:

Figure 2.40 – Edit space categories

Space categories will appear inside the **Categories** tab on your dashboard and as tabs in the space directory. They can be used to group together related spaces.

To see all the spaces we have created in an organized manner, follow the **Spaces** > **View all spaces** path from the menu at the top of the screen:

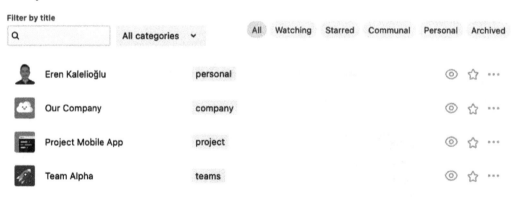

Figure 2.41 – Accessing spaces list

As you can see, we've created four spaces and determined the categories of each.

Summary

We recommend careful planning to establish a robust, secure, and flexible Confluence environment. This chapter presents the information architecture concept, providing transparent processes, checklists, and tips to assist you in your planning journey. You can now iteratively plan and build a Confluence environment from the ground up and set up the fundamental spaces for letting your teams collaborate remotely on Confluence.

In the next chapter, we will cover the core features of Confluence that will help you easily navigate within your collaboration environment. We will also discuss how to create and maintain dynamic content.

Questions

1. What is information architecture, and why does it matter?

2. What is a Confluence space, and how can it be used?

3. Explain the different types of administrators in Confluence.

4. Explain the technical contact role and the billing contact role.

5. What are the purposes of user management groups?

Answers

1. It's the discipline that focuses on the organization of information. You can build a better knowledge management system on Confluence with the help of information architecture.

2. Spaces are used to store and organize content within Confluence.

3. Space administrator, Confluence administrator, site administrator, and organization administrator.

4. Technical contacts are the people who will seek support directly from Atlassian. The primary technical contact's address information (including VAT) will appear on your invoices. Billing contacts are the people who will have access to billing-related sections. Here, you can add people who can see the invoice history.

5. It's easier to configure permissions with the use of user management groups.

Further reading

- `https://support.atlassian.com/confluence-cloud/docs/what-are-confluence-cloud-permissions-and-restrictions/`

- `https://support.atlassian.com/confluence-cloud/docs/what-are-space-permissions/`

- `https://support.atlassian.com/confluence-cloud/docs/assign-space-permissions/`

- `https://support.atlassian.com/confluence-cloud/docs/manage-global-permissions/.`

- `https://support.atlassian.com/confluence-cloud/docs/what-is-a-confluence-group/`

- `https://support.atlassian.com/user-management/docs/create-and-update-groups/`

- `https://www.atlassian.com/software/confluence/guides/get-started/set-up#step-5`

- `https://support.atlassian.com/confluence-cloud/docs/choose-a-space-key/`

3

Creating and Organizing Content

In the previous chapter, we looked at how to set up a Confluence environment. Now, we will cover **pages**, **attachments**, and other core features of Confluence that will help you quickly navigate within your collaboration environment. We will concentrate on every part of the Confluence **New Editor** area in this chapter. We will discuss how to create and maintain dynamic content and present practical collaboration examples on Confluence. By the end of this chapter, we'll be ready to create and organize content with Confluence.

We will cover the following topics in this chapter:

- Finding your way in Confluence
- Managing content
- Organizing content

Technical requirements

You will need the following software requirements to complete this chapter:

- An up-to-date web browser
- An active subscription to Confluence Cloud Premium

Finding your way in Confluence

Our goal here is to get to know the basic features and the interface of Confluence practically so that we can use this tool effectively. In this section, we'll talk about many text-processing features from other software you might be familiar with. We want to underline an important point: Confluence is a collaboration tool with powerful text-processing features. However, its main feature is not text processing. For this reason, you may realize that many features available in text processors are not in Confluence. Being aware that these features may have been left out on purpose can significantly increase the efficiency we get from Confluence. We aim to work together; hundreds of fonts, colors, and very detailed formatting features can easily distract us from this goal, and we can get lost in the details. That's why you'll find only the most essential features in Confluence; this simplicity. Although you may find it strange, this will allow you to focus on the content, communication, and teamwork so that you have less of a problem when working on the content as a team.

Discovering the global navigation bar

First, you'll need to master the navigation bar at the top of your screen. This bar is always visible, and that's why it is called the global navigation bar:

Figure 3.1 – Confluence navigation bar

As you can see, there are eight buttons on the navigation bar: the app switcher (the icon with nine squares at the left of the Confluence text), **Home**, **Recent**, **Spaces**, **People**, **Apps**, **Templates**, and **Create**.

Let's discover each button:

- **App switcher**: On the far left of the screen is a button consisting of nine small squares. With this button, you can switch between Atlassian products: Confluence, Jira, Bitbucket, and others.

- **Home**: Go to your Confluence home.

- **Recent**: You can easily access recent pages via this button. The available options are all pages, the pages you worked on, pages created by you, starred pages, and drafts.

- **Spaces**: You can browse existing spaces or create a new space.

- **People**: You can access your teams, invite a teammate, create a new team, and search for people and teams.

- **Apps**: You can access the applications installed on Confluence, Calendars, and Analytics. The options are **Your apps**, **Recommended apps**, **Find new apps**, **Manage apps**, and **View app requests**.

- **Templates**: You can discover the templates installed on Confluence.

- **Create**: You can create a new page.

Finding content within Confluence

Confluence has powerful searching capabilities. The search bar is located at the top right of the navigation area. There are two types of search tools in Confluence: quick and advanced. Here is a useful keyboard shortcut – press / on your keyboard to open the searcher:

Figure 3.2 – Quick search

As you can see, you can effortlessly search within Confluence and other Atlassian cloud products such as Jira and Bitbucket.

Confluence proposes recent pages, spaces, and other content when you select the search field.

Sometimes, you will need more powerful search capabilities to find what you are looking for, and that's where **Advanced Search** comes in.

There are two ways to access **Advanced Search**:

- Select the search field in the navigation bar and press the *Return* or *Enter* key on your keyboard.

- Select the search field in the navigation and click **Advanced Search**:

Find what you need in Confluence

Pro tip: Use Confluence search syntax (like operators) to further customize your search

Figure 3.3 – Advanced Search

As you can see, you can effectively search within Confluence using multiple filters.

Confluence search syntax

You can use the Confluence search syntax to focus your search. Here are some examples:

- To search results with an exact match, input " " – for example, `"hello world"`

- To search for content that contains the term "world" or "moon," use the `OR` operator in capital letters – for example, `world OR moon`

- To search for content that contains both the terms "world" and "mars," use the `AND` operator in capital letters – for example, `world AND mars`

- To search for content that contains "world" but *not* "virus," use the `NOT` operator in capital letters – for example, `world NOT virus`

- To search for content that must contain "atmosphere" but can contain either "mars" or "moon," use brackets to group the search terms – for example, `(mars OR moon) AND atmosphere`

- To perform a single-character wildcard search, use the `?` symbol – for example, `monda?`

- To perform a multiple-character wildcard search, use the `*` symbol – for example, `m**day`

Discovering the Home page

When launching Confluence, you can use the **Home** page feature as your starting point.

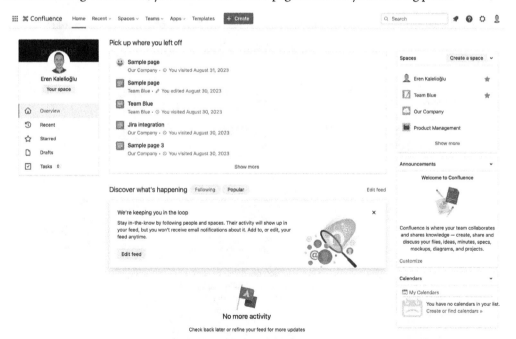

Figure 3.4 – Confluence Home page

As you can see, the **Home** page has different sections: **Pick up where you left off**, **Discover what's happening**, following spaces, **Spaces**, **Calendars**, and **Announcements**.

Now that we've reviewed the **Home** page on Confluence, it's time to talk about the space sidebar, which is located to the left of the screen.

Discovering the space sidebar

The space sidebar, as shown in the following screenshot, helps you navigate within a specific space:

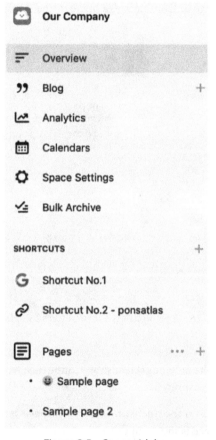

Figure 3.5 – Space sidebar

Let's discuss each button on the space sidebar shown in the previous screenshot:

- **Overview**: Click here to go to the space home page
- **Blog**: Click here to access blog posts
- **Analytics**: Click here to access space analytics

- **Calendars**: Click here to access space calendars, add a new calendar, or add an existing calendar
- **Space Settings**: Click here to access the space settings
- **Bulk Archive**: Click here to archive multiple pages at once
- **SHORTCUTS**: Add shortcuts to the sidebar
- **Pages**: All of your pages will be located here
- **Archived pages**: Click here to access the archived pages

We can add a shortcut to any page in Confluence or any external resources by pasting its link and (optional) display name:

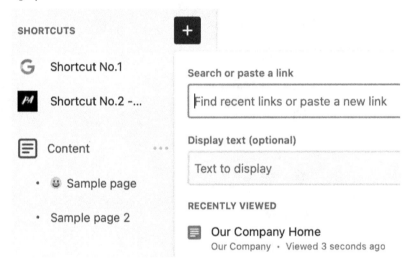

Figure 3.6 – Adding a new shortcut to the sidebar

You can add a new shortcut to the sidebar by pressing the + button on the right-hand side of the **Shortcuts** section. As shown in the previous screenshot, Confluence will offer you the chance to add your most recently visited pages as shortcuts.

You can hide some of the buttons on the sidebar by accessing **Space settings** | **Manage space** | **Edit sidebar**. The **Edit sidebar** interface is shown in the following screenshot:

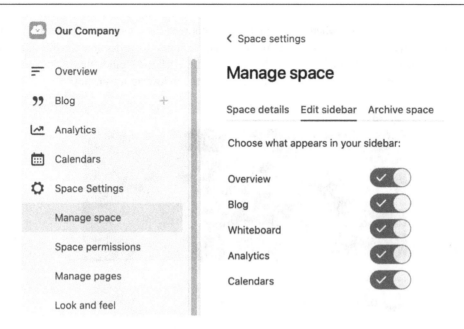

Figure 3.7 – Edit sidebar

Now that we've discussed how to find our way in Confluence, we are ready to think about how we can manage content.

Managing content

In Confluence, almost all content resides on pages, so it's essential to understand how to manage pages. Let's cover each function available to manage a Confluence page.

Discovering the differences between edit mode and view mode

There are two different content modes on Confluence:

- Edit mode
- View mode

When you visit a page on Confluence, view mode is activated by default, which will help you interact with the content on the page.

You need to switch to edit mode when changing the page's content. Press the pencil-shaped edit button from the menu above to switch to edit mode. You can make changes to the document while edit mode is active. After you've finished making your changes, you can click the **Update** button located at the top right. The fields that need your attention are shown in the following screenshot:

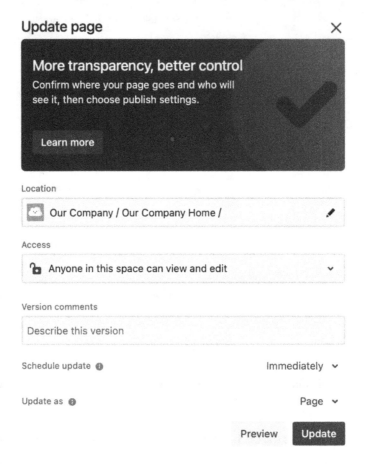

Figure 3.8 – The Update page dialog

Confluence will ask you to confirm where your page goes and who will see it. It's highly recommended that you describe the version for important pages.

You can update your page immediately or you can schedule the publication.

And finally, you have to publish your content as a page or as a blog post.

Click **Update** to publish the page. In this way, the most up-to-date version of the page, including all the changes you have made, can be seen in view mode.

You can also make changes later and choose not to publish the page. In this case, you can close the document by clicking the **Close** button. While in view mode, your most recent changes won't be visible. But don't worry – your current changes won't be lost or visible in view mode. It would be best if you switched back to edit mode to see these changes. You can revoke or publish the changed content later.

Confluence's interface changes quite a bit depending on the currently active mode. So, the buttons that appear in edit mode are drastically different from what you'll see in view mode.

Mastering view mode

The purpose of view mode is to display the content on the page in the most effective way. Any feature that does not serve this purpose will be turned off. You may view the document from a computer, tablet, or mobile phone. The entire interface is optimized for the best viewing experience.

This mode is similar to read-only mode, which is common in other software but not precisely the same. In this mode, the page is not inactive; therefore, you can interact with the content. We will get into the details of this later in this book.

When you look at a page in view mode, what you see will vary depending on your current device and browser settings. The interface adapts.

In this section, we will look at the components of view mode and what you can do while in it.

The following screenshot shows what a newly created Confluence page looks like in view mode:

Our Company

Sample page 3

Owned by Eren Kalelioğlu ···
Last updated: just a moment ago · 1 min read · 📈 1 person viewed

In Atlassian Confluence Cloud, there are different types of administrators, each with their own set of permissions and capabilities:

Site Administrators: They have the highest level of permissions and can manage global settings across all Atlassian products in the cloud instance (e.g., Jira, Confluence, etc.). They can manage users and groups, billing and subscriptions, and other site-wide settings.

Confluence Administrators: They have administrative rights specifically for Confluence. They can manage spaces, global permissions, and configure Confluence settings, but they don't have access to site-wide settings or other Atlassian products.

Space Administrators: They have administrative rights for a specific Confluence space. They can manage pages, permissions, and settings for that space only.

Organization Administrators: They can manage Atlassian accounts, security settings, and domain verification for the entire organization, but they don't have administrative rights in Confluence or any other Atlassian product unless explicitly granted.

my-first-label ×   my-second-label ×   sample-label-01 ×   sample-label-02 ×   + Add label

😊 Be the first to add a reaction

Write a comment...

Figure 3.9 – A page in view mode

As you can see, view mode consists of multiple sections:

- Menu section
- Header section
- Main section
- Bottom section

Let's take a closer look at each section.

Menu section

You can interact with your page using various features accessible via the menu at the top right of the page's content:

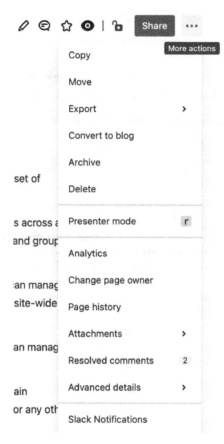

Figure 3.10 – Menu available in view mode

As you can see, the menu in view mode has many features. We'll briefly cover each component from left to right and then from top to bottom.

Status

Here, you can see the status of your page. Please note that the page's status can only be modified in edit mode.

Edit mode

You can enable edit mode by pressing the edit button (in the form of a pencil). This button will only be available if you have edit permission for this space and for this page.

You can enable edit mode by using the *e* keyboard shortcut.

Show inline comments

Here, areas that contain inline comments are highlighted. These comments are not visible by default in view mode, and you must click these highlighted areas to see inline comments behind them.

You also have another option to make inline comments visible. To do this, click the **Inline Comments** button:

Figure 3.11 – Showing inline comments on a Confluence page

As you can see, there are two inline comments on this page. By clicking the **Show inline comments** button, you can easily make them visible.

Star this page

You can put a star on a page to quickly go back to it without searching for it later or using browser bookmarks. Starring a page has other benefits, which will be covered later.

Watching/unwatching a page

Some pages are more important than others. You will want to discover what's happening on these pages quickly via comments, replies, mentions, modifications, and task assignments.

You can mark a page as watched or unwatched by clicking the eye-shaped watching button. When you start watching a page, you will receive updates about changes made to this page:

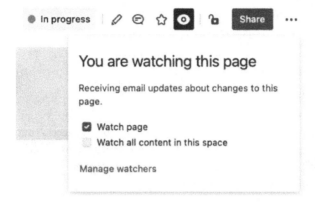

Figure 3.12 – Watching a page or a space

As you can see, you can manage the watchers of a page if you have permission to do so. To do this, click the **Manage watchers** button.

It is possible to watch an entire space by checking **Watch all content in this space**. You'll receive email updates about all changes to this space when you watch it.

Restrictions

You can set view and edit restrictions on a Confluence page. This way, you can precisely define who can view and edit your page:

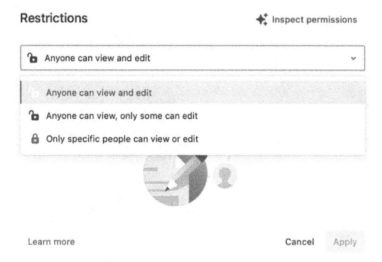

Figure 3.13 – Restricting viewers and editors of a page

As you can see, there are three options:

- **Anyone can view and edit**
- **Anyone can view, only some can edit**
- **Only specific people can view or edit**

You can precisely define the users and groups who can view and edit a page here.

At some point, you may have many pages in Confluence, with many restrictions on them. Sometimes, you will encounter access problems related to the page restrictions. People will be complaining about not being able to access the content. You will also have people who can access confidential information, even if they are not allowed to access it. You must troubleshoot these access problems effectively without disturbing people's work. At this point, you'll need a systematic way to troubleshoot the case. This is where the **Inspect permissions** feature comes in, which will help you determine whether someone is allowed on a page:

Figure 3.14 – Inspecting page permissions for troubleshooting

As you can see, you can search for different types of permissions (view and edit) for a user.

Share

You can share a page with a user, a group, a team, or even an email account. Confluence will send an email to recipients, including the page's title and, optionally, your message.

You can copy the link to this page via the **Copy link** button:

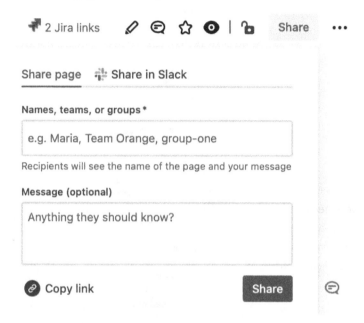

Figure 3.15 – Sharing a page with teammates

As you can see, you can customize the notification message that's sent to recipients by adding a message.

More actions

At the very end of the menu bar, there's a button marked with ... (three dots) that will present you with more features. The **More actions** section is shown in the following screenshot:

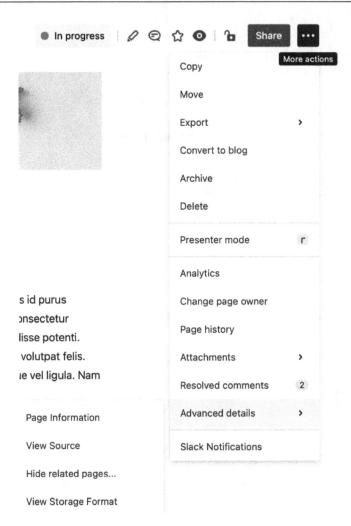

Figure 3.16 – More actions

As we can see, there are several operations here:

- **Copy**
- **Move**
- **Export** (to Word, to PDF)
- **Convert to blog**
- **Archive**
- **Delete**

- **Presenter mode**
- **Analytics**
- **Change page owner**
- **Page history**
- **Attachments** (files, custom contents)
- **Resolved comments**
- **Advanced details** (page information, view source, hide related pages, view storage format)
- **Slack Notifications**

Depending on the permissions you have on the space, you may not be able to see all the buttons here.

In this section, we will briefly cover each action.

Copy

You can easily duplicate a page with this button, and you should give the copied page a unique title.

Move

You can move a page to another location with the help of the **Move** button. You can also change the parent page of your page:

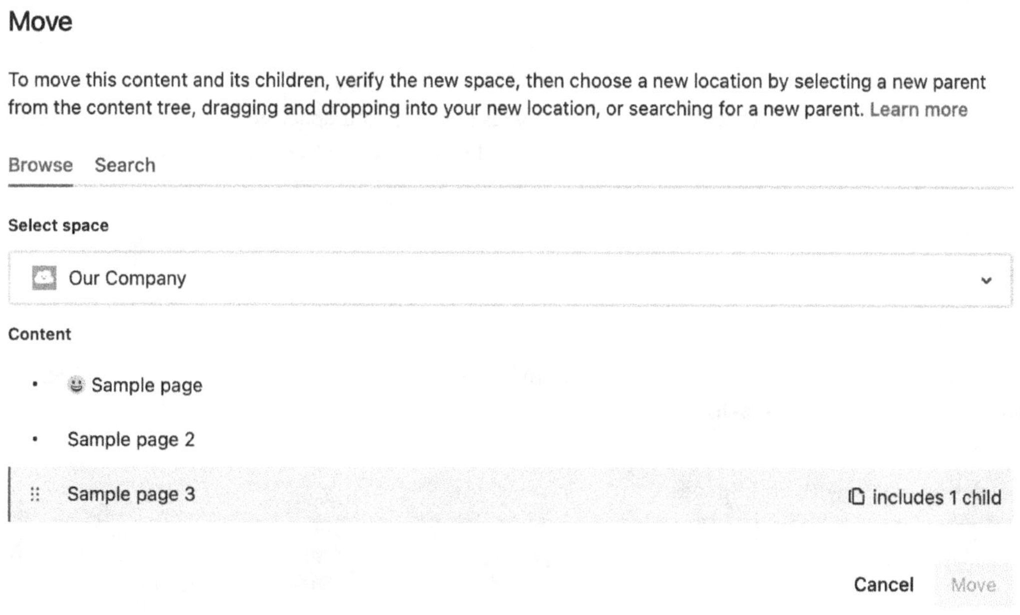

Move

To move this content and its children, verify the new space, then choose a new location by selecting a new parent from the content tree, dragging and dropping into your new location, or searching for a new parent. Learn more

Browse   Search

Select space

🖼 Our Company	⌄

Content

- 😊 Sample page
- Sample page 2
- ⠿ Sample page 3   📄 includes 1 child

Cancel   Move

Figure 3.17 – Moving a page to another location

As you can see, moving a page to another space is possible.

Export

You can easily export a Confluence page into different formats:

- Microsoft Word
- PDF

You can customize the exporting options here.

Convert to blog

There are two types of pages in Confluence:

- Standard pages
- Blog pages

Standard pages and blog pages have many features in common. However, they are different and were created for other purposes. We'll cover blog posts in detail later.

Typically, you should explicitly create blog pages. Sometimes, you'll need to convert a standard page into a blog post. This is why we need the **Convert to blog** feature, which allows you to easily convert a page into a blog post without the need to copy the content of the source page into a newly created blog post.

Archive

One of the most critical use cases of archiving a page is keeping your space clean and up-to-date, by making outdated or inaccurate content invisible from the page tree an the quick search.

You can always find archived pages via the **Archived pages** section.

Delete

You can delete a page if you are sure you won't need it later.

Deleted pages are stored in the space's trash and can be restored. You can find trash by going to **Space settings | Manage pages | Trash**.

> **Deleting a page with child pages**
> Child pages are not deleted when you delete their parent page; they move up to the nearest page instead.

Presenter mode

Presenter mode adapts your Confluence page to your presentation needs and hides all outside contents and almost all of the buttons of view mode:

Sample page 3

In Atlassian Confluence Cloud, there are different types of administrators, each with their own set of permissions and capabilities:

Site Administrators: They have the highest level of permissions and can manage global settings across all Atlassian products in the cloud instance (e.g., Jira, Confluence, etc.). They can manage users and groups, billing and subscriptions, and other site-wide settings.

Confluence Administrators: They have administrative rights specifically for Confluence. They can manage spaces, global permissions, and configure Confluence settings, but they don't have access to site-wide settings or other Atlassian products.

Space Administrators: They have administrative rights for a specific Confluence space. They can manage pages, permissions, and settings for that space only.

Organization Administrators: They can manage Atlassian accounts, security settings, and domain verification for the entire organization, but they don't have administrative rights in Confluence or any other Atlassian product unless explicitly granted.

Figure 3.18 – Presenting page content in an elegant and distraction-free way

As you can see, you can also show a QR page that will help your audience quickly access the page you're presenting within their device.

Also, you can easily navigate the different parts of your page using the **Selective focus** feature, which you can access via the small menu item at the top right of the **Presenter mode** screen.

> **No need to prepare time-consuming presentation materials**
>
> You don't have to prepare additional presentation materials (Microsoft PowerPoint, Google Slides, and others) for your presentation needs.
>
> It's highly recommended that you use this mode during meetings, standups, and where needed.

Analytics

You can get detailed analytics on page views and attachments if you are on the Premium plan:

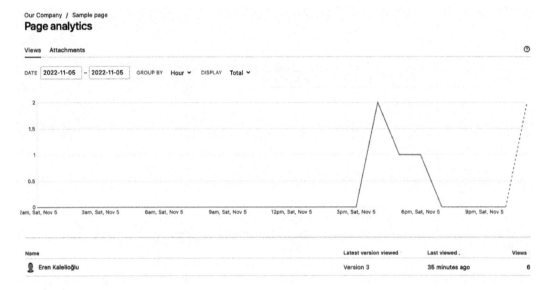

Figure 3.19 – Getting page insights via Page analytics

As you can see, you can quickly get insights into how your page and attachments perform between intervals you define.

Page history

There is a robust version control system within Confluence where you can easily track the changes to your page over time. This can be useful for troubleshooting or getting insights into how your team contributes to this page:

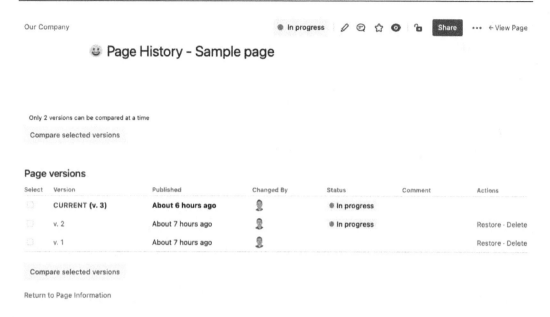

Figure 3.20 – Tracking changes to a page

As you can see, you have some powerful tools here:

- Restore a previous version

- Delete a version that is not needed anymore

- Compare two versions

Attachments

Here, you can upload attachments to your page. All of the attachments can be managed within the **Attachments** section.

You can also see your attachments and their details, such as size, creator, creation date, and comments.

You can manage them like so:

- Adding or removing their labels

- Deleting them

- Deleting their versions:

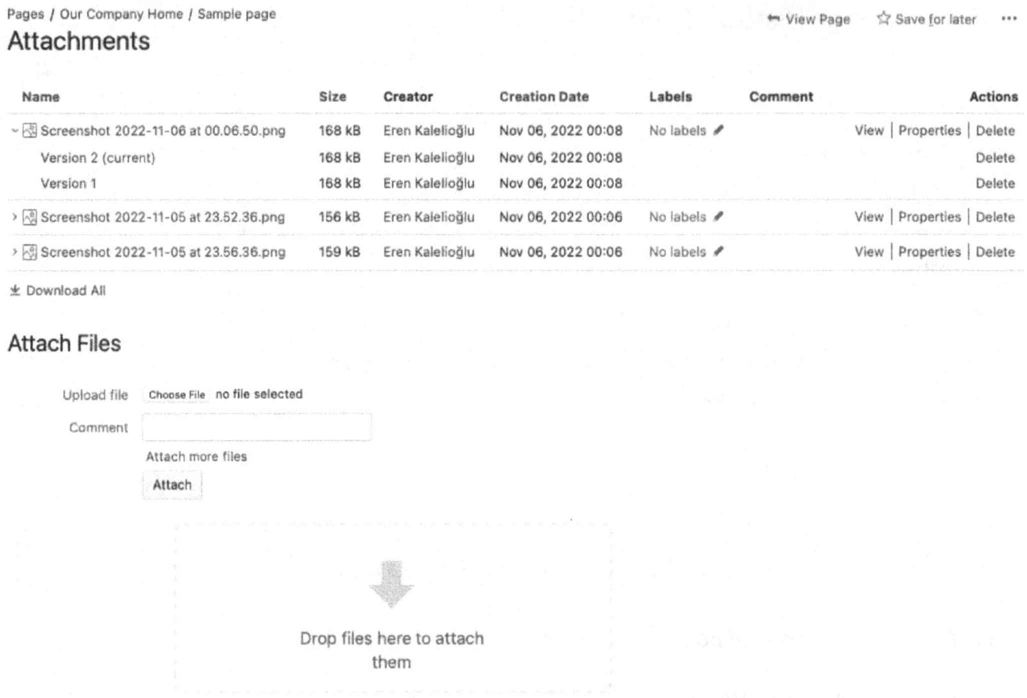
Pages / Our Company Home / Sample page
View Page
Save for later
Attachments
Name
Size
Creator
Creation Date
Labels
Comment
Actions
Screenshot 2022-11-06 at 00.06.50.png
168 kB
Eren Kalelioğlu
Nov 06, 2022 00:08
No labels
View | Properties | Delete
Version 2 (current)
168 kB
Eren Kalelioğlu
Nov 06, 2022 00:08
Delete
Version 1
168 kB
Eren Kalelioğlu
Nov 06, 2022 00:08
Delete
Screenshot 2022-11-05 at 23.52.36.png
156 kB
Eren Kalelioğlu
Nov 06, 2022 00:06
No labels
View | Properties | Delete
Screenshot 2022-11-05 at 23.56.36.png
159 kB
Eren Kalelioğlu
Nov 06, 2022 00:06
No labels
View | Properties | Delete
Download All
Attach Files
Upload file
Choose File
no file selected
Comment
Attach more files
Attach
Drop files here to attach them

Figure 3.21 – Managing a page's attachments

As you can see, there are two main sections here:

- **Attachments**
- **Attach Files**

> **Controlling the attachment's version**
>
> We already discussed the version control of pages, and here, we can see how Confluence controls the versions of an attachment.
>
> Confluence creates a new version when you upload a file with the same name as the attachment. This way, you don't have to explicitly deal with versions within filenames, such as `report-version-01.pdf` and `report-version-02.pdf`. Confluence takes care of the versioning without complicating the filename.

You can access and modify the attachment's properties by clicking **Properties**:

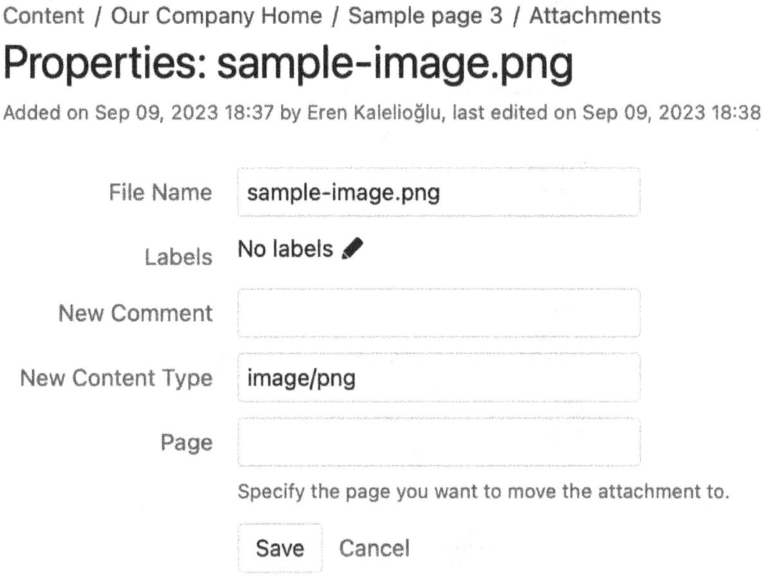

Content / Our Company Home / Sample page 3 / Attachments

Properties: sample-image.png

Added on Sep 09, 2023 18:37 by Eren Kalelioğlu, last edited on Sep 09, 2023 18:38

File Name	sample-image.png
Labels	No labels ✏
New Comment	
New Content Type	image/png
Page	

Specify the page you want to move the attachment to.

Save   Cancel

Figure 3.22 – Modifying the attachment's properties

As you can see, you can easily comment on an attachment and move it to another page.

Resolved comments

As we mentioned previously, active inline comments are highlighted in yellow. An active comment means that the discussion continues and is still ongoing:

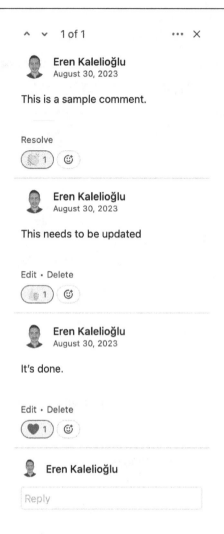

Figure 3.23 – Discussing with inline comments

As you can see, you can discuss different parts of the page with your teammates. They can react or reply to your comments.

When people are done with comments, they can click on **Resolve comments** to mark this thread of comments as resolved. Resolved comments are not highlighted in yellow anymore and are not visible by default, but they are not lost. You can access resolved comments whenever you need them by using the **Resolved comments** button:

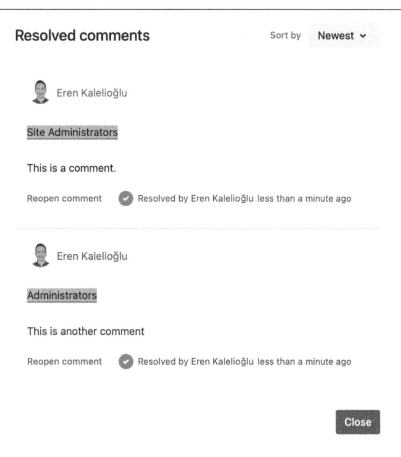

Figure 3.24 – Discovering resolved comments

As you can see, you can always reopen a resolved comment.

Advanced details

You have five choices in this section:

- **Page Information**
- **View Source**
- **Hide Related Pages**
- **View Storage Format**
- **Import Word Document**

Page Information gives an overview of all the information on the page, such as **Recent Changes**, **Outgoing Links**, **Hot Referrers**, and many more:

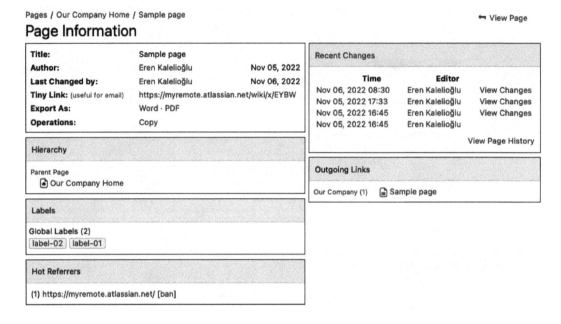

Figure 3.25 – Page Information

As you can see, the **Page Information** dialog provides inaccessible information, such as **Outgoing Links**.

> **Tip for minimizing side effects when archiving or deleting a page**
> We recommend accessing the **Page Information** section before deleting or archiving a page.

Slack Notifications

Typically, Confluence sends two types of notifications:

- Confluence notifications
- Email messages

Note that you can receive notifications via Slack as well. The configuration is relatively straightforward, and you should select the workspace and channel where messages will be sent. You can see how to add a Slack subscription in the following screenshot:

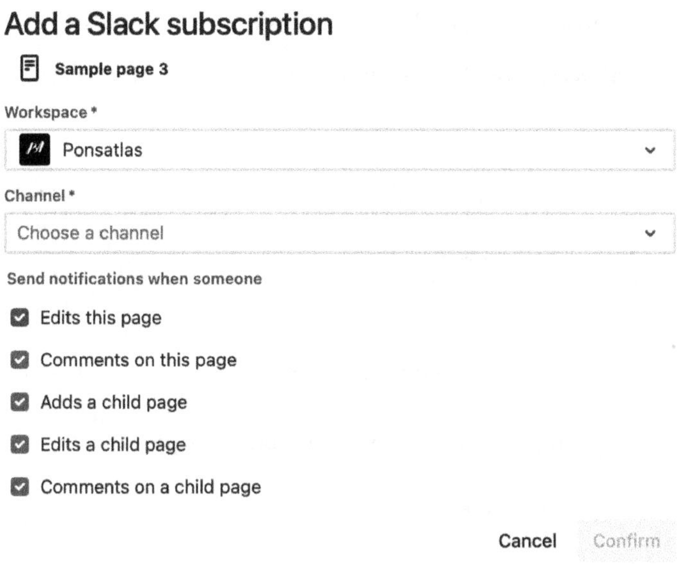

Add a Slack subscription

📄 **Sample page 3**

Workspace *

| 🅼 Ponsatlas | ⌄ |

Channel *

| Choose a channel | ⌄ |

Send notifications when someone

☑ Edits this page

☑ Comments on this page

☑ Adds a child page

☑ Edits a child page

☑ Comments on a child page

Cancel   Confirm

Figure 3.26 – Configuring a Slack subscription to a page

As shown in the previous screenshot, you can precisely define which actions will send a Slack notification. You can also configure notifications on child pages.

In addition, it is possible to add more than one Slack subscription to a Confluence page:

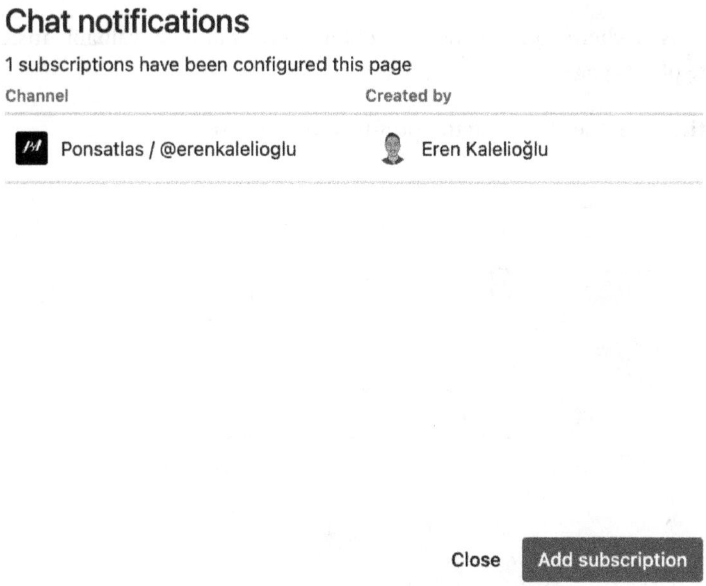

Chat notifications

1 subscriptions have been configured this page

Channel	Created by
🅼 Ponsatlas / @erenkalelioglu	👤 Eren Kalelioğlu

Close   **Add subscription**

Figure 3.27 – Adding multiple Slack subscriptions to a page

As you can see, you can manage different subscriptions easily.

That's all for the **More actions** section. Next, we'll cover the header section of view mode.

Header section

The header section is shown in the following screenshot:

Figure 3.28 – The header section of a page

Let's look at the areas of this section in more detail:

- **Emoji**: You can add an emoji to your page title.
- **Page title**: This is the page title. Give your page a unique (in its space), relevant, and easy-to-remember title. Avoid special characters in the page title.
- **Owned by**: This is the owner of the page.
- **Last updated**: This was when the page got its latest update.
- **Estimated reading time**: Confluence gives you an idea of how much time it takes to read this page.
- **Analytics**: This is where you can check essential metrics and get valuable insights about the performance of this page.

By clicking **Analytics**, you'll see the analytics pop-ups shown here:

Figure 3.29 – Checking the performance of the page via its analytics details

Here, you can see the total number of views and the unique number of viewers. You can get more insights about this Confluence page via the **Analytics** feature, which will be covered later.

Main section

The contents of your page are shown in the main section of the view mode.

Bottom section

There is a section at the bottom of every page in Confluence:

Figure 3.30 – Bottom section of a page

As you can see, there are three areas in the bottom section:

- Labels
- Reactions
- Comments

Labels

Here, you can see the labels on this page. You can also give this page new labels, even if you are in view mode.

Labels are handy when you're organizing your content in Confluence. We'll study labels in more detail in future sections.

Reactions

People can react to pages using emojis. Here, your teammates can respond to your page using emojis, and you can see how your teammates reacted to your page.

Comments

This is where you and your teammates will discuss the content of this page. Confluence has many valuable features for collaborative commenting on a page, and we'll cover this collaboration feature in more depth later.

In this section, we covered all the view mode elements. Now, we will dive into edit mode.

Mastering edit mode

As mentioned previously, you can turn on edit mode to make changes to a Confluence page. There are three methods of turning edit mode on:

- Using the *e* keyboard shortcut
- Clicking the **Edit** button within the top menu
- Clicking the **Edit** button within the page tree:

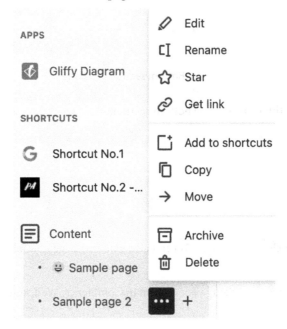

Figure 3.31 – Turning edit mode on using the page tree

View mode and edit mode are quite different. While view mode is optimized for quickly viewing and experiencing a page, edit mode is optimized for editing a page collaboratively:

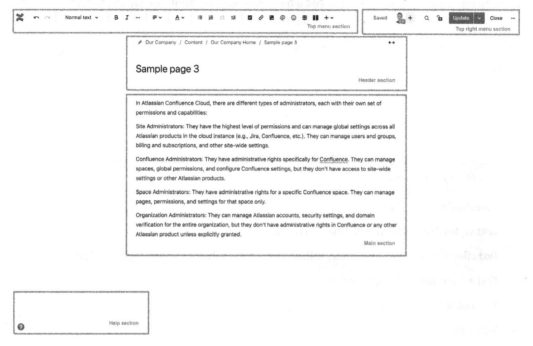

Figure 3.32 – Editing a page

As you can see, many features are available in edit mode. That's why we will categorize and examine the features in edit mode according to the sections they are in:

- Top menu section
- The top-right menu section
- Main section
- Header section
- Help section

Top menu section

The editing top menu is shown when you edit a page. Although we think you are already familiar with the buttons from most word processors, we'll go over them briefly here:

Figure 3.33 – Discovering the top menu in edit mode

As you can see, there are many buttons here. We will list all of them, but we will only explain the ones that are unique to Confluence:

- **Undo/redo**
- **Text styles**: Normal text, heading 1 to heading 6
- **Text effects**: Bold, italics, underline, strikethrough, code, subscript, superscript, and clear formatting
- **Text alignment**: Left, right, or center
- **Text color**
- **Bullet list**
- **Numbered list**
- **Indent/outdent**
- **Action item**: Insert a task
- **Link**: Insert a link to another page or an external resource
- **Files and images**
- **Mention**: Notify a colleague
- **Emoji**
- **Table**
- **Layouts**: Insert a layout module into a page
- **Insert**: Insert a macro into a page

Press the + button to insert a macro into a page:

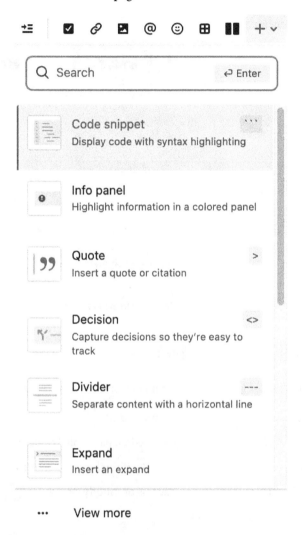

Figure 3.34 – Discovering the actions within the top menu in edit mode

As you can see, you can easily add a macro to a page. We will cover this later.

The top-right menu section

Let's explain the top-right menu section:

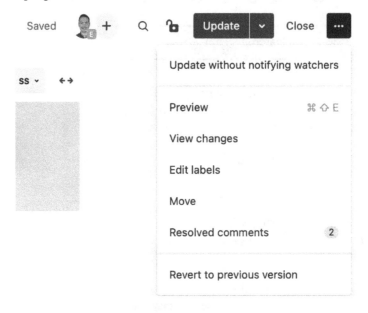

Figure 3.35 – Discovering the top-right menu of edit mode

As you can see, the menu bar comprises seven components:

- **Saved**: This appears when changes have been saved
- **Invite to edit** (plus icon): Invite a colleague to edit a page collaboratively
- **Find and replace** (loop icon): Find a specific text within the page and replace it with another text
- **Restrictions** (lock icon): Define who can access or modify a page
- **Publish**: Save changes and publish a page
- **Close**: Saves changes without publishing
- More (…)

The more (…) button hides multiple components in it. Let's go over them:

- **Update without notifying watchers**: Publish the page without sending a notification to people watching the page or the space
- **Preview**: See what the page will look like when it is published
- **View changes**: See the changes since the last save

- **Edit labels**: Edit the labels of the page
- **Move**: Move the page to another location
- **Resolved comments**: Make the inline comments that were resolved visible
- **Revert to previous version**: Close the page and discard any changes since the previously published version

Main section

The content of your page is shown in the main section of edit mode. You can edit the content of your page within the central area.

Header section

Let's take a closer look at the header section:

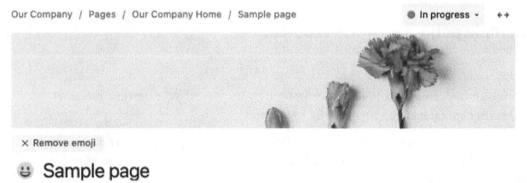

Figure 3.36 – Discovering the page header in edit mode

There are five features here:

- Path (breadcrumb)
- Add status
- Page width
- Add emoji
- Add header image

The path feature allows you to navigate different hierarchical levels up to this page.

Path

Here is the path for this page:

```
Our Company / Pages / Our Company Home / Sample page
```

We can check the exact location of a page by examining its path. Here, we can see that we are currently working on a page called **Sample page** located on another page called **Our Company Home** in a space called **Our Company**.

Add status

Here, you can set a status for your Confluence page. This way, the audience will know the page's status. This can help reduce misunderstandings in your team:

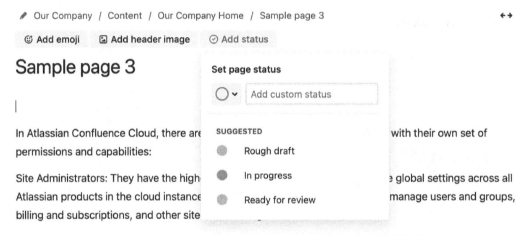

Figure 3.37 – Setting a page status

As you can see, you can use default statuses (**Rough draft**, **In progress**, and **Ready for review**) or create a custom status.

Page width

You can make a page full-width or fixed-width.

Add emoji

You can add an emoji to a page. This emoji will be visible next to the name of the page.

Add header image

You can add a header image to a page by searching from Unsplash or uploading the file from your computer. The Unsplash dialog is shown in the following screenshot:

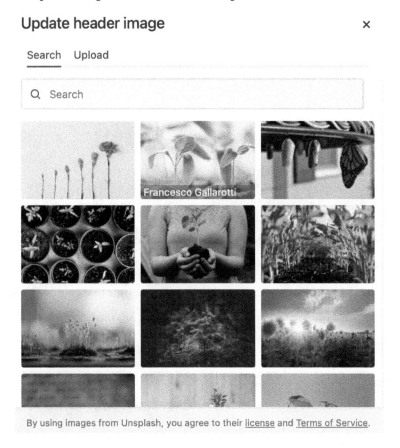

Figure 3.38 – Adding an image from Unsplash

As shown in the preceding screenshot, you can easily search for images from Unsplash to use them as header images for your page.

Help section

Here, you can consult the most needed resources quickly. This area is located at the bottom left of edit mode:

Editing keyboard shortcuts ⌘/
Editing updates
Use page templates
Tutorial
Feedback

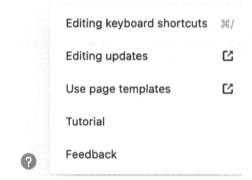

Figure 3.39 – Discovering the help menu of edit mode

Let's look at these options in more detail:

- Upon clicking **Editing keyboard shortcuts**, you will get a list of all keyboard shortcuts, which will help boost your editing experience in Confluence
- **Editing updates** is a shortcut to the documentation page on creating and editing content
- **Use page templates** is a shortcut to the documentation page on creating a page from a template
- The **Tutorial** area provides quick onboarding tips for first-time users of Confluence
- Finally, you have the **Feedback** button, which helps you give Atlassian feedback about Confluence:

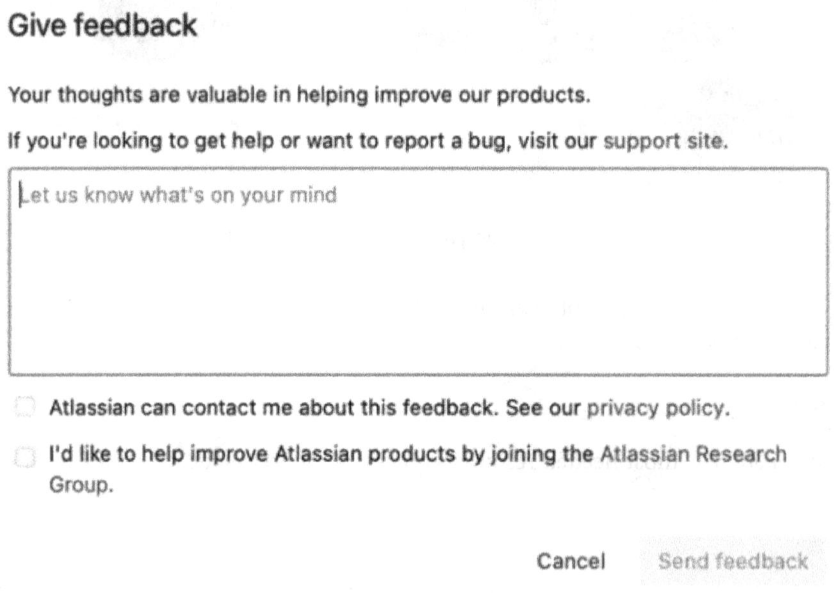

Give feedback
Your thoughts are valuable in helping improve our products.
If you're looking to get help or want to report a bug, visit our support site.
Let us know what's on your mind
Atlassian can contact me about this feedback. See our privacy policy.
I'd like to help improve Atlassian products by joining the Atlassian Research Group.
Cancel
Send feedback

Figure 3.40 – Giving feedback to Atlassian

At this point, we have mastered view mode and edit mode. We studied almost all of the features present in these modes together. At this point, we are ready to proceed with essential tips on managing and organizing content.

Organizing content

Your Confluence environment, in which many people work, can turn into complete chaos in a short period if you are not organized. In such an environment, no one knows where to record new information or where to find the information they are looking for. The information here stays out of date, which results in wasted efforts. Things soon turn for the worse, and gradually people stop using Confluence.

Now, let's put pessimism aside and see how we can keep the environment clean with effective habits. The aim is to provide an environment where new information is quickly recorded and easily found. In addition, we want this environment to be up-to-date, complete, and fun at all times.

This section will explain how we can keep spaces and pages organized.

Organizing spaces

Here are some tips on how you can keep your Confluence spaces tidy:

- Avoid constantly creating new spaces and create a new space only when necessary.
- Archive unused spaces.
- When creating a new space, name it carefully and choose its space key carefully.
- Keep consistency when naming a space and defining a space key.
- Space logos can be very useful when used effectively. A good logo provides visually distinctive information about the space it belongs to. Therefore, make the logos self-consistent.
- Categorize the spaces using labels. In this way, you can see the related spaces grouped. To assign categories to the spaces, you should follow the **Space settings** > **Manage space** > **Space details** path.
- Set a simple and effective description for each space. In this way, people who visit this space can quickly grasp its purpose and scope.

It can be challenging to implement these simple suggestions we have mentioned. These suggestions will help you avoid many risks, especially when it comes to communication accidents and an increased number of spaces.

Now that we've given many suggestions on how to organize spaces; it's time to organize the pages and attachments inside these spaces.

Organizing pages and attachments

Pages are the most crucial concept of Confluence, and all content comes to life either as a page or inside a page.

Many of the suggestions we will give for pages also apply to attachments. For this reason, we will start from the general and move toward the specific.

You want users to stay aware of your space when they come to your space. For this reason, it is beneficial to prepare a brief overview page for each space. This welcome screen can include the following:

- The purpose of the space
- A guide on how the space is organized
- Latest updates
- Links to the most important pages

Understanding the fundamental differences between pages and blog posts will help you significantly. Here, one can ask: In which case will I create and publish the content as a blog post or page? Here's a tip: If the content you create will be valid for long periods and, therefore, will be subject to regular updates, you should create it as a page. If the content you create will only be used actively for a certain period and will not receive any updates afterward, you can prepare it as a blog post. Using the page and blog post concepts intentionally will help you organize your space.

We recommend doing the following:

- Promptly correct or delete incorrect content to retain pages and attachments.
- Archive outdated content.
- Name pages and attachments carefully according to a certain standard. Please note that a field cannot have more than one page with the same name.

There is no folder concept in Confluence that we are used to when it comes to operating systems. You can use pages like folders by placing a page below another page, and you can see and organize the pages you have added under the other via the page tree. Note that this tree structure always requires maintenance.

Giving labels to pages and attachments will help you organize this content. For example, with labels, you can do the following:

- Group pages and attachments
- Easily find the pages and attachments you are looking for
- List pages and attachments with a specific label
- Access other pages related to a page

Summary

In this book, our primary goal is to ameliorate our team's collaborative ability using Confluence. Although this is not an easy task, we can achieve it by mastering the interface and the basic concepts of Confluence.

In this chapter, we tried to convey all the features of Confluence's interface. We examined the concepts of a space, page, blog post, and attachment together. Following these basic concepts, we explored how we can keep them organized. This chapter should have provided you with the necessary technical background on using the basic functions of Confluence and helped you focus on content. Now, we are ready to explore how we can collaborate with our team in the next chapter.

Questions

Answer the following questions to test your knowledge of this chapter:

1. When do you use a blog post? When do you use a page?
2. How can you keep your space organized?
3. Can you attribute more than one label to a page?
4. What are the benefits of attributing a label to a page?
5. What are the three options within page restrictions?

Answers

Here are the answers to this chapter's questions:

1. You can use blog posts for time-sensitive content. On the other hand, you can use a page for content that is independent of time.
2. You can keep your space organized by avoiding creating a new page only when necessary, archiving unused pages, and naming pages carefully.
3. Yes, you can add multiple labels to a page.
4. Labels make it easier to reuse pages.
5. The three options are: **Anyone can view and edit**; **Anyone can view, only some can edit**; **Only specific people can view or edit**.

Further reading

To learn more about the topics that were covered in this chapter, take a look at the following resources:

- `https://support.atlassian.com/confluence-cloud/docs/search-for-pages-and-posts/`

- `https://support.atlassian.com/confluence-cloud/docs/confluence-search-syntax/`

- `https://support.atlassian.com/confluence-cloud/docs/use-home-to-jump-into-work-and-see-whats-happening/`

- `https://support.atlassian.com/confluence-cloud/docs/delete-restore-or-purge-a-page/`

- `https://support.atlassian.com/confluence-cloud/docs/add-or-remove-page-restrictions/`

- `https://support.atlassian.com/confluence-cloud/docs/use-labels-to-categorize-spaces/`

- `https://support.atlassian.com/confluence-cloud/docs/use-labels-to-organize-your-content/`

- `https://support.atlassian.com/confluence-cloud/docs/organize-your-space/`

- `https://support.atlassian.com/confluence-cloud/docs/create-and-edit-content/`

- `https://support.atlassian.com/confluence-cloud/docs/archive-pages/`

- `https://support.atlassian.com/confluence-cloud/docs/present-your-page-with-presenter-mode/`

- `https://support.atlassian.com/confluence-cloud/docs/view-insights-on-pages/`

- `https://support.atlassian.com/confluence-cloud/docs/create-edit-and-publish-a-page/`

- `https://support.atlassian.com/confluence-cloud/docs/manage-uploaded-files/`

- `https://support.atlassian.com/confluence-cloud/docs/create-a-page-from-a-template/`

- `https://support.atlassian.com/confluence-cloud/docs/move-copy-and-hide-pages/`

4
Collaborating with Your Team

In this chapter, we'll create a team space using what we've learned so far. First, let's get to know the team. The team consists of five people who work from different countries in different time zones. It is not easy for them to come together physically, and they need a productive, collaborative workspace. Just like a physical office, they want to come together to discuss and share information. We will create this space virtually and put it at the team's service. We will learn how to create a space and configure it properly, so that you can configure all team spaces within your company. In this chapter, we will cover the following topics:

- Preparing a team space
- Collaborating with your team
- Managing meetings
- Managing decisions
- Inspiring ideas for your team space

Technical requirements

You will need the following software and requirements to complete this chapter:

- An up-to-date web browser
- An active subscription to Confluence Cloud Premium

Preparing a team space

Here, we will create a space in which a team can collaborate. This virtual space is similar to a physical office where people can communicate with each other and work together. We need this space because it will be the home for all the content that your team will need.

We also want this space to have the following properties:

- We want transparency. All content must be accessible to everyone unless specifically indicated.
- All information should be collaboratively recorded, shared, and updated.
- This space must be a single source of truth for our team.
- This area should accelerate the adaptation of newcomers to the team.
- It should contribute to fostering trust between team members.
- We ought to minimize outdated information or do parallel work.
- We need to switch between tools to find documents.

Meanwhile, we want this space to contain the following content:

- A home page to welcome the team
- Contact information of team members
- Information about the team (mission, rules, etc.)
- Goals
- Announcements
- Recently updated content
- Meeting notes
- Decisions
- Shortcuts

To create a new space, follow the path from the top menu of Confluence. Click on **Spaces** and then **Create space**. Select **Team space** from the pop-up window and click **Next** as shown:

Figure 4.1 – Choosing a space template

As you can see, there are a number of space templates that you can choose. They are similar, but it is helpful to be aware of the minor differences. Here, we choose **Team space** because we want to collaborate and share resources with our team.

In the opened window, there are three things you must do:

1. Add an icon for your space. You can choose it from the icon library or upload an image.

2. Create and enter the name of your space. Team Blue is an example.

3. Identify this space with a key. By default, Confluence proposes you with one. You can also set a custom key. Enter a value that contains only A-Z, a-z, or 0-9 characters here. For example, this could be TeamBlue or TB.

Here are some tips on space keys:

- Space keys may only consist of ASCII letters or numbers (A-Z, a-z, 0-9)

- This is used in your space URL

- You cannot change the space key once it is set

So, choose your space key carefully. Now, we are ready to create a team space:

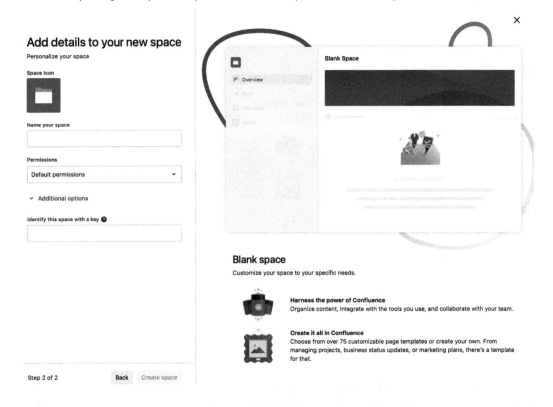

Figure 4.2 – Configuring your team space

As you can see, Confluence gives you options for space permissions. We want this space to be visible to the whole team, so let's choose the second option, **Default permissions** (use the space permissions set by your admin). Now, let's hit the **Create space** button.

Your team space is almost ready. It's time to deep dive into this newly created space:

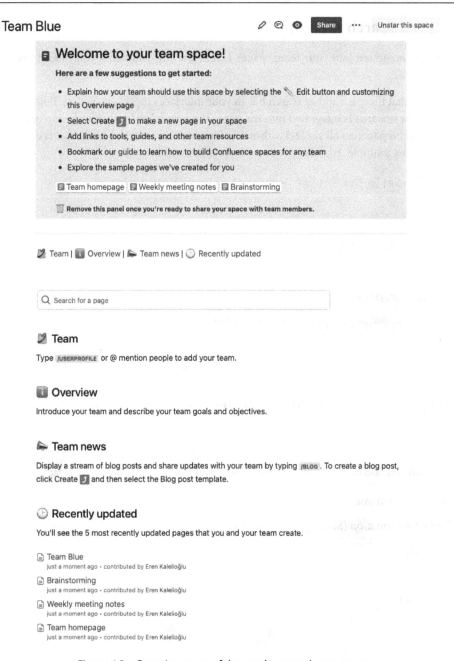

Figure 4.3 – Overview page of the newly created team space

As you can see, Confluence has created and populated an **Overview** page inside your team space. This is what people see first when they view your team space. The **Overview** pages include all the titles, shortcuts, links, and guiding notes, which are customizable according to your needs.

Search (live search macro)

A search bar is integrated into your team space's **Overview** page, allowing you to find knowledge within your space.

You may notice that there is another search bar in your interface's top-right section. But this is quite different from the one that is integrated into the page. The search bar located at the top of the screen is for global searching (across all spaces) within Confluence. This powerful search bar is even capable of searching across multiple Atlassian products such as Jira and Bitbucket:

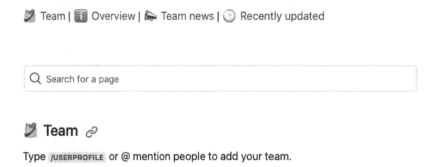

Figure 4.4 – Searching for a page

As seen in *Figure 4.4*, there is a search bar on the **Overview** page of your space.

Team

We recommend you add the following information about the whole team to this area:

- Name and surname
- Contact information (Slack, phone, email, city, etc.)
- Photograph
- Title/role
- Team news

Blog

There is a blog feature within your space. You can use it to manage your team's news. Note that you should prepare a separate blog post for each piece of news. You can then have these blog posts automatically listed on the home page. Note that the blog feature can be easily disabled in the space settings:

Team Blue
Overview
Blog
Analytics
Create a blog b
Calendars
Space Settings
Bulk Archive

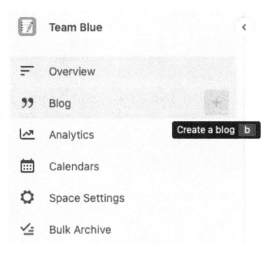

Figure 4.5 – Creating a blog post

You may have noticed that it is possible to easily create a blog post with the **Create a blog** button on the sidebar of your team space.

Recently updated

Here, Confluence automatically lists recently updated content. This way, you won't miss the team's latest updated content:

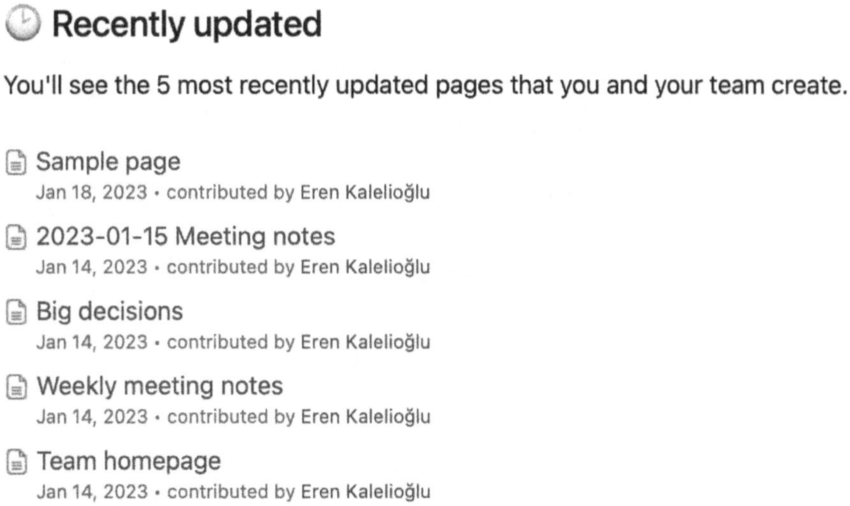

Recently updated
You'll see the 5 most recently updated pages that you and your team create.
Sample page
Jan 18, 2023 • contributed by Eren Kalelioğlu
2023-01-15 Meeting notes
Jan 14, 2023 • contributed by Eren Kalelioğlu
Big decisions
Jan 14, 2023 • contributed by Eren Kalelioğlu
Weekly meeting notes
Jan 14, 2023 • contributed by Eren Kalelioğlu
Team homepage
Jan 14, 2023 • contributed by Eren Kalelioğlu

Figure 4.6 – Recently updated

In *Figure 4.6*, you can see that there is a list of the five most recently updated pages in your space. You can customize this section by clicking the pencil-shaped **Edit** button at the bottom of this macro. The Edit interface is shown in *Figure 4.7*:

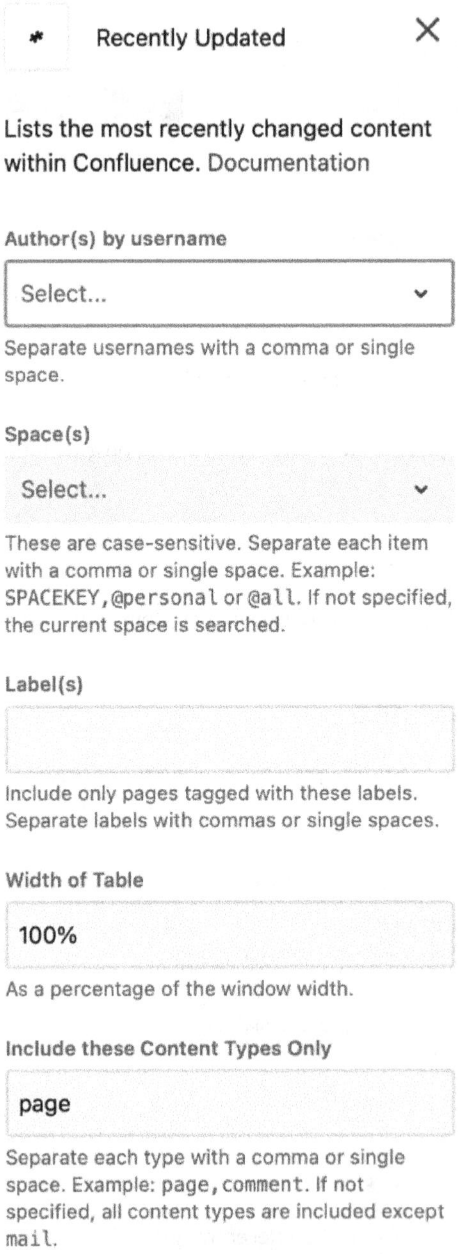

*   Recently Updated   ✕

Lists the most recently changed content within Confluence. Documentation

Author(s) by username

| Select...   ⌄ |

Separate usernames with a comma or single space.

Space(s)

| Select...   ⌄ |

These are case-sensitive. Separate each item with a comma or single space. Example: SPACEKEY,@personal or @all. If not specified, the current space is searched.

Label(s)

| |

Include only pages tagged with these labels. Separate labels with commas or single spaces.

Width of Table

| 100% |

As a percentage of the window width.

Include these Content Types Only

| page |

Separate each type with a comma or single space. Example: page,comment. If not specified, all content types are included except mail.

Figure 4.7 – Editing the recently updated macro

As seen in *Figure 4.7*, you have many options for customizing the **Recently Updated** macro. You can set which spaces' pages will be shown by the macro or which pages updated by certain users will be displayed. Also, you can ensure that only pages with specific labels are listed by this macro.

Now that we have created a space, configured it according to the basic needs of the team, and covered the different elements of the space, we are now ready to collaborate on the content.

Collaborating with your team

At first, Confluence may seem like a typical text processor, but it has a unique philosophy: Confluence is entirely based on cooperation. The priority here is not just to store the text in a cloud but also to manage information collaboratively. The interface and the features are designed according to this philosophy. In Confluence, all of the content is created, updated, and developed collectively. It is visible and collectively shared unless stated otherwise.

In Confluence, each element (pages, attachments, comments, etc.) is optimized for collaborative work. Many of the features that enable collaboration on Confluence are quite simple yet very powerful so that you can use the interactions here in a small team of 5 people or a large company of 10,000 people.

In Confluence, you can do the following:

- Develop content collaboratively
- Discuss an entire document
- Brainstorm on a specific region of a document
- Send a specific part of a document to your team
- Present on a document
- Get instantly informed about the changes on a page and notify others
- Refer to a colleague or the entire team in a specific section of a document

You can perform these actions synchronously (simultaneously) or asynchronously (at different times).

While providing an effective collaboration environment, Confluence quietly manages many technical processes in the background such as backup, automatic recording, monitoring of changes, versioning, and analytics. This allows you to concentrate primarily on collaboration.

Mastering commenting on a Confluence page

There are two types of comments:

- Page comments
- Inline comments

Before diving into the details, let's first create a sample page and add sample content. To start with, click the **Create** button on the top navigation.

Let's set the page's name as `Sample page`. Now, add sample content and press the **Publish** button:

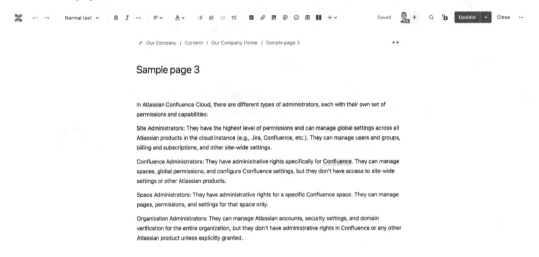

Figure 4.8 – Creating a sample page

As you can see, we now have a page on which we can add comments. Note that only users with comment permission can add a comment on a Confluence page.

Page comments

You can add comments to a page or blog post, and your colleagues can react to your comments or reply to them.

Let's add a comment to the page:

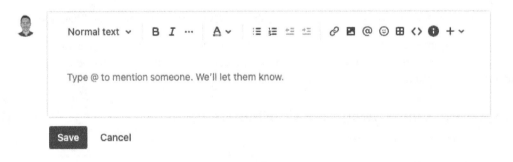

Figure 4.9 – Adding a page comment

Note that the content you can add to the comment area includes images, links, other Confluence pages, Jira links, tables, and files. You can even refer to your teammates here:

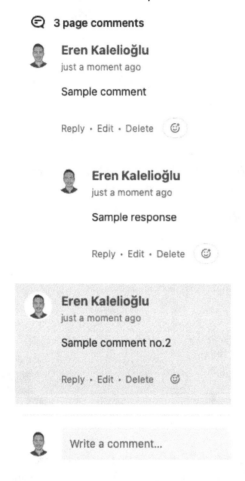

Figure 4.10 – Page comments

As seen in *Figure 4.10*, page comments are visible at the bottom of the page. Remember, comments can only be viewed in view mode, they are not visible when you're in edit mode. This is where inline comments become practical.

Inline comments

You can comment by selecting any part of the page or blog content. Let's see how.

First, let's select a word, a sentence, or a paragraph on the page and press the **Comment** button in the window that opens:

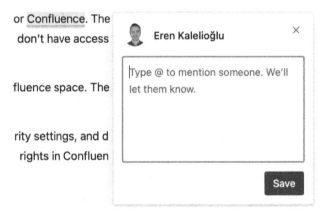

Figure 4.11 – Creating a comment

As you can see, we just selected a word and we want to add a comment on that word. We can type our comments in the window that opens. We can also add links and refer to teammates:

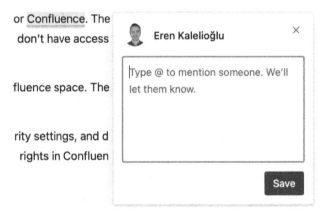

Figure 4.12 – Creating a comment (continued)

As you can see, Confluence highlights the selected word, making comments easily noticeable. Typically, all comments are hidden when the page is opened. To make them visible, you should click on the highlighted section of the content:

Confluence. The

lon't have access

ence space. The

ty settings, and d

ights in Confluen

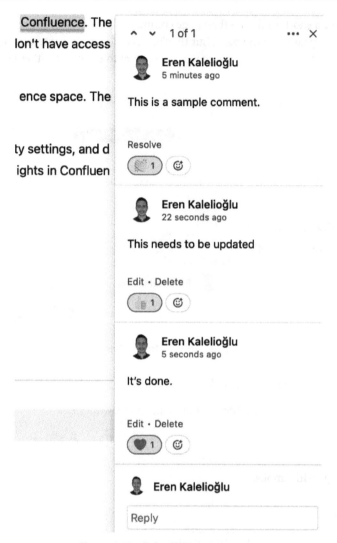

Figure 4.13 – Reacting to a comment

As you may have noticed, all comments are listed in chronological order. Once you and your teammates have finished discussing a highlighted section of the page, you can archive your comments by pressing the **Resolve** button. This way, resolved comments become invisible. You can always access them when you need them. You can access resolved comments by clicking the **Show resolved comments** button on the top right.

Inline comments have a shorter lifespan than page comments. When someone resolves a comment, they dissolve and disappear from the page, but they're never lost unless intentionally deleted. You can easily copy the link to a specific comment when you want to use it in another environment such as Jira or Slack.

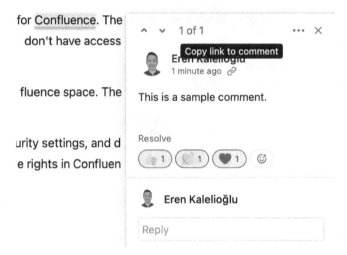

Figure 4.14 – Copying the link to an inline comment

Here, you can easily access and copy the link.

Inline comments can be viewed and added in both edit and view modes.

Reactions

You can react to a page with emojis.

Sharing page

Click the **Share** button at the top right of the display to share the page with your teammates:

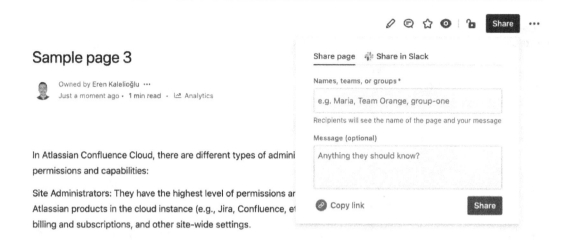

Figure 4.15 – Sharing a page

You can easily share the page with a colleague or an entire team so that they will receive an email notification including the page link and your message. You can also easily share your page with Slack. If you want to share the page from Teams, Jira, or any other platform, you can quickly get the link to the page by using the **Copy link** button.

Watching a page

You can start watching a page if you want to receive email updates about changes made on this page:

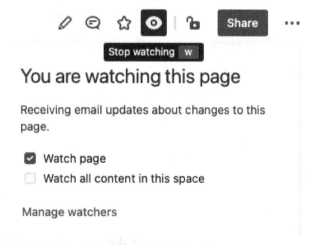

Figure 4.16 – Watching a page

As you can see, you can start watching all content in a single space with a single click. Once you decide not to get updates about a page, click the **Stop watching** button and simply stop watching.

You have now learned how to interact and collaborate with your teammates using Confluence. It's time to work on a practical scenario where we can apply what we've learned: facilitating meeting management with Confluence.

What is a Confluence macro?

Confluence Cloud offers a variety of macros to help users enhance their content and collaborate more effectively. Macros are small pieces of reusable content or functionality that can be added to a page or blog post. Here are some commonly used macros in Confluence Cloud:

- `Page Tree`: Displays a navigable hierarchy of pages. This is useful for creating a table of contents or sidebar navigation.
- `Table of Contents`: Generates a table of contents for a page based on the headings used.
- `Excerpt`: Marks a portion of a page's content to be reused in another page using the `Excerpt Include` macro.
- `Excerpt Include`: Displays content marked as an excerpt from another page.
- `Info, Note, Tip, Warning`: Used to highlight information, notes, tips, or warnings in a distinctive box.
- `Code Block`: Displays a block of code with syntax highlighting.
- `Gallery`: Displays a gallery of attached images.
- `Decision`: Allows you to record decisions made during a meeting.
- `Status`: Displays a colored lozenge (status) that you can customize.
- `Jira Issues`: Displays a list of Jira issues on a page.

Users can add macros to a page while editing it. To add a macro, click on the + icon at the bottom of the page editor and select the macro you want to add. Confluence Cloud also supports user-installed apps that may provide additional macros.

Keep in mind that some macros may not be available to all users as they may be restricted by the administrator or require a specific subscription.

Managing meetings

No matter how many participants there are, meetings, in different settings, will always exist in our lives. Whether you work in an office or with a distributed team, you must work on effectiveness.

Confluence can help you plan your meetings to be organized only when necessary to protect valuable time and reach goals faster.

Confluence can help you with the following:

- Reducing the number of meetings
- Organizing more productive meetings

Reducing the number of meetings

You can have fewer meetings using the features we learned about on Confluence. Let's look at how you can reduce the number of meetings through two different scenarios.

Scenario 1

You're dealing with an important contract that you need to finalize and are expecting full participation from your team.

The traditional solution, which we don't recommend, is, "Let's organize a meeting and distribute a copy of the contract to everyone. Let's get everyone's opinion during the meeting."

Our proposed solution, on the other hand, would be saying, "Let's not have a meeting. Let's turn the agreement into a Confluence page instead and ask the team to add comments within a specific time range. Let's use inline comments to discuss the document, resolve discussions, and make the necessary revisions."

Scenario 2

You want to make an important decision for the company, and you expect full participation from your team in this matter.

The traditional solution would sound like, "Let's organize a meeting and get everyone's opinion in turn at that meeting."

Instead, we recommend saying, "Let's not have a meeting. Let's gather all the information we need and the possible risks related to this decision in a Confluence document. Ask the team to add their comments on the decision as inline comments and review them within a specific timeframe. When the due date comes, then we'll make a decision as a team."

Organizing more productive meetings

With Confluence, you can make your meetings more effective and avoid wasting time and resources. We have three suggestions to make this possible.

Gather everything about the meeting in a single page

Create a Confluence page for each meeting and put everything we have about that meeting on this page. Then, share this page with the whole team before the meeting. Let's not waste time with cool presentation tools and programs; hold the meeting directly on this page. Also, update this page together during the meeting.

Use templates to get up to speed

The ready-to-use templates on Confluence are designed to help us save time and improve our meeting culture. It is also possible to build our own template library by developing existing templates or starting from scratch.

Confluence has six different meeting document templates in its template library. Most of them were designed by Atlassian while others were made by companies that are highly experienced in remote working, such as Miro.

Let's now explore three of the templates Confluence provides:

- **Meeting Notes**
- **Weekly Meeting Notes**
- **Sprint Planning Meeting**

Use the Meeting Notes template

This one is probably one of Confluence's most popular templates, and it can be used for many types of meetings. Let's see what this meeting template looks like:

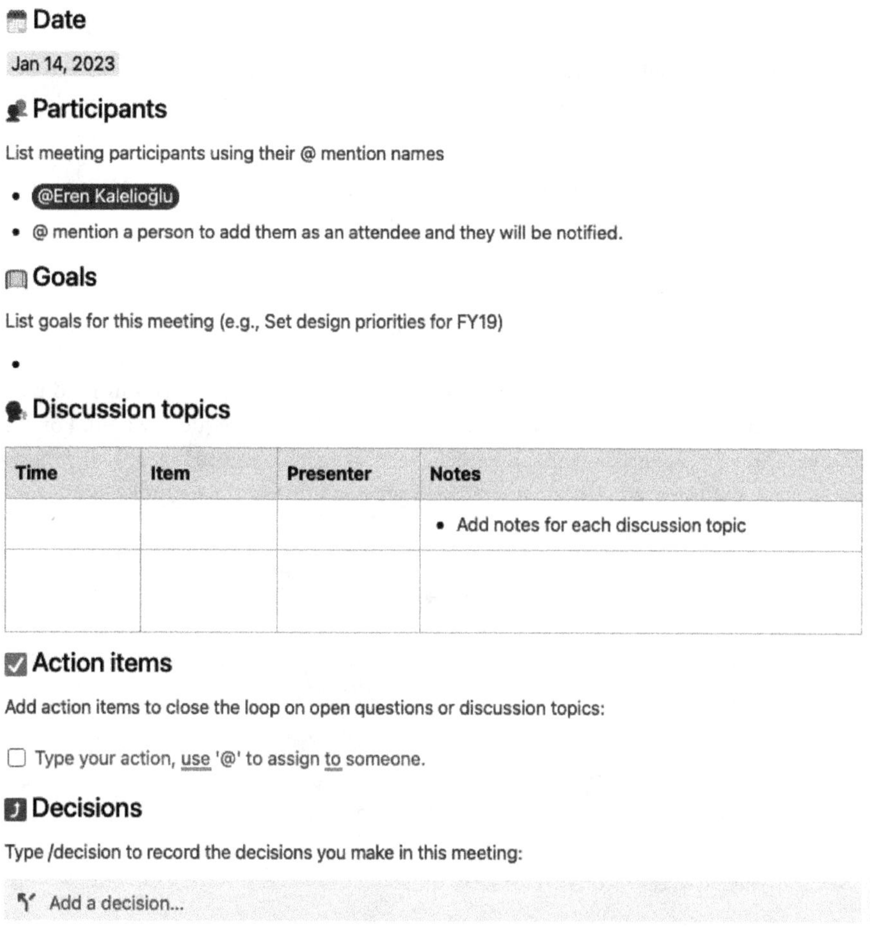

📅 Date

Jan 14, 2023

👤 Participants

List meeting participants using their @ mention names

- @Eren Kalelioğlu
- @ mention a person to add them as an attendee and they will be notified.

📖 Goals

List goals for this meeting (e.g., Set design priorities for FY19)

-

💬 Discussion topics

Time	Item	Presenter	Notes
			• Add notes for each discussion topic

✅ Action items

Add action items to close the loop on open questions or discussion topics:

☐ Type your action, use '@' to assign to someone.

🔲 Decisions

Type /decision to record the decisions you make in this meeting:

⌄ Add a decision...

Figure 4.17 – The Meeting Notes template by Atlassian

As you can see, this template consists of many different parts. Let's go over the essential elements of this template:

- **Date**: We can add the meeting date here using Confluence's **Date** macro.

- **Participants**: Here, we write down the names of the participants. If they have a Confluence license, Confluence will suggest their names after you enter a few letters. The people you add here will be notified immediately of all changes made to the document.

- **Goals**: Before the meeting, we agree on the goals and summarize these goals in two or three items at the most. This way, we can avoid long meetings and protect participants' time.

- **Discussion topics**: We add the topics that will be discussed at the meeting one by one. We determine the order in which these subjects will be covered, how much time we will devote to each topic, and who will present each topic. We can also add any content that could be useful before and during the meeting in the notes section.

- **Action items**: Here, we add the pieces of work that need to be done before, during, or after the meeting. We can also add a deadline and a responsibility for this job.

- **Decisions**: We record the final decisions in this area.

Discovering the weekly Meeting Notes template

Since creating separate documents for a meeting can be unsustainable, we recommend using this template, which can be very practical for the type of meetings that are frequently held. For example, this template can be handy for meetings that are held every morning because it keeps all your meeting notes in one place for the week, month, or sprint. Let's see what this template looks like:

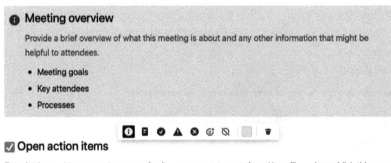

Figure 4.18 – The Weekly Meeting template

As you can see, this template has three parts: **Meeting overview**, **Open action items**, and **Meeting minutes**. As the first two areas are quite self-explanatory, we will only describe the last part.

We create a row for each agenda item. For each line, we add the following information: **Date**, **Attendees**, **Agenda**, **Notes**, **decisions**, and **action items**.

This section is similar to the **Discussion topics** section of the previous template, but there is a fundamental difference: this table is designed to organize many consecutive meetings in one table, and you can use an empty row with a gray background to separate the meetings visually.

Sprint Planning Meeting template

Since this is an advanced template designed by Atlassian, we will only introduce the modules that we find most important:

- Table of contents
- Sprint planning checklist
- Sprint team members
- Capacity planning
- Potential risks

Table of contents

You can see the table of contents of the template in the following screenshot:

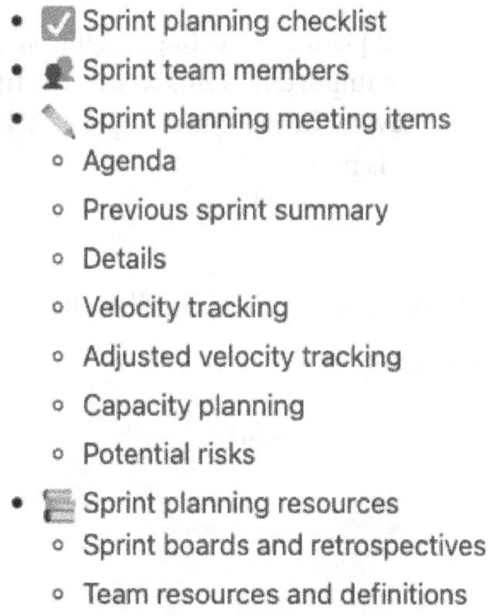

- ✅ Sprint planning checklist
- 👤 Sprint team members
- ✏️ Sprint planning meeting items
  - Agenda
  - Previous sprint summary
  - Details
  - Velocity tracking
  - Adjusted velocity tracking
  - Capacity planning
  - Potential risks
- 📚 Sprint planning resources
  - Sprint boards and retrospectives
  - Team resources and definitions

Figure 4.19 – Table of contents

As you can see, this template has a table of contents at the very beginning that automatically updates itself. At this point, one can ask, "Why would a meeting note have a table of contents?"

Sprint plannings are complex meetings; therefore, they require excellent preparation. Typically, critical information is shared during this type of meeting, and you do not want it to disappear. Thus, the notes of this meeting can be really long and intense. That's why a self-updating table of contents becomes handy to make the work more visible and practical for the team to navigate such a document.

Sprint planning checklist

You can utilize Confluence to make your sprint planning meetings with your team more effective. The table in this document section lets you visualize tasks that must be done before, during, and after the meeting. We recommend using the action item macros here.

Sprint planning checklist

Keep track of tasks you need to complete before, during, and after your sprint planning meeting. Follow up by updating and adding Jira tickets to your template.

Preparation	Meeting	Follow up
☐ e.g., organize the backlog and close the last sprint	☐ e.g., present velocity and confirm team capacity	☐ e.g., update JIRA tickets
☐ Type your action, use '...	☐ Type your action, use '...	☐ Type your action, use '...

Figure 4.20 – Sprint planning checklist

Figure 4.20 displays the checklist. As sprint planning meetings require serious planning, it is beneficial to use a checklist to avoid forgetting the important items in the meeting. The macro used here to capture work items is the same one we saw in the previous templates. Also, note that you can also set deadlines or assign responsibilities for this part.

Sprint team members

In this section, you should list all the team members who will participate in the sprint:

Sprint team members

Name	Role
@ mention team member	e.g., Scrum Master

Figure 4.21 – Sprint team members

Here, you can also define team members' roles. Once you type your teammates' names starting with @, they will be immediately notified of every change in this document.

Capacity planning

You can keep the capacity metrics of the current sprint in this section:

Capacity planning

✔ You can customize this template to change or add capacity measurements. You can also review older sprints by adding columns.

	Current sprint	Previous sprint
Total days	e.g., 10 days	
Team capacity	e.g., 80%	
Projected capacity	e.g., 50 points	
Individual capacity	@ member	

Figure 4.22 – Capacity planning

Keeping the capacity metrics visible for the previous few sprints can be practical.

Potential risks

In this section, you can display a basic risk assessment of the sprint:

Potential risks

Risk	Mitigation
e.g., The team has a smaller buffer than they expected	e.g., The team might need to move low priority work to the backlog

Figures 4.23 – Potential risks

As you can see in *Figure 4.23*, there are two columns in this table. While the risk is defined in the first column, the mitigation plan is displayed on the right side.

Atlassian's other resources for meetings

Atlassian has created many valuable resources for meetings. You can find some of them at the end of this chapter.

In this section, we discussed how to organize effective meetings with Confluence and suggested that meeting-related content be compiled into a single document. We also introduced templates to make this all possible. Now, we are ready to manage decisions with Confluence.

Managing decisions

Teams have to consistently make decisions for different objectives, and we are aware that recording, announcing, archiving, and managing these decisions is not always easy. At this point, Confluence has features that will help a distributed team carry out the decision-making process with full participation. In this section, we'll talk about two macros (`Decision` and `Decision Report`) to keep track of both small and complex decisions and to make them more manageable and effective.

Using Decision for simple decisions

You can easily capture and keep track of your simple decisions using the `Decision` macro. You can access this macro in two ways:

- Press the + button from the menu located at the top of your page editing screen, then click on **Decision** from the drop-down menu.

- Use the `/decision keyboard` shortcut:

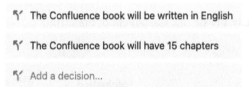

Figure 4.24 – Adding a decision

As you can see, we just captured two decisions.

Using Decision Report to list decisions

You can use the `Decision Report` macro to list decisions scattered across different documents in your team space in one place. You can add this macro to the page in two ways:

- Press the + button from the menu on top of your page and click on **Decision Report** from the drop-down menu.

- Use the /Decision Report keyboard shortcut:

Page Title	Decisions
📄 2023-01-14 Meeting notes	⤷ The publisher of the Confluence book will be Packt
📄 2023-01-15 Meeting notes	⤷ The Confluence book will be written in English ⤷ The Confluence book will have 15 chapters

Figure 4.25 – Decision Report

As you can see in *Figure 4.25*, decisions from different pages are displayed in a single table. On the left side, you can see on which page the decision is. On the right, you can see the decision itself.

When you press the pencil-shaped **Edit** button at the bottom of the Decision Report macro, you will reach the **Edit 'Decision report' Macro** interface, which can be seen in *Figure 4.26*:

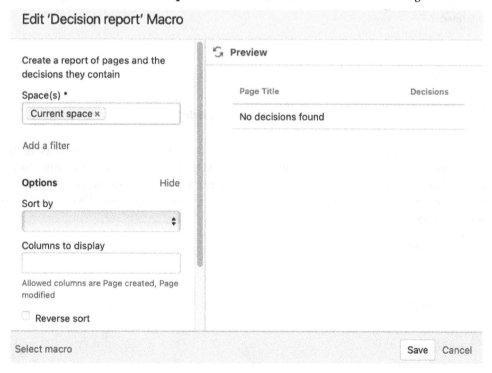

Figure 4.26 – Edit 'Decision report' Macro

As seen in the previous screenshot, you can customize the Decision Report macro according to your needs. You can set how many decisions will appear in the report or which spaces' decisions will be displayed in this report.

Using templates for managing complex decisions

There are three templates on Confluence to prepare for complex decisions. Here, we will examine the template named DACI: Decision documentation.

At the beginning of this template, there is a table where we keep a record of the essential information about the decision:

Status	NOT STARTED / IN PROGRESS / COMPLETE
Impact	HIGH / MEDIUM / LOW
Driver	@ mention driver
Approver	@ approver
Contributors	@ contributors
Informed	@ stakeholders
Due date	Type // to add a date
Resources	Type /link to add links to relevant research, pages, and related decisions

Figure 4.27 – Decision properties

As you can see, you can add names to the relevant table to involve the decision stakeholders. In this way, responsibilities become more visible and it is ensured that all stakeholders are immediately informed of changes to this document. This template also has a section where you can add relevant data and background information to provide context when making decisions. You can add rich content to this area:

Relevant data

Add any data or feedback the team should consider when making this decision.

Background

Provide context on a decision the team needs to make and include information about constraints and challenges.

Figure 4.28 – Relevant data and Background for a decision

When evaluating a complex decision, you may want to assess the alternatives in a table and compare them. You can use the **Options considered** section to do so:

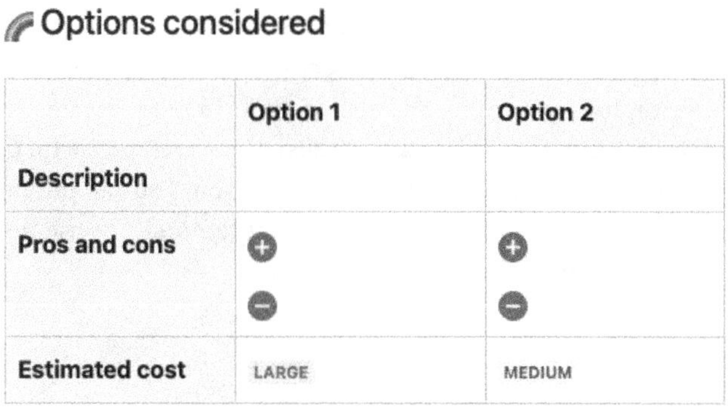

Figure 4.29 – Options considered

This table looks simple enough, but it can assist you in more complicated scenarios.

In this section, we discussed how you can contribute to interactive decision management in your team using Confluence. The two macros and three templates we mentioned here can help you to quickly set up a simple and effective decision-management system for your team. Also, please note that these templates are just reference points; you can always adapt them to your ever-changing needs.

Inspiring ideas for your team space

You can add a lot of content other than meeting notes and resolutions to the team area. "What can we put in?" we hear you ask. You can add any content the team will probably need. Let's take a look at some examples:

- Team goals and objectives (OKRs)
- Team rules
- Team metrics (KPI's)
- Roadmap
- Frequently used links
- Links to other software you use such as Miro, Canva, Google Workspace
- All kinds of files such as `.ppt`, `.excel`, `.pdf`, `.word`, or `.zip`
- Brainstorming notes

Summary

In this chapter, we saw how Confluence can support a distributed team in collaboration. First, we created a team space containing all the information the team will need. Then, we provided a brief **Overview** page in this space and learned how to interact with our teammates, including important topics such as collaborative capturing, editing, and sharing information. Finally, after discussing how to manage meetings and decisions with Confluence, we also discovered powerful Confluence features such as templates and macros. Now, using all this new information, you can provide your teams with a solid workspace where they can collaborate while working remotely. In the next chapter, we will learn how to use macros to easily manage dynamic content.

Questions

1. What should you do to be notified of updates on all space pages?

2. What are the main differences between inline comments and page comments?

3. What benefits do Confluence templates bring to your meetings?

4. How do you get a list of all decisions in a space?

5. How do you increase meeting effectiveness with Confluence?

Answers

1. You have to watch the space.

2. Page comments are visible only in View mode. You can resolve inline comments.

3. You can prepare for meetings effectively using templates. Templates allow you to be more organized and save time during and after the meeting.

4. You can use the `Decision Report` macro to get a list of all decisions in a space.

5. By setting the meeting agenda clearly, you contribute to making everyone ready for the meeting. You can make your team more involved with a meeting note that can be updated by anyone and is easily accessible from different devices. By using macros, you can reuse your content both in Atlassian products and in other systems.

Further reading

- `https://www.atlassian.com/work-management/project-collaboration/team-meetings`
- `https://www.atlassian.com/blog/inside-atlassian/how-to-facilitate-successful-offsite-meetings-human-dynamics`
- `https://www.atlassian.com/work-management/project-collaboration/team-meetings/how-to-go-meetless`
- `https://www.atlassian.com/work-management/project-collaboration/team-meetings/codelime-saves-time-meets-less`
- `https://www.atlassian.com/software/confluence/templates/meeting-notes`
- `https://www.atlassian.com/software/confluence/templates/weekly-meeting-notes`
- `https://www.atlassian.com/software/confluence/templates/sprint-planning-meeting`

5

Mastering Dynamic Contents

If you have decided to collect and organize all company information on Confluence, you will need to master some skills. The foremost of these is the ability to use dynamic pages effectively.

Pages whose content is automatically updated according to specific rules or contain rich content other than text and images are called dynamic pages. They interact with other pages on Confluence.

By making the pages dynamic, you can easily organize your knowledge base and find what you seek. Dynamic pages interact with other pages in the environment, and this way, you can reuse content from one page to another.

In this chapter, you will learn how to make static pages dynamic. You can be sure that what you learn here will greatly benefit you.

We will cover the following topics in this chapter:

- Labeling pages
- Getting to know the macros
- Exploring macros that use labels
- Discovering macros that interact with pages
- Adding more macros to Confluence
- Discovering Smart Links

Technical requirements

You will need the following software and requirements to complete this chapter:

- An up-to-date web browser
- An active subscription to Confluence Cloud Premium

Labeling pages

You can add one or more labels to a Confluence page. With these labels, you can make the pages dynamic. In addition, thanks to the labels, you can effortlessly find the specific page you are looking for in an environment with hundreds or thousands of pages. For example, you can filter pages that have a specific label. You can also utilize filters while searching.

You can see the page's labels at the bottom of that page. You can assign one or more previously created labels to the page. However, you can also add a brand new label to a page. When you do this, a new label is created. This label can also be used on other pages within your Confluence site. This way, your newly created label will be available for other spaces too.

We suggest that you follow these practices:

- Give multiple labels to each page.
- Set a standard rule for naming the labels – for example, `my-first-label` or `my-second-label`.
- Remember that there is no way to manage labels on Confluence, so we recommend choosing them carefully.
- It is not practical to leave the responsibility of labeling pages to one person; doing this as a team is beneficial. You can ensure that all pages have at least one label.

Labels can't have any spaces, so if you add a space, it is automatically replaced by –

Labels can be found at the bottom of a Confluence page. If no label has been given yet, you will only see the + **Add label** button:

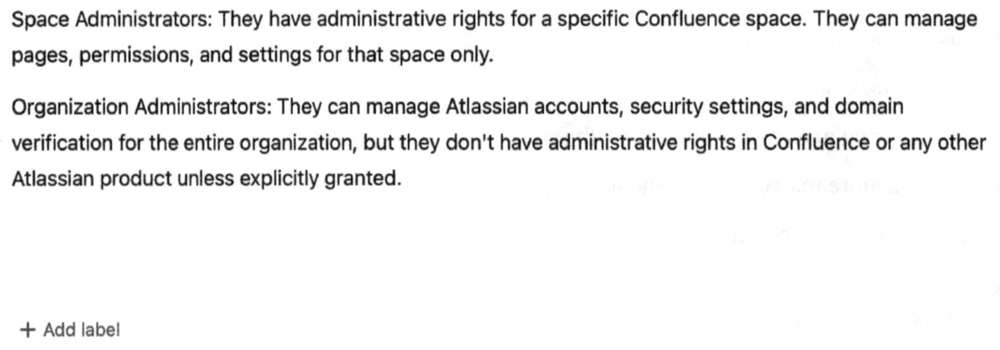

Space Administrators: They have administrative rights for a specific Confluence space. They can manage pages, permissions, and settings for that space only.

Organization Administrators: They can manage Atlassian accounts, security settings, and domain verification for the entire organization, but they don't have administrative rights in Confluence or any other Atlassian product unless explicitly granted.

+ Add label

Figure 5.1 – Page labels (this page currently has no label)

As you can see, there are no labels on the page. Let's click on the + **Add label** button.

You can easily add an existing label in the **Labels** section. It is also possible to create a new one:

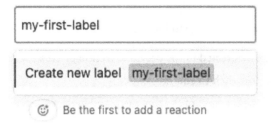

my-first-label

Create new label my-first-label

☺ Be the first to add a reaction

Figure 5.2 – Creating a new label

As you can see, Confluence allows you to save the new label that you entered, called **my-first-label**.

Note that you can enter multiple labels on a page, as shown in the following screenshot:

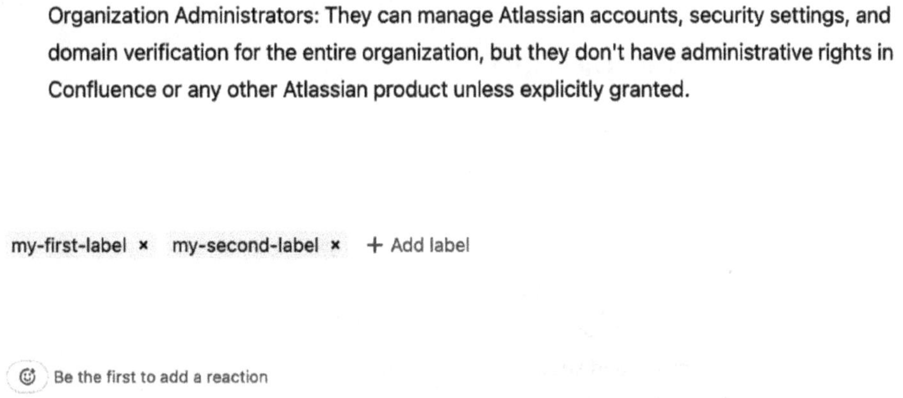

Organization Administrators: They can manage Atlassian accounts, security settings, and domain verification for the entire organization, but they don't have administrative rights in Confluence or any other Atlassian product unless explicitly granted.

my-first-label ×   my-second-label ×   + Add label

☺ Be the first to add a reaction

Figure 5.3 – Page labels

As you can see, this page has two labels – **my-first-label** and **my-second-label**.

This section taught us about labels, an essential concept in Confluence. We learned to see labels on a page, add labels to a page, and create a new label. We also acknowledged how important effective label management is for the health of your Confluence environment. Now, it's time to review the macros on Confluence. You will see that a significant number of these macros use labels.

Getting to know macros

Adding a macro is one of the most effective ways to make dynamic Confluence pages. By adding one or more macros to a page, we can make that page dynamic. In other words, macros serve to make pages much more resourceful. Confluence offers us many macros for different purposes. In this and the following sections, we'll examine macros closely.

Adding a macro to a page is easy. First, we want to teach you this skill. Next, we'll go over the macros one by one.

Let's see how we can add a macro to a page following these steps:

1. Open the sample page we created in the previous section or create a new one.

2. Click the **Edit** button to switch to edit mode.

3. Click the + button on the far right of the top menu and look at the options. The screen should look like this:

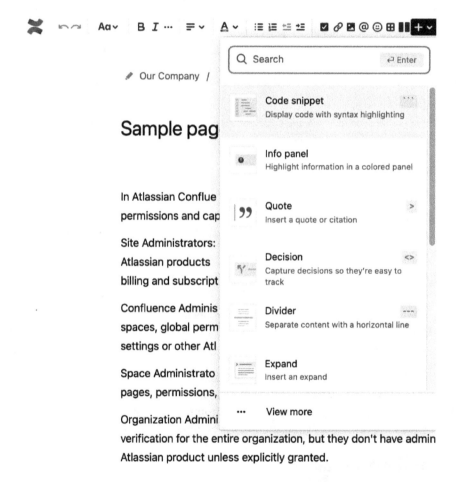

Figure 5.4 – Inserting a macro

We can also type / on a page to find macros.

4. As you can see, many macros can be added to the page. Let's see the macro list by clicking the **View more** button.

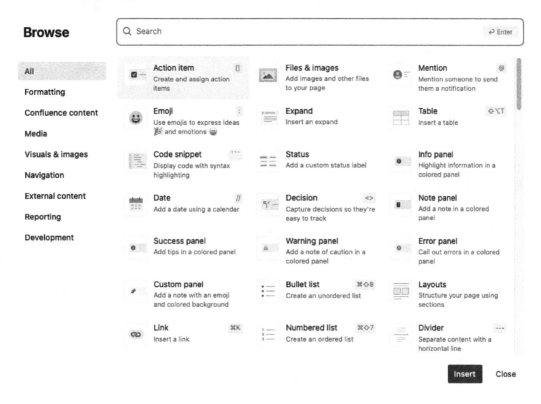

Figure 5.5 – A list of all the macros

5. As you can see, the list of macros you can add to the page is extensive and divided into eight categories. Press the **Insert** button to add the macro you chose for the page.

After looking at our list of macros and learning how to add a macro to the page, we are now ready to review the macros individually. We will examine macros in two separate groups:

- Macros that use labels
- Macros that interact with pages

Exploring macros that use labels

In the previous pages, we introduced the basics of making pages dynamic with labels. In this section, we will deep dive into this. Now, let's go over the important macros that use labels:

- Related Labels
- Content by Label
- Labels List
- Popular Labels
- Content Report Table

Related Labels

This macro fetches labels from other pages that share a label with the page the macro was added to. Thus, it allows you to list the related labels on your page.

You can see the output of this macro in the following screenshot:

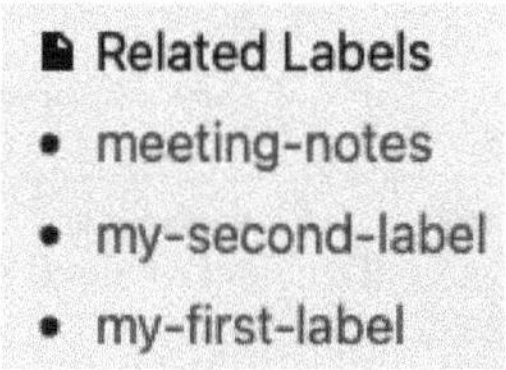

Figure 5.6 – The Related Labels macro

As you can see, this simple macro lists labels that might be relevant to this page.

Content by Label

Using this macro, you can list all content (pages, blog posts, and attachments) with specific labels of your preference.

You can see the macro settings on the left side of the following screenshot. On the right side, you can preview the output of the macro.

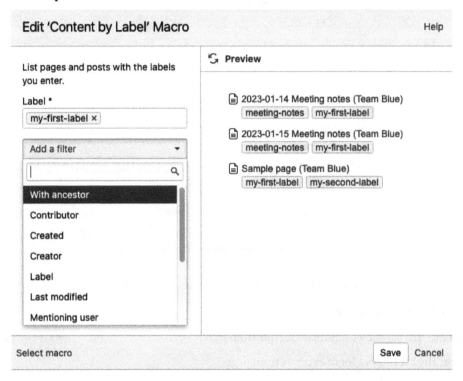

Figure 5.7 – Edit 'Content by Label' Macro

As you can see, adding a filter to this macro allows you to be more specific about the pages that will be listed. On the right, you can see how the macro will appear on the page. Sticking to the current settings, the following information will be shown for each page in the list:

- The space that the page is in
- The page labels

You can set which information will appear in the list this macro produces:

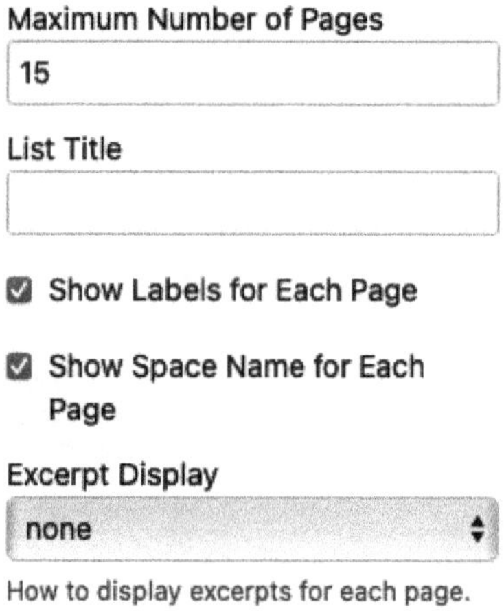

Maximum Number of Pages

15

List Title

☑ Show Labels for Each Page

☑ Show Space Name for Each
   Page

Excerpt Display

none ⬍

How to display excerpts for each page.

Figure 5.8 – Configuring the Content by Label macro

Also, **Excerpt Display** has three drop-down options – **none**, **simple**, and **rich**:

- **none**: The list does not show any excerpt from pages
- **simple**: The list shows minimal excerpts from pages
- **rich**: The list shows a lot of excerpts from pages

In the next screenshot, you can see what the screen output looks like when the **Excerpt Display** setting is set to **none**.

Figure 5.9 – The output of the Content by Label macro

In the previous screenshot, we can see that pages with the **my-first-label** content from different spaces are listed here.

Labels List

With this macro, you can dynamically add a list of all labels to a page. You can see the settings of this macro in the following screenshot:

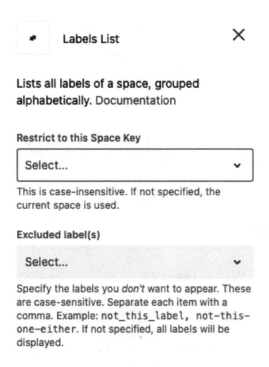

Figure 5.10 – The Labels List macro

As you can see, you can list labels solely in the space of the active page or all spaces on the page.

You can see what output this macro produces in the following screenshot:

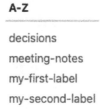

Figure 5.11 – The output of the Labels List macro

This macro sorts all the labels alphabetically. You can easily access the pages with the relevant label by clicking on them.

Popular Labels

With this macro, you can list the most popular labels on the Confluence site or a specific area on a page.

You can see the settings of this macro in the following screenshot:

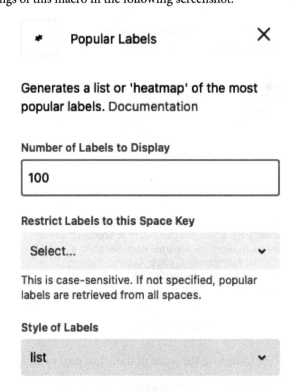

Figure 5.12 – The Popular Labels macro

As you can see, listing the labels in the currently active space is possible. You also have the option to list the labels from the entire Confluence site.

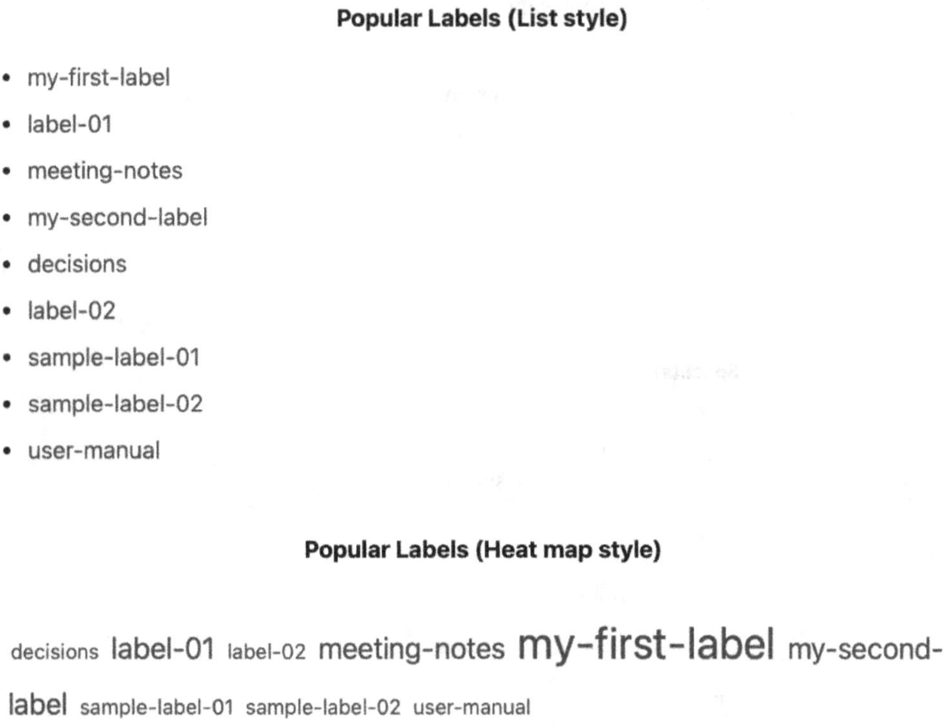

Popular Labels (List style)

- my-first-label
- label-01
- meeting-notes
- my-second-label
- decisions
- label-02
- sample-label-01
- sample-label-02
- user-manual

Popular Labels (Heat map style)

decisions label-01 label-02 meeting-notes my-first-label my-second-label sample-label-01 sample-label-02 user-manual

Figure 5.13 – Popular Labels

As seen in the preceding screenshot, the Popular Labels macro can format its output with two style options – **List** and **Heat Map**.

Content Report Table

You can use this macro to report pages with a specific label in a table.

The settings of this macro should look like this:

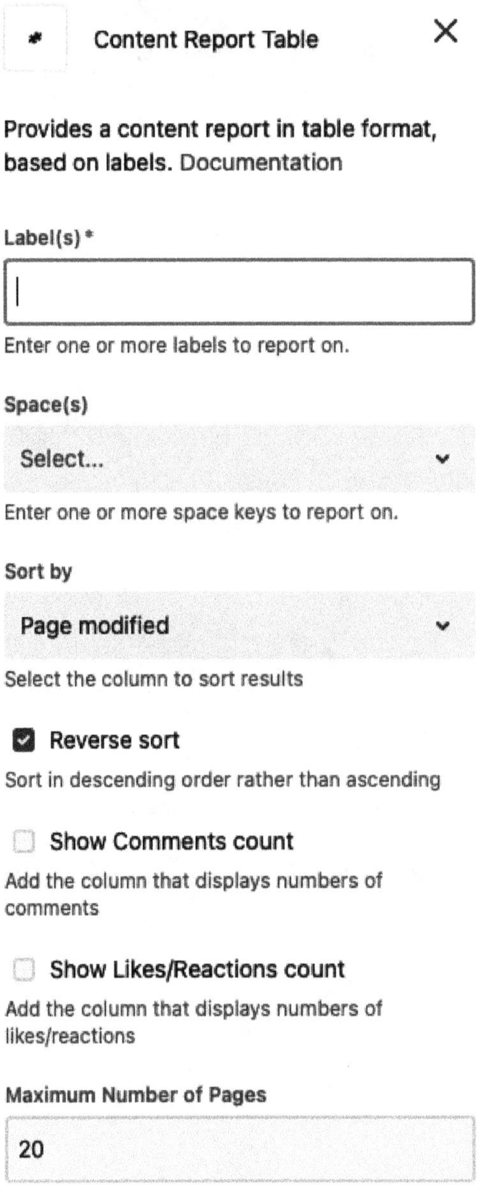

Figure 5.14 – The Content Report Table macro

As you can see, it is possible to generate this report based on one label or more. You can see the output of this macro in the following screenshot:

Content Report Table		
Title	**Creator**	**Modified**
Sample page	Eren Kalelioğlu	20 minutes ago
2023-01-15 Meeting notes	Eren Kalelioğlu	Jan 14, 2023
2023-01-14 Meeting notes	Eren Kalelioğlu	Jan 14, 2023

Figure 5.15 – The output of the Content Report Table macro

As you can see, this report currently includes the name of the page, the creator, and the date it was last updated. By changing the settings of the macro, you can add additional columns and change the order of this list.

In this section, we've reviewed macros that use labels. Now, it's time to examine the macros that interact with the pages.

Discovering macros that interact with pages

This section will explore macros that allow you to interact with other pages. The number of macros you can use for this purpose is quite large. Let's now cover the six macros we think are the most important ones:

- Include Page
- Children Display
- Excerpt and Excerpt Include
- Recently Updated
- Recently Updated Dashboard
- Table of Contents

Include Page

Sometimes, you may need to reuse content from one page over and over on others. In this case, the Include Page macro will come in handy. With this macro, you can display a page inside another page.

There are two scenarios where this macro is very practical:

- You can reuse content from one page over and over on other pages. When a section that appears on several pages is changed on one page, you do not need to update individual pages that display that content. You can update the content from one place and only once, and all pages that show this content will be updated.

- You can use this macro when you want a certain part of a page to be seen or modified only by authorized people, using page restrictions. You can create the section you want to hide as a separate page and embed this page inside the main page.

Children Display

Using this macro, you can list pages under a specific page.

You can see the settings of this macro in the following screenshot:

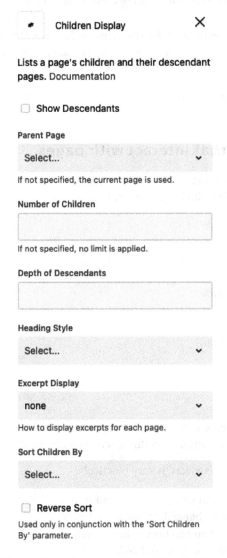

Figure 5.16 – The configuration parameters of the Children Display macro

As you can see, this macro has many settings. First, you need to select the page where you will list the child pages. If you skip this selection, the child pages where you placed the macro will be listed instead.

You can adjust the level of detail of the resulting list using settings such as the number of child pages and the depth of descendants. Thanks to the **Excerpt Display** setting, you can make the summary sections of the child pages in the list.

You can customize the list's order and heading styles to wrap everything up.

Excerpt and Excerpt Include

Occasionally, you will want to reuse only a part of a page on another. In this case, there are two macros you can benefit from:

- **Excerpt**: You can determine which part of a page will be reused using the Excerpt macro
- **Excerpt Include**: Using the Excerpt Include macro, you can bring the section you determined a step ago into the page

Now, let's get to know these two macros better.

You can see the settings page of the **Excerpt** macro in the following screenshot.

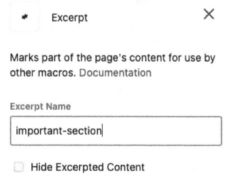

Figure 5.17 – The Excerpt macro

As you can see, there are only two parts here. In the first part, we need to give this field a name. If you wish, you can activate the **Hide Excerpted Content** option so that this special region does not appear on the page. Note that this section will be visible in edit mode and hidden in view mode.

Let's see what this macro looks like on a page:

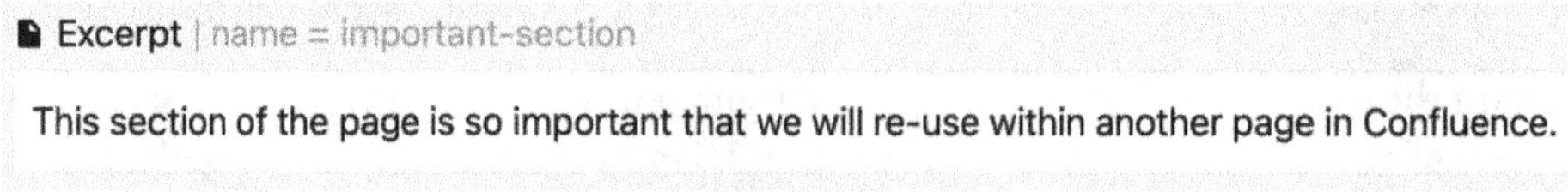

📄 **Excerpt** | name = important-section

This section of the page is so important that we will re-use within another page in Confluence.

Figure 5.18 – The Excerpt macro on a page

As you can see in the previous screenshot, we selected the contents from a section of the page and named this section `important-section`. We will be able to access any content that we add in this section from another page.

Notably, you can add more than one Excerpt macro to a page.

Now, it's time to look at the Excerpt Include macro. First, let's discover the configuration parameters of this macro, as shown in the following screenshot:

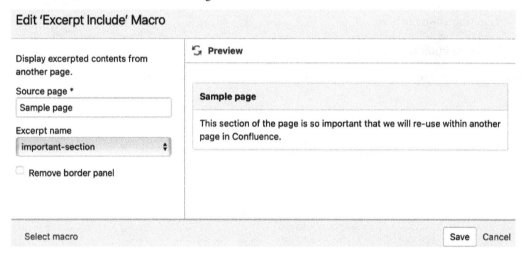

Figure 5.19 – The configuration parameters of the Excerpt Include macro

As you can see, there are two sections on the configuration page of this macro. On the left section, firstly, it is necessary to specify the page from which we will draw a section. Then, you need to choose the excerpt name. In the right section, you can preview this macro's output.

Once you activate the **Remove border panel** option, the section added to the page will appear as if it's a part of that page. It won't be noticeable that this section was brought from another page.

Recently Updated

This macro lets you dynamically generate a list of the latest updated content in your selected fields. You can see the settings of this macro in the following screenshot:

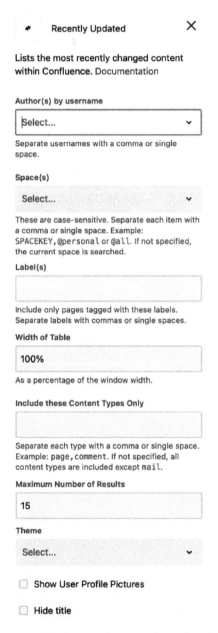

Figure 5.20 – Configuring the Recently Updated macro

There are many settings where you can customize the output of this macro. The most important setting to pay attention to is the list of spaces to monitor. If you don't select any fields here, only the updated pages in the space of the page you inserted the macro into will be listed.

This macro can list many types of content, such as comments, not just the pages. Note that you can limit which types of content will be listed.

Also, you can filter the contents using labels.

The output of this macro is shown in the following screenshot:

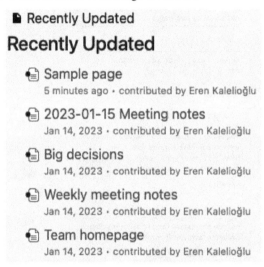

Figure 5.21 – The output of the Recently Updated macro

As you can see, this macro lists all recently updated content. The content's title, the date it was updated, and the person who last edited it are displayed here.

Recently Updated Dashboard

This macro is a slightly more advanced version of the previous macro. Let's look at the output of this macro, which will be significantly helpful when the number of people working in the Confluence environment increases:

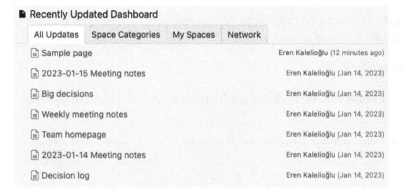

Figure 5.22 – The Recently Updated Dashboard output

As you can see, the listed content is organized by tabs. You can see the settings of this macro in the following screenshot:

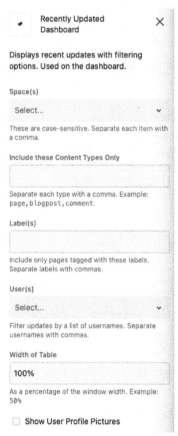

Figure 5.23 – The configuration parameters of the Recently Updated Dashboard macro

The settings of this macro are very similar to the previous one. The difference is that you can specify which user's updates you want to see.

Table of Contents

With this macro, which you will probably use frequently, you can add a dynamic table of contents to a page.

This macro has several settings; let's examine them now.

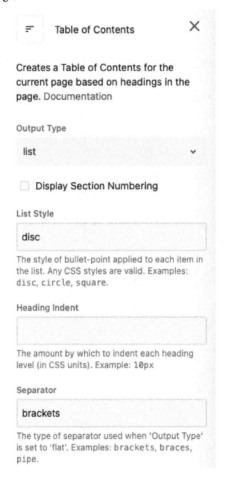

Figure 5.24 – The configuration parameters of the Table of Contents macro

You can see the first part of the settings page, which will help you to adjust how the dynamic content section will appear. You can also apply section numbering to the headings and set the structural properties of the table of contents in the following screenshot.

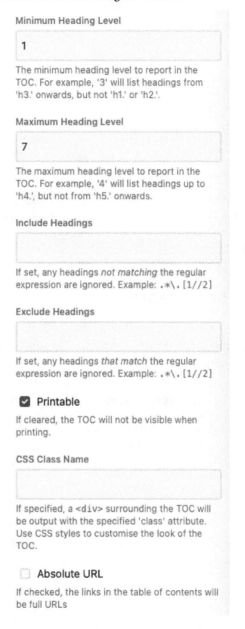

Figure 5.25 – The configuration parameters of the Table of Contents macro (continued)

Also, note that it is possible to change the appearance of the table of contents using **Cascading Style Sheets (CSS)**:

- Heading 1
    - Heading 1.1
    - Heading 1.2
- Heading 2
    - Heading 2.1
- Heading 3

Figure 5.26 – The output of the Table of Contents macro

As you can see, Confluence creates a dynamic table of contents based on the page titles.

In this section, we have examined the most critical macros that Confluence offers us. There are many more macros on Confluence than we've seen here, and we encourage you to explore them.

You may decide that the macros on Confluence are not enough for you; if so, you have options. In the next section, we'll discuss adding new macros to Confluence.

Adding macros to Confluence

It is possible to add macros to Confluence. There are two ways to do this – the first is to add a macro through the Atlassian Marketplace, and the other is to develop your macro from scratch. In this section, we will share practical information about both options.

Adding macros via the Atlassian Marketplace

You can find many Confluence macros on the Atlassian Marketplace, and you can upload the ones you like to your environment and start using them immediately. The following are a few recommendations that will be useful when evaluating macros:

- Make sure that you trust the producer of the macro
- Make sure that the macro is sufficient for information security
- Atlassian puts so much effort into ensuring that the content on this platform is world-class, but remember – the primary responsibility here is yours

Develop a new macro

You may want to develop your macro for various reasons. Maybe you couldn't find such a macro on Marketplace, didn't like the macros you found, or had reservations about information security. Whatever the reason, knowing you can develop your macro is reassuring.

Developing a new Confluence macro is beyond the scope of this book. However, we would like to share a few notes that will be useful:

- The essential information required to develop a macro is available on Atlassian's websites
- You can develop the macro yourself
- The macro you develop needs to go beyond operating error-free; it must be world-class regarding information security
- Remember that you will have to update the macro you develop constantly

Discovering Smart Links

In this section, we will discuss Smart Links, a relatively new feature. Smart Links make integrating a Confluence page with other systems straightforward. By using Smart Links, viewing content from supported programs as if you were inside the Confluence page is possible. For example, you can safely add a Miro visual to a Confluence page. Smart Links allow you to work with other programs without using any plugins. They are also very effective in making Confluence pages dynamic if used well. This is why we recommend you experiment a lot with Smart Links.

Smart Links is a new feature. While there was no Smart Links feature, we used to use plugins downloaded from the Atlassian Marketplace or develop software from scratch for such integrations. Smart Links have largely made these plugins and software development efforts unnecessary.

Smart Links work on the following principle – when you add a link to a Confluence page, the content where that link goes is examined. If Atlassian supports the system hosting the content, that content can be viewed as if it were inside the Confluence page. Many problems related to this integration, especially information security, are solved thanks to Smart Links.

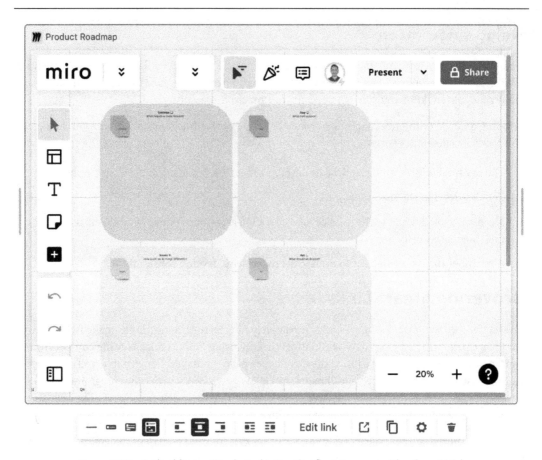

Figure 5.27 – Embedding a Miro board into a Confluence page with a Smart Link

As seen in the preceding screenshot, Smart Links seem very simple, but they have a serious infrastructure behind them. Major platforms, such as Google Drive and Miro, are supported by Smart Links. Although it is unlikely, not all links you add may be supported by Smart Links. However, knowing that Atlassian is increasing the amount of systems supported by Smart Links is helpful. Behind Smart Links lies a fundamental feature of Confluence (and all Atlassian products) – Atlassian products emphasize safe and easy integration with other products.

Summary

In this chapter, we gained significant experience with Confluence. First, we talked about dynamic content. We've seen different ways to make pages dynamic. We learned the concept of labels, the purpose of labels, and how they are used. Then, we covered macros. We saw the basic logic of macros, and then we examined the selected macros individually. Finally, we discovered different ways to enrich Confluence's rich macro library.

Thanks to what you have learned in this chapter, you can comfortably carry out the work in the following parts of the book. In the next chapter, you will learn how to manage a software development project using Confluence by applying the concepts we've seen here.

Questions

1. What are the macros that use labels?
2. Explain the Related Labels macro.
3. Explain the Content Report Table macro.
4. Can more macros be added to Confluence? How?
5. Explain Smart Links.

Answers

1. Related Labels, Content by Label, Labels List, Popular Labels, and Content Report Table.
2. This macro fetches labels from other pages that share a label with the page the macro was added to. Thus, it allows you to list the related labels on your page.
3. You can use this macro to report pages with a specific label in a table.
4. Yes. You can add new macros to Confluence via Atlassian Marketplace.
5. Using Smart Links, viewing the contents from supported programs as if they were inside the Confluence page is possible. For example, you can safely add a Miro visual to a Confluence page. Smart Links allow you to work with other programs without using any plugins.

Part 2: Building a Real Confluence Site

This part will present tangible solutions using Confluence for four crucial issues often encountered in companies. First, you'll discover how to utilize Confluence effectively during software and product development. Next, we'll delve into creating a robust knowledge base with Confluence and how to provide your employees with a personalized space. Lastly, we'll discuss strategies to design a space in Confluence that addresses the needs of multiple teams within your company.

This part contains the following chapters:

- *Chapter 6, Creating a Space for a Software Project*
- *Chapter 7, Creating a Space for Product Management*
- *Chapter 8, Setting Up a Knowledge Base*
- *Chapter 9, Setting Up a Personal Space*
- *Chapter 10, Connecting All Teams with Confluence*

6

Creating a Space for a Software Project

In the previous chapter, we delved deep into the workings of Confluence by exploring various aspects of dynamic content creation. We learned about the critical role of labels, their purposes, and their applications. Additionally, we embarked on a journey through macros, starting from understanding their fundamental logic to a detailed examination of selected macros, ultimately uncovering different ways to maximize the potential of Confluence's extensive macro library.

As the world has witnessed a significant shift toward remote work, the challenges associated with managing software projects for distributed teams have multiplied. Effective communication, collaboration, and project management tools have become the linchpin of remote operations. This is where Confluence shines bright as an indispensable ally for remote software development teams, enabling them to manage projects successfully and foster robust collaboration. It serves as a centralized content-sharing and collaboration platform, aggregating all project-related materials, such as designs, requirements, and user guides, into a single location that is easily accessible to all team members. With the necessity of having a centralized, up-to-date resource accessible to everyone, Confluence emerges as the perfect solution for remote teams' specific needs.

Furthermore, Confluence comes packed with features that streamline project tracking and management. Its integration with Jira facilitates task tracking, workflow management, and project progress monitoring, allowing teams to generate reports, gain insight into the project's development, and engage with team members on tasks. Since effective communication and collaboration are the bedrock of remote teams' productivity, Confluence aids in promoting these by facilitating information sharing, clarifying responsibilities across teams, and centralizing project documentation.

In this chapter, we will guide you on how to utilize Confluence effectively to create project spaces, leverage document management features, collaborate seamlessly, and track projects. The goal is to empower remote software development teams to manage their projects successfully. This information is pivotal as Confluence not only enhances team collaboration and streamlines project workflows but also ensures everyone has access to the most current project information.

By the end of this chapter, you will have a comprehensive understanding of how to create a Confluence space tailored for a software project, which is a crucial step in managing remote collaboration effectively. The knowledge acquired here will be instrumental in helping you and your team navigate the challenges of remote work, ultimately leading to more successful project outcomes.

In this chapter, we will cover the following topics:

- Discovering different roles in a software development project
- Creating a single source of truth for a software development project
- Discovering the software project space template
- Customizing Confluence's software development template for project-based needs
- Using Confluence as a hub with external tools
- Using Confluence and Jira together for software project management
- Using the step-by-step guide to create a software project space on Confluence

Discovering different roles in a software development project

In a remote software development team, there are several roles, known as "personas" or "stakeholders," each with their own unique needs and ways they can benefit from a Confluence space. Here are a few examples:

- **Software developers**: Being at the core of the team, software developers create and test the code that makes up your software product. They need easy access to technical specifications, design documents, coding standards, and project plans. They also need a way to communicate effectively with other team members. A Confluence space can serve as a central repository for all this information, making it easy for developers to find what they need. They can also use Confluence's commenting features to ask questions, discuss problems, and share ideas.

- **Product managers**: These individuals are responsible for guiding product development, making decisions about what features to include, and prioritizing tasks. They need a holistic view of project progress, as well as the ability to drill down into details when necessary. Confluence can help with this need through pages dedicated to project plans, progress tracking, and task lists. Product managers can also use Confluence to communicate their decisions and gather feedback from the team.

- **Quality assurance (QA) engineers**: QA engineers test the software for document bugs. They need access to test plans, bug reports, and sometimes design documents or technical specs. They can use Confluence pages dedicated to test plans and bug tracking. QA engineers can also use Confluence to report bugs, discuss them with the team, and track their resolution.

- **DevOps engineers**: They focus on the systems and processes that support the development team, such as version control systems, **continuous integration/continuous deployment (CI/CD)** pipelines, and infrastructure. DevOps engineers need access to technical documentation and system specs. At this point, Confluence can serve as a central source of information, to document their processes and procedures, which is crucial for effective DevOps practices.

- **UX/UI designers**: They are responsible for user experience and interface design, having the need to share their design and gather feedback. In this case, UX/UI designers can benefit from a Confluence space where they share their material, discuss it with the team, and track changes and updates.

Creating a single source of truth for a software development project

Creating a single source of truth on Confluence for a software project involves organizing and centralizing all relevant information in a structured and accessible manner. Here's a step-by-step guide on how to achieve this goal:

1. **Define the structure**: Plan how you will organize your Confluence space to reflect the structure of your software project. Consider creating a hierarchy of pages and sub-pages that align with different aspects of the project, such as a project overview, requirements, design, development, testing, and documentation.

2. **Project overview**: Create a page dedicated to providing an overview of the project, including the objectives, scope, stakeholders, and timeline. This page can serve as a North Star for team members and stakeholders to understand the project's context.

3. **Requirements**: Document the project requirements in detail. Use Confluence's formatting options to structure and categorize the requirements. Also, consider using tables, bullet points, or checklists to better organize and track requirements, and make sure the material is easy to follow.

4. **Design and architecture**: Create pages to capture the design and architecture of the software. Include diagrams, wireframes, UI mockups, and any other visual representations that help communicate the design decisions. Provide explanations and annotations to clarify the design choices made.

5. **Development**: Use Confluence to track the development progress and make updates visible. Create pages or use templates to document user stories, development tasks, and backlog items. Use tables or task management macros to track task status, assignees, and due dates. Encourage team members to provide regular updates on their progress.

6. **Testing**: Document the testing strategy, test plans, and test results within Confluence. Create pages to outline the testing approach, define test cases, and track test results. Include any relevant screenshots or logs to provide context for failed tests and bug reports.

7. **Documentation**: Use Confluence as a central hub for all project-related documentation, which includes technical documentation, API references, user manuals, and release notes. Ensure that the documentation is up to date and easily accessible to team members and stakeholders.

8. **Collaboration and communication**: Leverage Confluence's collaborative features to encourage team members to share their insights, ask questions, and provide feedback. Utilize commenting, @mentions, and notifications to facilitate discussions and keep everyone informed.

9. **Version control and history**: Use Confluence's version control capabilities. Track changes in pages, review them, and revert to previous versions to maintain a progress record if needed. This feature also boosts transparency through the project's evolution.

10. **Promote adoption and governance**: Encourage team members to use Confluence consistently. Provide training and support to ensure everyone understands how to use Confluence effectively and master the best practices. Establish governance practices to ensure the accuracy, quality, and currency of the information in the Confluence space.

By following these steps, you can create a reliable single source of truth on Confluence for your remote software project. These steps will assist your team in streamlining collaboration, improving transparency, and ensuring that team members are aligned and working with the most up-to-date project information.

Discovering the software project space template

There is a ready-made space template on Confluence. In it, you can have Confluence ready for your project. In this section, we'll review this template and discuss the content you can work on.

To start with, let's create a new space:

1. Click **Spaces** from the menu at the top.

2. Click **Create a space**.

You can see this dialog in the following screenshot.

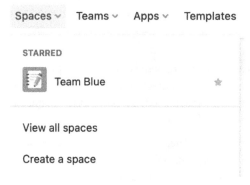

Figure 6.1 – Creating a space

As seen in the previous screenshot, you can list all the spaces in the Confluence environment from the **Spaces** menu.

Now, let's choose a template to get started quickly with your new space. For this, follow this set of instructions:

1. Choose the **Software project** template to populate your space with useful content for a software project.

2. Click **Next**.

This interface is shown in the following screenshot.

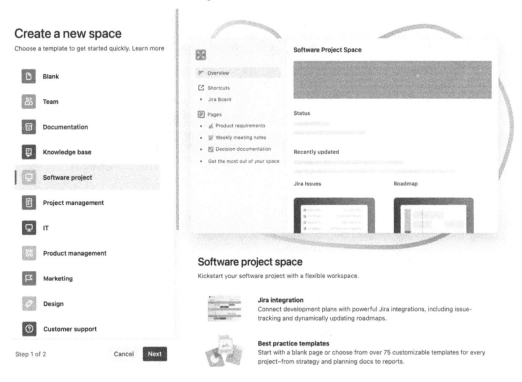

Figure 6.2 – Choosing the Software project template

As you can see in the previous screenshot, Confluence offers a number of space templates. You can preview the template you selected on the left from the right side of the interface.

At this stage, Confluence will ask you to add details to your new space. Follow these instructions to personalize your space:

1. Choose a space icon.
2. Name your space.
3. Select a Jira instance (if you use Jira).
4. Select a Jira project (if you use Jira).
5. Choose **Default permissions** for space permissions.
6. Define a space key to uniquely identify this space.
7. Click **Create space**.

You can see all the things we mentioned here in the following screenshot.

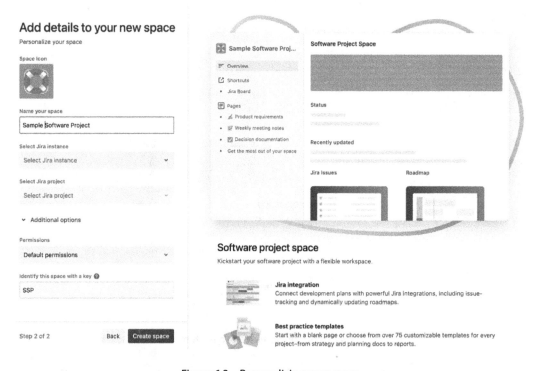

Figure 6.3 – Personalizing your space

As you can see in the previous screenshot, we provided all the information Confluence needed to create our new space.

Congratulations, now you have a space and four pages in it:

- Template – **Product requirements**

- Template – **Meeting notes**

- Template – **Decision documentation**

- Get the most out of your software project space

Now, you have an overview page that acts as the home page of your space. You can see this newly created space in the following screenshot.

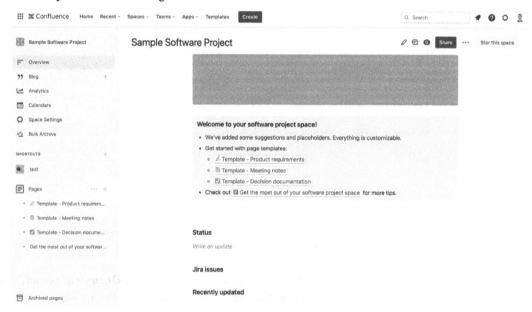

Figure 6.4 – Overview page of the Software project space

We are now ready to discover each of the four pages.

Product requirements template

The **Product requirements** template in Confluence is a crucial tool for remote teams working on software development. For a remote team, clearly defined product requirements are essential to ensure that everyone is aligned on the project's goals, features, and constraints, despite being physically apart. It provides a single source of truth that everyone can refer to, minimizing misunderstandings and communication gaps. For a software development team, well-defined product requirements are the foundation upon which the entire project is built. It helps in setting clear expectations for what needs to be developed, the features and functionalities that are essential, and the constraints that need to be considered. The **Product requirements** template in Confluence provides a structured format to document all these details, making it easier for the team to understand and work toward the common goal. By centralizing all the project-related information in an easily accessible location, Confluence's **Product requirements** template not only streamlines the development process but also fosters better collaboration and communication among remote teams.

As with almost all templates on Confluence, Atlassian has included a table with the basic information of the document as the first content in this template. You can see this table in the next screenshot.

Target release	Type // to add a target release date
Epic	Type /Jira to add Jira epics and issues
Document status	DRAFT
Document owner	@ mention owner
Designer	@ designer
Tech lead	@ lead
Technical writers	@ writers
QA	

◎ Objective

Figure 6.5 – Product requirements template

As you can see in the previous screenshot, you can add your teammates to the **Document owner**, **Designer**, **Tech lead**, and **Technical writers** fields. You can customize this table as you wish.

The Objective section

The **Objective** section in the **Product requirements** template is a pivotal element when documenting product requirements. Clearly defining the objectives is crucial for several reasons. First, it sets the direction for the entire project by outlining the goals that the product is intended to achieve. This helps in aligning the team and ensuring that everyone is working toward the same end goal. Second, it provides a basis for decision-making throughout the project. When faced with different options or when making trade-offs, the objectives serve as a guide to making decisions that are in the best interest of the product. It is important to note that objectives are different from requirements. Objectives are the overarching goals that the product aims to achieve, whereas requirements are the specific functionalities and features that the product must have to meet those objectives. For example, an objective could be "Improve user engagement on the platform," while a requirement could be "Implement a recommendation algorithm to suggest personalized content to users." By clearly defining the objectives and differentiating them from the requirements, the Product requirements template in Confluence helps in creating a well-structured and comprehensive document that serves as a roadmap for the entire development process. You can put the project objectives on your page. Here are some objective ideas:

- **Develop a robust and scalable enterprise chat program**: The primary objective is to create a chat program that meets the needs of businesses, providing secure and efficient communication channels for employees.

- **Ensure seamless integration with existing enterprise systems**: The chat program should seamlessly integrate with other enterprise systems commonly used by companies, such as email clients, project management tools, and document collaboration platforms. This integration will enhance productivity and streamline workflows for users.

- **Deliver a user-friendly and intuitive interface**: The chat program should have a user-friendly interface that is intuitive and easy to navigate. Users should be able to quickly adapt to the platform, minimizing the learning curve.

After completing the **Objective** section, let's review the next three sections of the template: **Success metrics**, **Assumptions**, and **Milestones**. You can see these three sections in the next screenshot.

📊 Success metrics

Goal ↓	Metric

👥 Assumptions

⭐ Milestones

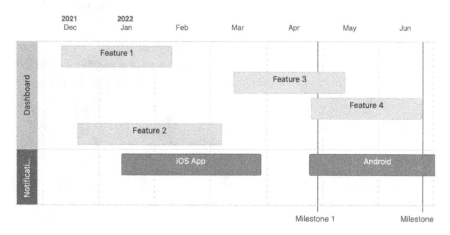

Figure 6.6 – Success metrics, Assumptions, and Milestones

Now, let's examine the three sections seen in the previous screenshot one by one and give realistic examples of each.

The Success metrics section

The **Success metrics** section in the **Product requirements** template is another crucial component that should be clearly defined when documenting product requirements. Specifying success metrics is essential as it provides a clear definition of what success looks like for the project. It sets the criteria that will be used to evaluate the success of the product once it is developed and implemented. This not only helps in setting clear expectations for the team but also provides a basis for evaluating the product post-implementation.

Success metrics are different from both objectives and requirements. While objectives define the overarching goals of the product, and requirements specify the functionalities and features needed to achieve those objectives, success metrics define the criteria that will be used to evaluate whether the objectives have been successfully met. For example, if the objective is "Improve user engagement on the platform," a requirement could be "Implement a recommendation algorithm to suggest personalized content to users," and a success metric could be "Increase the average session duration of users by 20%."

By clearly defining the success metrics, along with the objectives and requirements, the **Product requirements** template in Confluence helps in creating a comprehensive document that not only guides the development process but also sets the criteria for evaluating the success of the product post-implementation.

Here, we provide three sample assumptions:

- **Performance and scalability**: The chat program should be capable of handling a large number of users and messages without significant performance degradation. It should be able to accommodate the needs of growing organizations and scale accordingly.

- **Integration success rate**: The success criteria for integration can be defined by the percentage of successful integrations with various enterprise systems. A high integration success rate indicates that the chat program effectively integrates with commonly used tools, facilitating seamless data exchange and collaboration.

- **User satisfaction and adoption**: User feedback and satisfaction surveys can be used to measure the success of the user interface. High user satisfaction scores and positive feedback show that the interface is intuitive and meets the needs of users, leading to higher adoption rates within the organization.

The Assumptions section

The **Assumptions** section in the **Product requirements** template plays an often underappreciated but vital role in the planning and execution of a project. Assumptions are essentially the conditions or facts that the team assumes to be true for the project to move forward successfully. These could be anything from the availability of certain technologies to market conditions or user behavior.

Clearly listing out assumptions is crucial for several reasons. First, it helps identify areas of risk early in the project, allowing for proactive risk management strategies. For instance, if an assumption doesn't hold true down the line, recognizing it early could save both time and resources. Also, it provides a basis for clarity and mutual understanding among team members and stakeholders. Everyone involved can refer back to these assumptions to align their efforts or to validate the viability of the objectives and requirements set forth.

By explicitly stating assumptions in the **Product requirements** template on Confluence, you can create a more robust roadmap for your project, one that accounts for potential risks and sets a common understanding for all parties involved.

Here, we provide three sample assumptions:

Assumption 1

The target companies have a need for an enterprise chat program.

Rationale1

Before embarking on the development of the chat program, it is essential to assume that there is a market demand for such a solution. Conducting market research or gathering feedback from potential clients can help validate this assumption.

Assumption 2

The development team has the necessary technical expertise to build the chat program.

Rationale 2

Assuming that the development team possesses the required skills and knowledge to develop a robust and scalable chat program is crucial. This assumption considers the team's proficiency in relevant programming languages, frameworks, and technologies.

Assumption 3

The integration with existing enterprise systems is feasible.

Rationale 3

Assuming that integrating the chat program with other enterprise systems commonly used by companies is technically feasible involves considering factors such as available APIs, documentation, and the compatibility of the systems to ensure smooth data exchange and collaboration.

The Milestones section

A milestone in the context of project management refers to a significant point or event in the project timeline. These are notable moments that signify some form of progress or achievement in the project. For example, completing the design phase, finishing the first prototype, or passing a critical review can all be considered milestones. Milestones are different from objectives as they serve as markers along the road to achieving an objective. While an objective is a broad and overarching goal that the project aims to achieve, a milestone is a specific and measurable point that marks progress toward that objective.

Clearly defining milestones in the **Product requirements** template is essential for several reasons. First, it helps in tracking progress during the project execution. By setting specific milestones, the team can monitor whether the project is moving as planned or whether any adjustments are needed. Second, it helps in setting clear expectations and keeping the team motivated. Achieving a milestone provides a sense of accomplishment and helps maintain momentum throughout the project. Lastly, it assists in effective communication with stakeholders by providing clear indicators of progress.

In summary, by clearly specifying milestones in the **Product requirements** template on Confluence, you can facilitate better project tracking, team motivation, and stakeholder communication, all of which are crucial for the successful execution of a project.

You can define your milestones in this section, where we provide three samples:

Milestone 1: Project Initiation

- **Start Date**: June 1, 2023
- **End Date**: June 15, 2023
- **Description**: This milestone marks the official start of the project and includes activities such as project planning, team formation, and setting up the development environment. Key deliverables may include a project charter, initial project plan, and team roles/responsibilities.

Milestone 2: Prototype Development

- **Start Date**: June 16, 2023
- **End Date**: August 15, 2023

- **Description**: This milestone focuses on developing a functional prototype of the enterprise chat program. The development team will work on implementing core features, designing the user interface, and conducting initial testing. By the end of this milestone, a working prototype should be available for evaluation and feedback.

Milestone 3: Beta Release and Testing

- **Start Date**: August 16, 2023

- **End Date**: October 15, 2023

- **Description**: This milestone involves refining the prototype based on user feedback and conducting comprehensive testing to ensure stability and usability. The development team will address any identified issues, optimize performance, and make the necessary adjustments based on user requirements. The beta version of the chat program will be released to a select group of users for further testing and feedback.

The Requirements section

Requirements are specific, detailed instructions or needs that must be fulfilled for a project or product to be considered complete. They are the essential functionalities, features, and constraints that define the final output. Requirements differ from objectives in that objectives are overarching goals or outcomes that the project aims to achieve, whereas requirements are the detailed specifications necessary to accomplish these objectives. For example, an objective might be to develop a mobile application that helps users manage their daily tasks, while a requirement would specify that the application should allow users to create, edit, and delete tasks.

It is crucial to clearly define requirements in the **Product requirements** document for several reasons. First, well-defined requirements set clear expectations for the team, helping to prevent misunderstandings or conflicts later in the project. Second, they serve as a basis for estimating the time and resources needed for the project, which is essential for planning and budgeting. Lastly, clear requirements are necessary for testing and validation purposes, as they serve as the criteria against which the final product will be evaluated. When writing requirements, it is important they are **specific, measurable, achievable, relevant, and time-bound (SMART)**. Also, involve all relevant stakeholders, including end users, to ensure that all perspectives are considered and that the final product will meet the needs of all parties involved.

In the next screenshot, you can see the three requirement examples we provided.

	Requirement	User stories	Importance	Notes
1	Real-time Messaging	1. As a user, I want to send instant messages to my colleagues to facilitate quick communication and collaboration. 2. As a user, I want to receive real-time notifications for new messages to stay updated on conversations. 3. As a user, I want the chat program to support group chats so that I can communicate with multiple team members simultaneously.	HIGH	This requirement focuses on enabling real-time messaging functionality within the chat program. It ensures sending and receiving messages instantly, providing users with efficient communication and collaboration. Supporting group chats enhances team collaboration by enabling seamless communication among team members.
2	Message Search and History	1. As a user, I want to search for specific messages within the chat program to find relevant information quickly. 2. As a user, I want to view and retrieve chat message history for reference and record-keeping purposes. 3. As a user, I want the chat program to provide advanced filtering options for searching messages based on specific criteria.	MEDIUM	This requirement focuses on providing robust search and history capabilities within the chat program. Users should be able to search for specific messages using keywords or filters to find relevant information instantly. Also, the chat program should maintain a comprehensive message history that users can access for reference and record-keeping purposes.
3	File and Media Sharing	1. As a user, I want to share files and documents within the chat program to facilitate collaboration on project-related materials. 2. As a user, I want to preview shared media files such as images and videos in the chat program. 3. As a user, I want to get notified when someone shares a file or media in a chat to stay informed about new content.	HIGH	This requirement focuses on enabling file and media sharing capabilities within the chat program. Users should be able to upload and share files, documents, images, and videos with their colleagues, promoting collaboration and knowledge sharing. Previewing shared media files within the chat program enhances the user experience. Real-time notifications about new shared files ensure that users are directly informed about the new content.

Figure 6.7 – Requirements section

As you can see in the previous screenshot, we identified several user stories for each requirement. We determined the importance level of the requirements, and finally, we wrote the notes about the requirements in detail. You can also write your own requirements in the format you want.

The User interaction and design section

In the **User interaction and design** section of your **Confluence** page, you can include various elements related to the user experience, interface design, and interaction patterns of your chat program. Here are some items you can consider adding to this section:

- **User interface (UI) design**: Provide an overview of the overall UI design of the chat program. This can include descriptions, screenshots, or mockups showcasing the visual elements, color schemes, typography, and layout of the UI. Let's add that you can benefit from Smart Links, which will display schemes from Miro or mockups from Figma. This way, everything will be in one place and you won't have to switch between tools.

- **User flows**: Present user flow diagrams or visual representations of how users navigate through different screens and interact with various features of the chat program. Highlight key user actions, transitions between screens, and decision points in the user journey.

- **Interaction patterns**: Describe the interaction patterns and behaviors implemented in the chat program. This can include details on how users initiate chats, send messages, navigate between chat groups, view notifications, or perform other common actions within the application. Explain any unique interaction patterns or gestures that enhance the user experience.

- **Wireframes and prototypes**: Include wireframes or interactive prototypes that illustrate the initial design concepts and layout of the chat program. These visual representations can help stakeholders and team members better understand the planned user interface and gather feedback early in the development process.

- **Usability testing and feedback**: Document the results of usability testing sessions conducted with potential users or stakeholders. Include feedback received during the testing process, insights gained, and any design iterations or improvements made based on the feedback. This demonstrates the iterative design process and user-centered approach adopted in the development of the chat program.

- **Design guidelines and style guide**: Provide a style guide or design guidelines that outline the visual and interaction principles to be followed in the development of the chat program. Include guidelines on typography, color usage, iconography, spacing, and other design considerations to ensure consistency across the application.

- **Accessibility considerations**: Discuss the accessibility features and considerations incorporated into the design of the chat program. Highlight how the user interface adheres to accessibility standards, such as support for screen readers, keyboard navigation, color contrast, and other accessibility related best practices.

- **Micro-interactions**: Describe any micro-interactions or subtle animations within the chat program that enhance the user experience and provide feedback on user actions. Examples include visual indicators for message sending, typing indicators, message delivery confirmations, or notifications.

By including these elements in the **User interaction and design** section, you can provide stakeholders, designers, and developers with valuable insights regarding the design principles, user experience considerations, and visual aesthetics of the chat program. Thus, you will have a cohesive and intuitive user interface that enhances user satisfaction and engagement.

The Open Questions section

As you manage the project, you and your team will have a lot of questions in mind. It is very important to identify these questions and record them on Confluence. As questions get answered, you can add answers to this section of the page. Having questions and answers transparently visible to the entire project team is invaluable to members of your remote team. In the next screenshot, we've given you three sample questions about the project.

	Question	Answer	Date answered
1	How can users invite new team members to join a chat group?	To invite new team members to a chat group, users can navigate the group chat settings and look for the Invite Members option. Clicking on this option will open a dialog where users can enter the email addresses or usernames of the team members they want to invite. Once the invitation is sent, the invited members will receive an email notification with instructions on how to join the chat group.	May 29, 2023
2	Can users delete or edit sent messages in the chat program?	In the chat program, users cannot directly delete or edit sent messages. However, they can utilize the Retract feature within a limited time frame after sending a message. The Retract option allows users to remove a message from the conversation within a window of time after it was sent. It's important to note that once the window expires, messages become permanent and cannot be modified or deleted.	Jun 19, 2023
3	How does the chat program handle message encryption and data security?		Not answered yet

Figure 6.8 – Open Questions section

As seen in the previous screenshot, some questions may not get answered right away. It is important that questions that remain unanswered stay visible to the entire team. We also recommend that you record the date the questions were answered.

The Out of Scope section

Out of Scope refers to any elements, features, or functionalities that will not be addressed or included in the current phase of a project. Clearly defining what is out of scope is as crucial as specifying what is in scope because it sets clear boundaries for the project and helps manage stakeholders' expectations. It also helps to avoid "scope creep," which occurs when additional work is added to the project without proper analysis, documentation, and approval, leading to delays, increased costs, and other potential problems. When defining what is out of scope, it is important to be as detailed and explicit as possible and to involve all relevant stakeholders to ensure that all perspectives are considered and that there is a mutual understanding and agreement on what will and will not be included in the project.

Identifying and documenting out-of-scope elements is particularly important for remote teams, as it helps to prevent misunderstandings and conflicts that can arise when team members are not co-located and may have different assumptions or interpretations about the project. Remote teams can identify out-of-scope elements by conducting virtual brainstorming sessions, using online collaboration tools, and continuously communicating and sharing feedback throughout the project. This helps to ensure everyone has a clear and shared understanding of the project boundaries, which is essential for coordinating work, managing expectations, and ultimately delivering a successful project.

In the following screenshot, you can see the sample contents that can be written to the **Out of Scope** section.

	Feature	Notes
1	Video Conferencing	The chat program will focus on text-based communication and messaging functionalities. It will not include built-in video conferencing capabilities. Users should use separate video conferencing tools or platforms for conducting video meetings and conferences.
2	File Sharing and Document Collaboration	While the chat program will support sharing of text-based messages and links, it will not provide extensive file-sharing and document collaboration features. Users will not upload and share files directly within the chat program or collaborate on document editing or version control. They should use file-sharing and collaboration tools dedicated to such purposes.
3	Voice Messaging	The chat program will not include voice messaging functionality. Users will not be able to send or receive voice messages within the chat program. The focus will primarily be on text-based communication and messaging.

Figure 6.9 – Out of Scope section

The out-of-scope topics you see in the previous screenshot will be much more numerous in a real project. You can use any format you want to record these topics. The important thing is that it is an easy-to-understand, sustainable format.

The Meeting Notes template

The **Meeting Notes** template in Confluence is an incredibly useful tool designed to optimize the way teams document and share information discussed during meetings. This template serves multiple purposes; it helps in organizing the meeting agenda beforehand, recording key discussions, decisions, and action items during the meeting, and sharing this information with team members after the meeting. Having a structured document that includes all the vital details discussed during a meeting is crucial for keeping all team members aligned, tracking progress, and ensuring accountability. It eliminates the chances of any misunderstanding or miscommunication and provides a clear and concise record of what was discussed, what decisions were made, and what the next steps that need to be taken are.

Moreover, the **Meeting Notes** template is highly customizable, allowing teams to tailor it to fit their specific needs and meeting formats. It usually includes sections for meeting attendees, agenda, discussions, decisions, and action items. After the meeting, the notes can be easily shared with the entire team, and because Confluence is a collaborative platform, team members can add comments, ask questions, and even update the document as required. This interactive and dynamic nature of the template ensures that everyone stays informed and engaged, even if they were unable to attend the meeting in person. Ultimately, the **Meeting Notes** template in Confluence is an essential tool for any team seeking to improve their communication, collaboration, and overall efficiency.

The **Meeting Notes** template in Confluence consists of six sections:

- Date
- Participants
- Goals
- Discussion topics
- Action items
- Discussions

You can use these sections as they are or modify them according to your preference. Now, we will explain how you can fill out the meeting template for a remote team with concrete examples.

Date

In this section, you can provide the date and time of the meeting: 29.5.2023, 19.00 - 21.00 UTC.

Note that including the time zone would be good practice, especially for remote teams.

Participants

You can include information on the participants of the meeting in this section, such as this:

- John Smith – john.smith@example.com
- Emma Johnson – emma.johnson@example.com
- Michael Davis – michael.davis@example.com

Goals

Every meeting has one or several objectives. It is critical to reflect on these objectives and make them visible to everyone for an effective meeting. This way, the entire team will be aligned on the meeting objectives; these could be goals, for example:

- Review the progress of the chat program development and discuss any challenges or roadblocks
- Brainstorm and make decisions regarding the user interface design and interaction patterns
- Assign tasks and responsibilities for the upcoming development sprint

As you can see, this meeting has three objectives, and they are visible to the entire team.

Discussion topics

It is a good idea to identify the discussion topics in advance. This way, you can save valuable time. You can also write notes in the table regarding the meeting topics, and define a time frame for each presenter. In the next screenshot, you can find examples of discussion topics we have prepared for you.

	Time (Minutes)	Item (Topic name)	Presenter	Notes
1	15	Progress update	John Smith	Review the completed tasks and the upcoming work
2	30	User interface design	Emma Johnson	Discuss wireframes and gather feedback
3	20	Sprint planning and task assignments	Michael Davis	Assign tasks and define priorities for the next sprint

Figure 6.10 – Discussion topics

As you can see in the previous screenshot, the duration in minutes, the name of the topic, the person responsible for the topic, and the notes on the topic are clearly defined for each discussion topic. You can add other information if you wish. We recommend that you update this table, which you created before the meeting, and fill it out to a large extent during and after the meeting.

Decisions

The **Decisions** section of the **Meeting Notes** template in Confluence is a critical component as it captures all the significant decisions made during a meeting. For remote teams, managing decisions made during a meeting is crucial as it ensures everyone is aligned and aware of the path forward. Documenting these decisions in the meeting notes is important as it creates a permanent record that can be referred to later, ensures accountability as it is clear who is responsible for what, and helps in keeping all team members, including those who could not attend the meeting, updated about the critical decisions made. When recording decisions, it is important to be clear and concise, specify who made the decision, and outline any next steps or actions that need to be taken as a result. Ideally, decisions should be recorded as they are made during the meeting by the designated note-taker – usually the person who organized the meeting or a designated scribe.

Recording decisions promptly during the meeting ensures that no critical information is lost or misunderstood, and it allows for any necessary clarification or additional discussion to occur in real time. It is the responsibility of the person designated to take the meeting notes to ensure that all decisions are accurately recorded and shared with the team as soon as possible after the meeting. This ensures that everyone has a clear and shared understanding of the decisions made and the next steps to be taken, which is crucial for the effective functioning of a remote team.

You can find examples of three decisions taken during the meeting in the next screenshot.

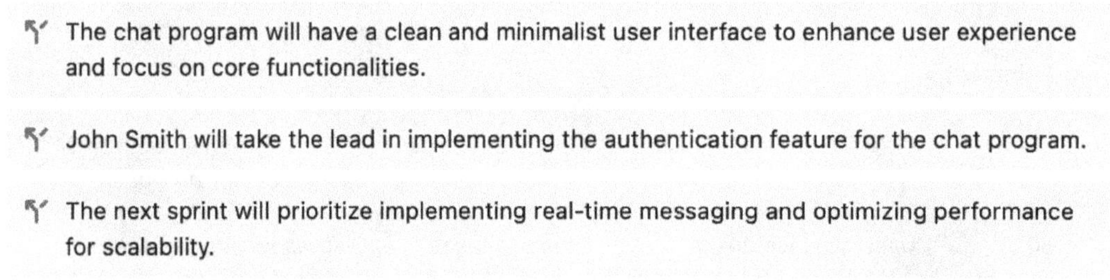

- The chat program will have a clean and minimalist user interface to enhance user experience and focus on core functionalities.

- John Smith will take the lead in implementing the authentication feature for the chat program.

- The next sprint will prioritize implementing real-time messaging and optimizing performance for scalability.

Figure 6.11 – Decision log

As seen, we use Confluence's decision tool to record each decision. We have seen this tool earlier in the book. Decisions recorded using this tool have an icon that looks like a green arrow at the beginning.

Let's remember that there is another macro called Decision Report, a macro that will help you summarize decisions from different pages in Confluence.

Action items

During the meeting, your team may define certain tasks to be completed. To ensure that these tasks are not overlooked, you can add them as action items in the **Action items** section of the meeting document.

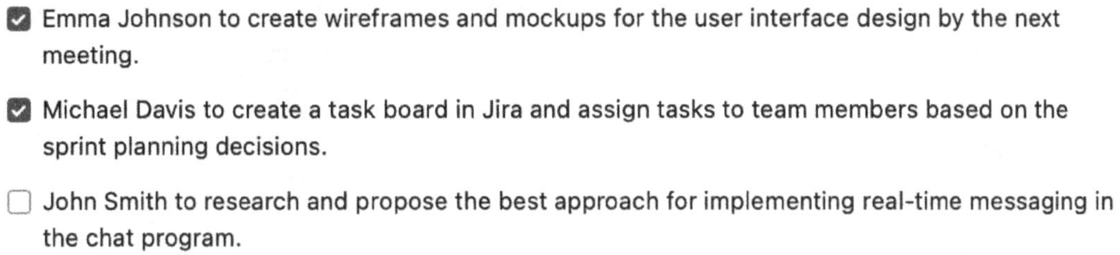

☑ Emma Johnson to create wireframes and mockups for the user interface design by the next meeting.

☑ Michael Davis to create a task board in Jira and assign tasks to team members based on the sprint planning decisions.

☐ John Smith to research and propose the best approach for implementing real-time messaging in the chat program.

Figure 6.12 – Action items

As you can see, three tasks were decided upon in the meeting. Two of these tasks have been completed, while one is still pending completion.

It's also a good practice to use the status macro to present statuses next to actions. The status macro is shown in the following screenshot.

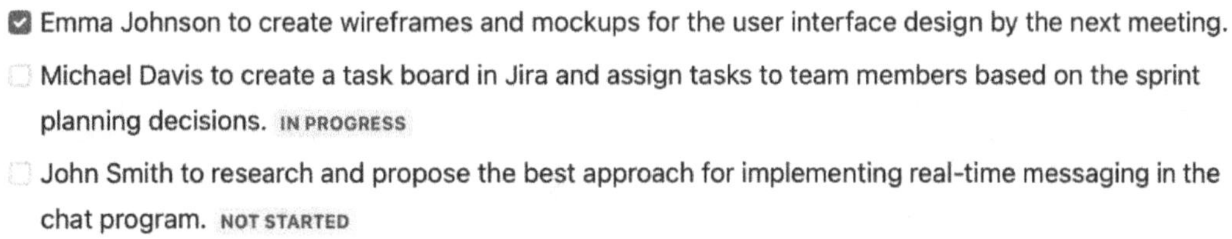

☑ Emma Johnson to create wireframes and mockups for the user interface design by the next meeting.

☐ Michael Davis to create a task board in Jira and assign tasks to team members based on the sprint planning decisions. IN PROGRESS

☐ John Smith to research and propose the best approach for implementing real-time messaging in the chat program. NOT STARTED

Figure 6.13 – Using status macro with action items

Decision document template

When making an important decision related to the project, using the **Decision Document** template in Confluence can be the practical option. Look at how this template may benefit your team:

- **Organization and structure**: The **Decision Document** template provides a structured format to capture and document key information related to the decision. It ensures that all relevant details are recorded in a consistent manner, making it easier to review and understand the decision-making process.

- **Clarity and transparency**: By documenting the decision in Confluence, team members and stakeholders can access and review the decision at any time. This promotes transparency and ensures that everyone is on the same page regarding the rationale behind the decision.

- **Accountability and ownership**: The template includes sections such as **Action Items** and **Outcome,** which help in assigning specific tasks and tracking the implementation of the decision. This fosters accountability and ensures that actions are taken to follow through on the decisions made.

- **Knowledge sharing and learning**: The **Decision Document** template becomes a valuable resource for future reference and learning. It captures the background information, options considered, and the decision-making process, allowing team members to understand the context and learn from past decisions.

- **Collaboration and input**: The template encourages collaboration by involving multiple stakeholders in the decision-making process. Team members can contribute insights, pros and cons, and alternative options for a more comprehensive and well-informed decision.

Overall, using the **Decision Document** Template in Confluence may help your team in documenting, communicating, and tracking decisions, leading to better alignment, accountability, and transparency within the project team and stakeholders.

As you can see in the following screenshot, you can fill in the essential information related to the decision at the beginning of the decision template.

Status	NOT STARTED / IN PROGRESS / COMPLETE
Impact	HIGH / MEDIUM / LOW
Driver	
Approver	
Contributors	
Informed	
Due date	
Resources	

📚 Relevant data

📖 Background

Figure 6.14 – Decision basic information

As seen in the previous screenshot, this template advises us to clearly transcribe many features related to big decisions. Examples of these characteristics are the status of the decision, the effect of the decision, and the people who are effective in making the decision. You can also add additional information to the fields you see in the figure. Here are two examples:

- **Decision impact**: Explanation of the potential impact of the decision, stakeholders, and overall success

- **Decision criteria**: List of the specific criteria or factors that will be considered in making the decision, such as cost, scalability, security, user experience, and so on

Relevant data

This section provides the relevant data that supports the decision-making process. Consider including concrete information related to the chat application project that is relevant to the decision at hand. For example, include data on the current user base, usage patterns, or technical infrastructure.

Here are some examples:

- **User feedback and requests**: Gather feedback from potential users or existing customers regarding their preferences and any specific requirements they may have for the chat application

- **Market research**: Conduct a thorough analysis of the current market trends, competitors, and existing chat applications to understand the landscape and identify potential opportunities or gaps in the market

- **Technical considerations**: Evaluate the technical requirements of the chat application, such as scalability, performance, security, and integration capabilities with other systems or platforms

Background information

This section provides the necessary background information for understanding the context of the decision.

Provide a paragraph that explains the background information specific to the chat application project. This could include details about the target audience, the purpose of the application, or any existing features or functionalities.

Here are some examples:

- **Project overview**: Provide a brief overview of the chat application project, including the objectives, target audience, and key features

- **Stakeholders**: Identify the key stakeholders involved in the project, such as project sponsors, clients, end users, and development team members

- **Project timeline**: Mention the timeline and milestones of the project, including any deadlines or time constraints that may influence the decision-making process

- **Existing chat solutions**: Describe any existing chat solutions or tools that are currently being used within the organization or by competitors, highlighting their strengths, weaknesses, and limitations
- **User requirements**: Summarize the user requirements and expectations gathered through user research, interviews, surveys, or feedback sessions

Options considered

This section compares and evaluates different options that were considered for the decision. Compare and evaluate three alternatives for the specific technical decision. For each alternative, include the following information:

- **Descriptions**: Provide a description of each alternative, such as different approaches, technologies, or frameworks
- **Pros**: List two advantages or positive aspects of each alternative, considering factors such as performance, scalability, or ease of implementation
- **Cons**: List two disadvantages or drawbacks of each alternative, considering factors such as complexity, compatibility, or potential risks

Now, let's take a look at the examples seen in the following screenshot.

	Option 1: Build a custom chat application from scratch	Option 2: Adopt an existing open-source chat solution	Option 3: Utilize a third-party chat API or service
Description	Develop a custom chat application tailored specifically to the project requirements and objectives.	Select and customize an open-source chat application that aligns with the project requirements.	Integrate a third-party chat API or service into the project, leveraging their pre-built chat functionality.
Pros and cons	➕ Full customization: Allows for complete control over the features, design, and functionality of the chat application. ➕ Scalability and flexibility: Can be designed to accommodate future growth and easily adapt to changing needs. ➖ Time and resource-intensive: Developing a custom chat application requires significant time, effort, and expertise from the development team. ➖ Higher development costs: Building from scratch may involve higher initial development costs compared to other options.	➕ Cost-effective: Open-source solutions are often available free of charge, reducing initial development costs. ➕ Established community and support: Access to an active community of developers and contributors can provide ongoing support and updates. ➖ Limited customization: While open-source solutions can be customized, they may have limitations compared to building a custom solution. ➖ Integration challenges: Integrating the open-source chat application with existing systems and workflows may require additional effort.	➕ Time-saving: Integration with a third-party service can expedite the development process, as the core chat features are already available. ➕ Expertise and reliability: Third-party providers specialize in chat solutions and can offer robust features, security, and reliability. ➖ Limited control: Depending on the service, there may be limitations on customization and flexibility compared to building a custom solution. ➖ Cost considerations: Third-party chat APIs or services may involve licensing fees or subscription costs.
Estimated cost	MEDIUM	HIGH	LOW

Figure 6.15 – Options considered section

When considering alternatives for the decision related to the chat application, you can evaluate the three options seen in the previous table.

These options can be evaluated when making the decision regarding the chat application. The final choice will depend on factors such as project requirements, budget, timeline, scalability needs, and the development team's expertise and resources.

Action items

The **Action items** section of the meeting template is one of the most critical parts of the document. During a meeting, various topics are discussed, decisions are made, and often, specific tasks or actions need to be assigned to individuals or teams. This is where the **Action items** section comes into play. It is a dedicated space for listing all the tasks or actions that are required to be taken following the meeting. Each action item typically includes a description of the task, the person responsible for completing it, and a deadline for its completion. By clearly defining and assigning these tasks during the meeting, it ensures that everyone is aware of their responsibilities, and there is accountability for completing them. It also helps in tracking the progress of these tasks after the meeting, as team members can update the status of their action items as they work on them. Ultimately, the **Action items** section is essential for transforming the discussions and decisions made during the meeting into concrete actions and ensuring that the necessary steps are taken to move the project forward.

This section outlines the actionable steps or tasks resulting from the decisions. Consider including specific action items that need to be taken based on the chosen alternative. For example, it could involve conducting further research, performing compatibility testing, or implementing the selected solution.

In the next screenshot, you can see three action item examples.

☐ Conduct a thorough evaluation of existing React and Node.js libraries and frameworks to identify the most suitable ones for implementing the chat application.

☐ Set up a development environment with the chosen technologies and establish coding standards and best practices for the project.

☐ Create a detailed project plan that includes milestones, deliverables, and timelines for implementing the chat application using React and Node.js.

Figure 6.16 – Action items

In the preceding screenshot, three tasks to be carried out have been added to the document as action items. An empty square signifies that the task has not been completed yet, while a filled square indicates that the task has been completed.

Outcome

This section describes the outcome of the decision-making process and the chosen option. Summarize the outcome of the decision-making process, including the option that was chosen and the rationale behind it. Also, explain how the selected alternative aligns with the project goals and requirements.

Here is an example:

After carefully considering the available options and evaluating their pros and cons, the decision has been made to select React and Node.js as the technology stack for the chat application. This choice aligns with the project's goals of delivering a highly interactive and scalable chat platform that provides a seamless user experience. React's component-based architecture and extensive ecosystem, coupled with Node.js's event-driven and non-blocking nature, will enable efficient real-time communication and boost responsiveness even under high user loads. Also, this technology stack offers a rich set of libraries, frameworks, and community support, which will facilitate rapid development, ease of maintenance, and future scalability. The chosen option provides a solid foundation for building a robust and feature-rich chat application that meets the requirements of both our internal team communication and customer support needs.

Atlassian's tips on managing your software project space

In Confluence, you will find a page titled *Get the most out of your software project space*, containing valuable tips on using your software space. This is one of the default pages automatically created when you create your space. Let's discover some of these best practices.

In the following screenshot, you can see Atlassian's advice on how to keep information accessible by using shortcuts.

Use shortcuts to keep information accessible

Next time someone asks for a status update, direct them to your space. Confluence makes it easy to give other teams a window into your world.

The space shortcuts highlighted below can be critical to navigation for both your team and your entire organization. Add team's roadmap, quarterly goals, meeting notes, important files, and decisions for easy access. You can even link to the work that's not in Confluence like tasks that are tracked in Jira Software or Trello. The homepage gives a snapshot, and the shortcut links make it easy to dive deeper into those pages.

Figure 6.17 – Atlassian tips: Use shortcuts to keep information accessible

In the following screenshot, you can see Atlassian's tips on using Confluence when working with sprints.

Manage your sprints

There's often a lot of material in Confluence that provides useful context for your team during a sprint. These might be requirements documents, designs, tech specs, customer research and more. By linking these pages to epics, you make them easy for your team to find during the sprint.

Here's how you can use Confluence to support your sprint from within Jira Agile:

- In Jira Software, create a Confluence page to plan your sprint. The page is created using the Meeting notes template and is automatically linked to the sprint.
- In an epic, link to useful Confluence pages, including requirements, designs, and more.
- Report on your progress to stakeholders using the Jira Report blueprint in Confluence.
- Use the Retrospective template in Confluence at the end of your sprint to take stock of what went well and not so well.

For people who work mostly in Jira Software, the integration means that useful Confluence pages are only a click away.

Your team doesn't work in a silo, so it's important to make it easy for anyone to find work you're currently working on.

Figure 6.18 – Atlassian tips: Manage your sprints

In the following screenshot, you will see Atlassian's tips on defining your requirements with Confluence.

Define your requirements

Confluence is the perfect place to start defining your requirements. You can use the Product requirements template to capture your requirements, then create your Jira epic and other issues right from the requirements page in Confluence.

Here's how it works:

1. Create a Confluence page using the Product requirements template.
2. Choose the placeholder text 'Link to Jira epic or feature' and choose **Create new issue** to create your epic in Jira.
3. Collaborate with your team to define your stories and save the page.
4. Highlight text on your requirements page and choose the**Create Jira issue** link to create stories in Jira, and automatically link them to your epic.
5. Track the progress of the stories from the Confluence page or from within Jira.

The tight integration between Confluence and Jira Software means you can easily access issues from the Confluence page and see their status at a glance, and from within Jira Software you can see links to related Confluence pages. All the information you need is right there.

Figure 6.19 – Atlassian tips: Define your requirements

Once you mastered the software project space template in Confluence, you can adapt it to your needs. Now, it's time for customizing your Confluence template.

Customizing Confluence's software development template for project-based needs

Confluence provides a ready-to-use software development template that offers useful content for software management projects. However, in most cases, it is necessary to tailor these pages to align them with the specific requirements of your project.

Now, we are ready to go through the process of customizing Confluence's software development template, ensuring you have a well tailored and effective project management environment:

1. **Assess your project requirements**: Start by understanding your project's unique requirements. Identify the specific information, processes, and workflows that are essential for your software development project. Consider aspects such as project documentation, team collaboration, task management, reporting, and any other specific needs.

2. **Review Confluence's software development template**: Take a close look at Confluence's software development template, which typically includes pages for project overview, requirements, design documentation, release planning, testing, and more. Assess each page's relevance to your project and determine which ones can be utilized as is and which ones require customization.

3. **Customize existing pages**: For the pages that need customization, edit and tailor the content to align with your project's specific requirements. Add or remove sections, modify headings, and adjust the content to reflect your project's terminology, processes, and standards. Consider incorporating specific guidelines, templates, or examples that are relevant to your project.

4. **Create new pages**: If the template does not include pages that address your project's unique needs, create new pages from scratch. Identify the areas where additional documentation or information is required, such as architecture diagrams, API references, user guides, or sprint planning. Create new pages to accommodate these specific needs and populate them with relevant content.

5. **Implement project-specific workflows**: If your project follows specific workflows, such as Agile or DevOps, adapt the existing template or create new pages to reflect these workflows. Customize the project planning, task tracking, and reporting sections to align with your chosen methodology. Include details on user stories, sprints, backlog management, and other relevant information specific to your project's workflow.

6. **Collaborative spaces and permissions**: Consider creating dedicated spaces within Confluence for different teams, stakeholders, or project phases. Set appropriate permissions to control access to sensitive information and ensure that team members have the right level of access and visibility based on their roles and responsibilities.

7. **Iterative improvement**: Keep in mind that customization is an iterative process. As your project progresses and evolves, regularly review and update the customized pages to reflect the latest project status, changes, and requirements. Encourage team members to contribute and provide feedback to continually improve the content and make it more relevant and useful.

You are now ready to effectively customize the Confluence software development template to match your specific needs. The result you'll get will be a well-structured project management environment that includes the necessary information, processes, and collaboration features required for the success of your software development project.

Example content you can add to your space

Here is some content you could add to your space.

Home page

This is the gateway to your team's work, which should be engaging and intuitive. You can include these contents in your home page:

- **Welcome section**: A brief overview of the team's purpose and goals, which could be especially helpful for new members

- **Quick links**: A section with links to frequently accessed pages such as project boards, the team directory, coding guidelines, or even external resources such as the company's intranet or a link to the team's communication platform

- **Calendar**: An embedded calendar that shows upcoming milestones, sprint timelines, team meetings, or even team members' time off. This can help everyone stay aware of important dates.

Project documentation

This is the heart of your team's work. Organizing this content effectively can save a lot of valuable time. Here, you can include the following:

- **Project pages**: Each project your team works on could have its own dedicated page, with sub-pages for different aspects of the project such as project plans, design documents, test results, and so on. Each page could include text, images, diagrams, or even embedded videos explaining complex concepts.

- **Version history**: Confluence automatically tracks changes made to each page, allowing you to see who made what changes and when. This can be very helpful in maintaining accountability and transparency.

Team collaboration and communication

Here, you can include the following:

- **Discussion pages**: These can be used for brainstorming, problem-solving, or decision-making. For example, you might have a discussion page dedicated to addressing bugs, where team members can post about any issues they encounter and discuss possible solutions.

- **Notifications**: Confluence allows users to watch pages or entire spaces. When a user watches a page, they receive email notifications about comments, page edits, and other updates. Encourage your team members to use this feature to stay up to date with areas of the project they're interested in or responsible for.

- **Labels**: Using labels effectively can make it much easier to find related content. For example, you might label all pages related to a specific project with the project's name or use a "meeting notes" label for all meeting notes.

Structure and updates

- **Page hierarchy**: Confluence allows you to structure pages in a hierarchical fashion, with parent pages and child pages. This can make it much easier to navigate the space. For example, you might have a parent page for a project, with child pages for the project plan, design documents, and other related content.

- **Regular updates**: Assign a person or a team with the responsibility of regularly updating the space. This can involve adding new information, updating existing pages, and archiving old content, ensuring that your Confluence space remains a reliable source of current information.

Also, please note that the key to a successful Confluence space is not just setting it up effectively, but also maintaining and updating it regularly. It should evolve with your team's needs over time.

Using Confluence as a hub with external tools

To configure Confluence as a hub for external systems, such as SaaS applications, you can utilize various integration capabilities and features available in Confluence. Here's a general guide on how to configure Confluence as a hub for external systems:

1. **Identify integration needs**: Determine which external systems or SaaS applications you want to integrate with Confluence. Consider the specific use cases and functionalities you want to achieve through these integrations. For example, you might want to embed content from external systems, display real-time data, or synchronize information between Confluence and other tools.

2. **Explore the Atlassian Marketplace**: Browse the Atlassian Marketplace, which offers a wide range of apps and integrations for Confluence. Look for apps that provide integration capabilities with your target external systems. Evaluate the available options based on functionality, user ratings, reviews, and compatibility with your Confluence instance.

3. **Install and configure integration apps**: Once you have selected the appropriate integration apps, install them in your Confluence instance by following the provided instructions. Configure the integration settings based on the requirements of the external systems you want to connect with. This typically involves providing authentication credentials, API keys, or configuring webhooks. It's good practice to test apps first using a sandbox environment without affecting your live Confluence environment. Remember that the sandbox option is only available in the Premium plan.

4. **Embed external content**: Many integration apps allow you to embed content from external systems directly within Confluence pages. For example, you can embed live dashboards, reports, or project boards from SaaS applications such as Jira, Trello, or Figma. This provides a centralized view of relevant information without needing to switch between different tools.

5. **Display real-time data**: Some integration apps offer the ability to display real-time data from external systems in Confluence. This can include metrics, status updates, or notifications. Configure the integration app to fetch and display the relevant data within Confluence, providing team members with up-to-date information without leaving the Confluence environment.

6. **Bi-directional data synchronization**: If you need to keep data synchronized between Confluence and external systems, look for integration apps that support bi-directional data synchronization. This can be useful when, for example, you want to sync Confluence pages with project documentation stored in a SaaS application or update Confluence content based on changes made in an external system.

7. **Customize Confluence with macros and APIs**: Confluence offers a variety of macros and APIs that allow for further customization and integration possibilities. Leverage these features to develop custom solutions or build specific integrations tailored to your unique needs. You can use Confluence's REST API, webhooks, or develop your own apps using the Confluence Connect framework.

8. **Test and monitor integrations**: After configuring the integrations, thoroughly test their functionality to ensure they are working as expected. Monitor the integrations over time to identify any issues, such as API compatibility, performance, or security concerns. Regularly update the integration apps and Confluence versions to ensure compatibility and access to new features and improvements.

By following these steps, it's possible to configure Confluence as a hub for external systems, allowing you to centralize information, streamline workflows, and enhance collaboration by integrating and leveraging data from various SaaS applications within Confluence.

Using Confluence and Jira together for software project management

Confluence and Jira are powerful tools that complement each other for software project management. Confluence is a collaboration and documentation platform, while Jira is a project management and issue-tracking tool. Here's a quick guide on how to use them together effectively:

1. **Define the purpose of each tool**: Understand the specific strengths and objectives of both tools. Confluence is ideal for collaborative documentation, knowledge-based articles, meeting notes, and design documents. Jira, on the other hand, is used for tracking tasks, managing issues, and facilitating project management workflows.

2. **Establish a project structure**: Create a Confluence space for each project. This space will serve as a central platform for project-related documentation, specifications, and other relevant information. Within Jira, set up a project and define its elements, such as epics, user stories, tasks, and sprints. Establish a clear connection between the Confluence space and the Jira project.

3. **Link Confluence pages to Jira issues**: Integrate Confluence and Jira to establish a seamless connection and enhance the power of each platform. Link Confluence pages to relevant Jira issues, epics, or user stories to allow your team members to easily access associated documentation directly from Jira and vice versa.

4. **Use Jira for task management**: Leverage Jira's issue-tracking and task-management capabilities to track and assign work. Create user stories, break them down into tasks, and assign them to team members. Use Jira's agile boards (Scrum or Kanban) to visualize the progress of tasks and manage workflows. Update task statuses, log work, and track progress in Jira.

5. **Document project information in Confluence**: Use Confluence to create and maintain project documentation such as requirements, meeting notes, and decision logs. Use Confluence's rich formatting options, templates, and collaborative editing mode to create and update content. Embed Jira dashboards or boards in Confluence pages to provide a visual overview of the project's progress.

6. **Use Jira macros in Confluence**: Make the most of Jira macros available in Confluence to display relevant Jira data within Confluence pages. Embed Jira filters, agile boards, or issue lists in Confluence pages to showcase real-time project information, task statuses, and progress to keep team members informed without switching between tools.

7. **Track discussions and decisions**: Utilize Confluence's commenting and collaboration features to facilitate discussions and decision-making. Encourage team members to leave comments, provide feedback, and ask questions on Confluence pages. Use @mentions to notify relevant stakeholders and keep everyone engaged.

8. **Track documentation changes**: Leverage Confluence's version control capabilities to keep a record of changes and enable effortless reverting to previous versions if needed. Encourage team members to review and update Confluence pages regularly to ensure all documentation remains accurate and up to date.

9. **Cross-reference between Confluence and Jira**: Establish cross-referencing between Confluence and Jira to maintain traceability. Link Confluence pages to related Jira issues and vice versa, allowing team members to easily navigate between documentation and task management, ensuring they have the necessary context and information.

10. **Regularly review and update**: Check for inconsistencies, outdated information, or missing documentation in both tools. Encourage team members to contribute to Confluence and Jira, ensuring that all knowledge and project statuses reflect the most accurate versions.

By leveraging the strengths of Confluence and Jira while establishing an effective workflow between the two, you can efficiently manage a software project, track tasks, maintain documentation, and foster collaboration among team members.

The step-by-step guide to creating a software project space on Confluence

Confluence is a powerful collaboration platform that can be used to manage software projects effectively. By creating a Confluence space dedicated to your software project, it is possible to centralize project documentation, facilitate team collaboration, and streamline task management. In this section, we'll walk you through the process of creating a software project space on Confluence to foster a productive project environment with a step-by-step guide:

1. **Creating a space**: Click on the **Spaces** button on the Confluence home page and select **Create Space**. Name your space `Software Project` and provide a brief description. Click **Create** to create the space.

2. **Designing the home page**: The home page of your software project space should provide an overview of your project. Include essential components such as project goals, objectives, team members, timeline, priorities, and relevant links and resources.

3. **Documentation and knowledge base**: Create pages within the space for a documentation and knowledge base. Include documents such as project requirements, design specifications, user guides, API references, and other relevant materials.

4. **Team collaboration**: Foster collaboration among team members by creating pages or sections dedicated to communication and interaction. Include features such as meeting notes, discussion forums, and announcements to facilitate effective communication and information-sharing.

5. **Task management with Jira integration**: Integrate Confluence with Jira, a powerful issue-tracking and project management tool. Create a project in Jira and link it to your Confluence space. Utilize Jira for defining tasks, tracking progress, and generating reports, while linking relevant Jira issues to Confluence pages.

6. **Training and help resources**: Develop training materials and helpful resources to support your project team. These resources can include user guides, workflow instructions, video tutorials, and help pages to assist team members in navigating Confluence and Jira effectively.

Note that this guide provides a general framework. You can always customize the process for your project-specific needs. By following these steps, you can create a well-organized and collaborative environment for managing your software project on Confluence.

Summary

In this chapter, we learned that Confluence is a collaboration and project management tool, particularly beneficial for remote software development teams. It provides a centralized platform for storing project-related documents, facilitating effective communication and collaboration. It integrates with Jira, allowing teams to track tasks, manage workflows, and monitor project progress. It also caters to various roles within a software development project, such as software developers, product managers, quality assurance engineers, DevOps engineers, and UX/UI designers. By using Confluence, we saw how teams can create a single source of truth for their projects, customize templates to meet specific needs, and enhance collaboration and productivity.

Questions

1. What is Confluence? How can remote software development teams benefit from it?
2. What are some of the roles in a remote software development team that can benefit from Confluence?
3. How can Confluence be used to create a single source of truth for a software development project?
4. How can remote teams benefit from the Confluence-Jira integration?
5. What is the role of the overview page? What does it include?

Answers

1. Confluence is a collaboration and project management tool that helps remote software development teams to effectively manage projects while facilitating collaboration. It provides a centralized platform for storing project-related documents and enables direct communication among team members.
2. Software developers, product managers, quality assurance engineers, DevOps engineers, and UX/UI designers can benefit from Confluence in a remote software development team. Confluence provides many features and capabilities to meet the specific needs of each role.
3. Confluence allows teams to centralize and organize all relevant project information in a well-structured place. By creating different pages dedicated to project overview, requirements, design, development, testing, and documentation, teams can ensure that each member of the team has access to the most up-to-date project information.
4. Confluence integrates with Jira, a project management tool to track tasks, overview workflows, and monitor project progress. This integration allows teams to have a comprehensive view of their projects and streamline their management processes.
5. The home page of your software project space should provide an overview of the project. You can include essential components such as project goals, objectives, team members, timeline, priorities, and relevant links and resources.

7
Creating a Space for Product Management

As remote work is becoming more prevalent, maintaining efficient communication and collaboration among teams, especially product management teams, can be challenging. Confluence was built to address these challenges, offering a shared workspace where teams can collaborate, create, and manage all their work in one place.

Product management teams are responsible for guiding the success of a product and leading the cross-functional team responsible for improving it. This involves planning, forecasting, producing, and marketing a product or products at all stages of the product life cycle. With team members potentially spread across different locations and time zones, having a centralized platform for collaboration is crucial.

Confluence is a content collaboration tool used to help teams collaborate and share knowledge efficiently. With Confluence, your remote product management team can create, share, and collaborate on projects in one place to keep its work organized and accessible. The platform allows teams to develop product requirements, project plans, meeting notes, and so on, all while integrating seamlessly with Atlassian's other product, Jira, to track tasks and manage projects.

Whether it's planning a new product feature, outlining marketing strategies, or detailing product requirements, Confluence provides a single source of truth for your product management team. It encourages active collaboration by enabling team members to comment on pages, contribute to discussions, and give real-time feedback. This helps ensure everyone stays on the same page, reducing misunderstandings and keeping work flowing smoothly.

Furthermore, Confluence's robust set of features can be tailored to your team's specific needs. Spaces can be created for individual teams or projects and structured according to different needs; thus, Confluence becomes a flexible tool for your team where each space is a central hub for related pages, keeping work organized and easy to find.

In other words, Confluence can be the backbone of your remote product management team, fostering effective collaboration and ensuring everyone stays aligned and informed. We are now ready to discover how.

Exploring product management roles

A product management team typically has several roles with different responsibilities and needs. Here are some common roles and how Confluence can address their specific needs:

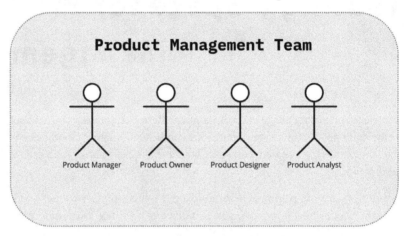

Figure 7.1 – Different roles on a typical product management team

Product manager

The product manager is responsible for setting the product's strategic direction while defining a roadmap and working with other teams to bring a product to market. Their needs include the following:

- **Communication**: They need to communicate the product vision and roadmap to the rest of the team. Confluence can be used to create and share detailed product plans and roadmaps.

- **Collaboration**: They must work closely with other roles, including engineers, designers, and marketers. Confluence's collaborative editing and commenting features make it easy to work together on documents.

- **Documentation**: They must document product requirements, user stories, and other information. Confluence can be used to create, store, and share these documents.

Product owner

The product owner is usually responsible for managing the product backlog, writing user stories, and working with the development team to ensure they understand the requirements. Their needs include the following:

- **Backlog management**: They need a place to manage and prioritize the product backlog. Confluence can be used to create and maintain a product backlog, with the ability to easily update priorities and statuses. Confluence can be more powerful if used with Jira; this way, Confluence pages can easily be linked with Jira issues.

- **Requirement documentation**: They need to document detailed user stories and acceptance criteria. Confluence provides a platform to write and share these details with the development team.

Product designer

The product designer is responsible for creating the product's user interface and user experience. Their needs include the following:

- **Design sharing and feedback**: They need a place to share their designs and mockups and get feedback. Confluence allows designers to share their designs and gather feedback directly on a Confluence page.

- **Design documentation**: They need to document design guidelines and principles. Confluence can be used to create a design system or style guide easily accessible to the rest of the team.

Product analyst

The product analyst is responsible for analyzing data related to a product's performance and usage. Their needs include the following:

- **Data sharing**: They need a place to share their analyses and reports. Confluence can be used to publish reports and share data with the rest of the team.

- **Documentation of analysis**: They need to document their analysis methods and findings. Confluence provides a platform for detailed documentation.

By providing a centralized space for communication, collaboration, and documentation, Confluence can meet the diverse needs of various roles within a product management team.

Remote product management challenges

There are a lot of challenges specifically faced by remote product management teams. Let's discuss on some of them and how Confluence Cloud can help mitigate these issues.

Prioritization and roadmap visibility

Remote product teams can struggle with keeping everyone aligned on product priorities and upcoming features. The absence of an in-person environment can lead to misunderstandings and misalignments. Confluence Cloud can aid in maintaining the visibility of a product roadmap. You can create a dedicated page for your roadmap where priorities are clearly defined and regularly updated. This ensures everyone in the team is on the same page.

Cross-functional collaboration

Product managers often work closely with various departments such as engineering, design, marketing, and sales. Remote work can make cross-functional collaborations more challenging, so Confluence Cloud provides a platform where all these departments can collaborate and share their work. Each department can have its page within the product space, making it easier to share updates and collaborate effectively.

Customer feedback collection

For product teams, collecting and analyzing customer feedback is crucial. However, in a remote setup, centralizing this feedback can be difficult. Confluence Cloud can serve as a centralized repository for all customer feedback. It can be categorized and tagged for easier analysis, ensuring all voices are heard and considered in product decisions.

Knowledge transfer

In product management, there's often a lot of information to be shared regarding the product, market, competitors, and so on. In a remote environment, this pool of knowledge transfer can be challenging. Confluence Cloud can be used as a knowledge base where all important product and market information is stored, ensuring that all team members can access the same information, regardless of location.

Product releases and change management

Coordinating product releases and managing changes remotely can be challenging due to the lack of real-time communication. Confluence Cloud can help you manage product releases and changes more efficiently. You can create detailed release plans and change logs, assign tasks, set deadlines, and track progress all in one place. By creating a space on Confluence Cloud, you can centralize communication, facilitate cross-functional collaboration, streamline customer feedback collection and analysis, enhance the transfer of knowledge, and manage product releases and changes more effectively.

Cloud-based tools used by product managers

Product management teams working remotely and asynchronously often utilize cloud-based tools to facilitate their work. These tools typically span several categories – project management, communication, collaboration, documentation, and prototyping. Here's a list of standard tools for each function:

- **Project management**: Tools such as Jira and Trello help teams track tasks, manage backlogs, and coordinate project progress. These tools are essential to manage workflows, assign tasks, and monitor progress.

- **Communication**: Tools such as Slack, Microsoft Teams, and Zoom are used for instant messaging, video conferencing, and maintaining regular communication within a team.

- **Collaboration and documentation**: This is where Confluence excels. Confluence is a workspace where teams can create, share, and collaborate on documents in real time, making it ideal for creating project plans, meeting notes, product requirements, and so on.

- **Prototyping and design**: Tools such as Sketch, Figma, and Adobe XD are commonly used to create product designs and interactive prototypes.

- **File sharing**: Dropbox, Google Drive, and OneDrive are used to store and share files across a team.

Confluence integrates seamlessly with many of these tools, especially those within the Atlassian ecosystem such as Jira and Trello. For instance, you can embed Jira issues directly into your Confluence pages or link Confluence pages to Jira issues, allowing a seamless transition between planning, documenting, and tracking work. Also, you can integrate Confluence with communication tools such as Slack. For example, you can set up notifications in your Slack channels for updates to Confluence pages, making sure your team stays informed about changes to important documents.

These integrations make Confluence a central hub for product management teams working remotely, allowing them to maintain transparency, collaborate effectively, and keep all necessary documentation in one accessible place. This can lead to improved productivity and alignment across a team, regardless of where team members are physically located.

Exploring the product management templates in Confluence

As of June 2023, there are 131 templates on Confluence. When you filter them, you will see that there are 19 templates for product management, as shown in the following screenshot. In this section, we will give you a summary of these templates. Also, note that this number may have increased by the time you read this book.

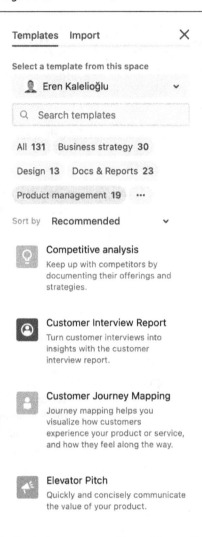

Figure 7.2 – Product management templates on Confluence

This is the list of the templates in the product management category:

- **Competitive analysis**: Document the offerings and strategies of competitors to stay ahead

- **Customer interview report**: Transform insights from customer interviews into a detailed report

- **Customer journey mapping**: Visualize the experience of customers as they interact with your product or service

- **Elevator pitch**: Communicate your product's value in a clear and concise manner

- **Goals, signals, measures**: Utilize this template to separate relevant signals from noise when setting team objectives

- **MVP ideation**: Use this framework to thoroughly develop your **Minimum Viable Product (MVP)** idea

- **OKRs**: Apply this template to set ambitious and quantifiable milestones

- **Premortem**: Implement this template to conduct a premortem session to identify and strategize for potential risks

- **Product launch**: Organize and document your product launch strategy and activities

- **Product requirements**: Detail, monitor, and define the requirements for your product or feature

- **Product roadmap**: Outline your team's comprehensive product roadmap

- **Project kickoff**: Initiate projects efficiently by setting aligned expectations and objectives with your team

- **Project plan**: Detail, define, and schedule milestones for your upcoming project

- **Project poster**: Utilize this template to clarify your problem, suggest a solution, and prepare for execution

- **SMART goals**: Implement the SMART goals framework to maintain your team's focus and direction

- **Strategic plan**: Document and share your business strategy with the executive team and board of directors

- **Team poster**: Ensure your entire team understands the tasks they need to focus on and the reasons behind them

- **Vision to values**: Articulate your company's vision to develop actionable business strategies

- **Voting table**: Survey your team to prioritize tasks, agree on a strategy, or make other important decisions

These templates will give you a good starting point. You can develop these templates or create your own from scratch. Now, let's get to know some of these templates a little more closely.

MVP ideation

This template has five sections:

- **Problem to solve**: Describe the problem you want to solve

- **MVP solution**: Describe the core concepts of MVP

- **Target Market**: Define the user groups that apply to MVP

- **Value proposition**: Enumerate the unique selling propositions of the MVP

- **Competitors**: Identify the current competitors in the market and why their product doesn't solve the problem

MVP Ideation

⚑ Problem to solve

Succinctly define the problem you plan to solve and why it is needed.

⅄ MVP solution

Describe the broad concepts of the MVP.

◎ Target Market

Name the specific users groups for the MVP.

1.
2.
3.

✦ Value proposition

Enumerate the unique selling propositions of the MVP.

1.
2.

🖾 Competitors

Identify the current competitors in the market and why their product doesn't solve the problem.

Company name	Product name	Pros and cons
		➕ ➖

Figure 7.3 – The MVP ideation template

As shown in the previous screenshot, the most basic features of Confluence, such as layout and table, are used in this template. Although it may not seem technically complex, it is certainly a very useful template.

Product launch

This one can be considered a big template. Therefore, we will only discuss some areas of it. First, we will discuss the **Product release roadmap** section. Here, the Confluence macro named **Roadmap Planner** is used. With this macro, you can create a basic roadmap for your team.

📌 Product release roadmap

Use the roadmap planner (/roadmap) to help your team stay on track. To edit workstreams or dates, select the placeholder below and tap the pencil icon.

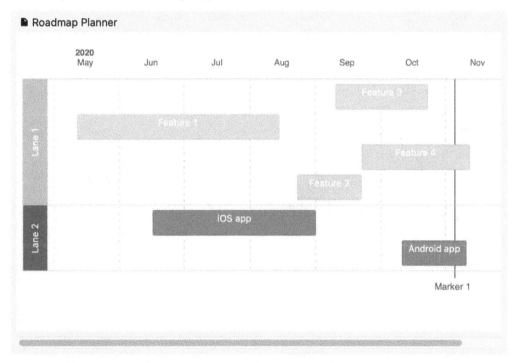

Type /trello to add a card or board to this page or /jira to include a Jira issue, chart, or project.

Figure 7.4 – The Product release roadmap section from the Product launch template

As you can see, adding Trello or Jira content to Confluence is possible. In the following figure, you can see the **Distribution channels & launch activities** section. Here, you can plan your launch-day activities day by day.

Distribution channels & launch activities

Plan your launch-day activities and communications using the table below. Put each activity on its own row, @mention activity owners, and type /date to add due dates.

Activity	Owner	Due date	Status	Notes
Internal comms				
e.g., Write a blog post to announce the launch			NOT STARTED	
PR				
e.g., Send press release to TechCrunch and WIRED				
Email				
Blog				
Social				

Figure 7.5 – The Distribution channels & launch activities section from the Product launch template

As you can see in the previous screenshot, a table is used in this section. Some cells of the table are merged and colored.

Product requirements

This is a great template that begins with an imprint section. In it, you can add stakeholders to this document, and it is worth remembering that all stakeholders added here will be notified of updates to the document. In this section, the macro named **Page Properties** is used. Thanks to this macro, we can easily access the information in this part of the page from another page.

Page Properties

Target release	Type // to add a target release date
Epic	Type /Jira to add Jira epics and issues
Document status	DRAFT
Document owner	@ mention owner
Designer	@ designer
Tech lead	@ lead
Technical writers	@ writers
QA	

Figure 7.6 – The Page Properties section from the Product requirements template

As you can see in the preceding screenshot, there is a natural integration between Jira and Confluence. This template shows that epics and issues from Jira can be added to this document.

In the **Requirements** section, you can define the product requirements in detail.

Requirements

Requirement	User Story	Importance	Jira Issue	Notes
e.g., Must be mobile responsive	e.g., John is a PM who wants to check on his team's progress from the train station	HIGH		

Figure 7.7 – The Requirements section from the Product requirements template

As you can see in the previous screenshot, a simple table is also used in this section. However, this table includes a status macro (the element currently marked as **HIGH**). Also, the template invites us to integrate with Jira. We must clarify all the details about the requirements in this section of Confluence, then transfer each requirement as an issue to Jira, and track it there.

Then, there is the **User interaction and design** section. This area currently appears to be quite small. However, it can quickly become an area that takes up a lot of space. You can add various formats of content to this area. You can even enable embedding content from Miro, Google Drive, and so on. This way, you can easily view your content on different platforms through this Confluence template.

You might be wondering what a Jira issue that has been added to a Confluence page looks like. If so, we recommend examining the next screenshot.

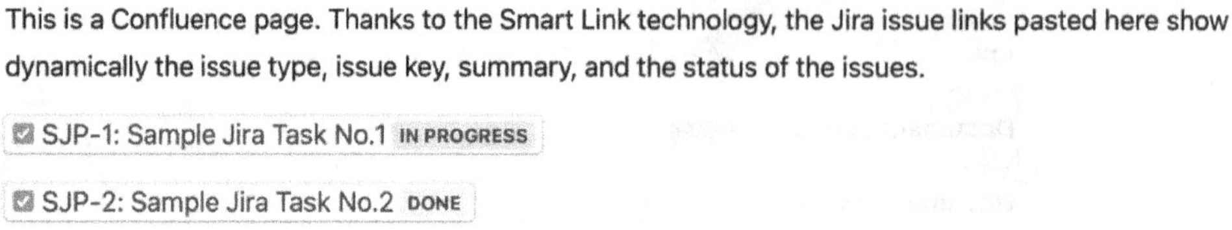

> This is a Confluence page. Thanks to the Smart Link technology, the Jira issue links pasted here show dynamically the issue type, issue key, summary, and the status of the issues.
>
> ☑ SJP-1: Sample Jira Task No.1 **IN PROGRESS**
>
> ☑ SJP-2: Sample Jira Task No.2 **DONE**

Figure 7.8 – Jira issues embedded on a Confluence page

You can see that the appearance of the added link has changed, and it dynamically brought many details of the Jira issue to the Confluence page. You can easily view any fields of a Jira issue while you are on Confluence.

🎨 User interaction and design

Type /image to add mockups, diagrams, and screenshots related to the requirements.

Figure 7.9 – The User interaction and design section from the Product requirements template

As you can see, you can add diagrams and screenshots to this section.

When determining product requirements, you may encounter numerous questions that need to be answered. A simple table can record, track, and answer these questions.

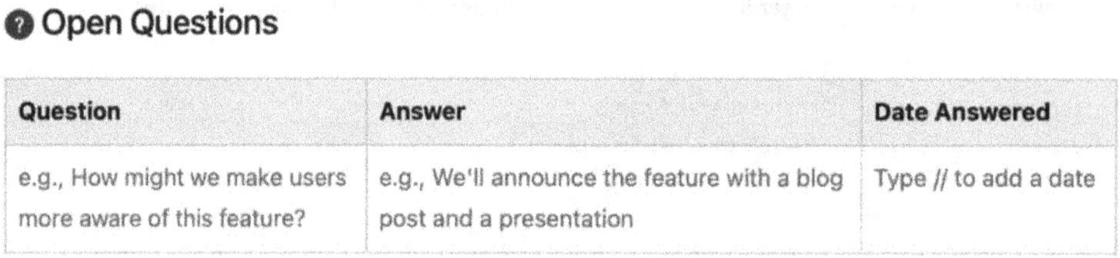

❓ Open Questions

Question	Answer	Date Answered
e.g., How might we make users more aware of this feature?	e.g., We'll announce the feature with a blog post and a presentation	Type // to add a date

Figure 7.10 – The Open Questions section from the Product requirements template

As you can see in the previous screenshot, a simple table is used here as well. Tables are among the frequently used macros on Confluence for various purposes.

We have examined three templates in a row. We are now ready to explore other templates to help you create your own.

Creating a single source of truth for product management

A **Single Source of Truth (SSOT)** refers to having one primary, authoritative data source that all users agree is the real, trusted number. This concept is widely used in information systems and data management, especially in complex environments where multiple teams, departments, or stakeholders need access to the same information.

Why do product managers need an SSOT?

For asynchronous and remote product management, an SSOT is particularly crucial for several reasons:

- **Consistency**: With an SSOT, everyone on the team works from the same information. This eliminates discrepancies or conflicts in data, ensuring everyone is on the same page, regardless of location or time zone.

- **Efficiency**: An SSOT reduces the time spent searching for information, clarifying misunderstandings, or reconciling conflicting versions of data. When everyone knows where to find the right information, work can proceed more smoothly and efficiently.

- **Collaboration**: An SSOT facilitates collaboration by providing a common ground for all team members. It simplifies the exchange of information and the coordination of tasks, especially in remote settings where face-to-face interactions are limited.

- **Decision-making**: Reliable and consistent data is fundamental for informed decision-making. With an SSOT, decision-makers can trust their decisions to be based on accurate and up-to-date information.

How to create an SSOT optimized for product management using Confluence

Let's look at how to create an SSOT optimized for product management using Confluence:

- **Set up a dedicated Confluence space**: Create a dedicated space in Confluence for your product management activities. This will be the central location where all product-related information is stored and updated.

- **Emphasize important information**: Ensure key information, such as team goals and project milestones, are prominently displayed on the space home page so that important details are immediately visible to anyone accessing the space.

- **Use shortcuts and the page tree**: To keep information accessible, use the page tree feature in Confluence. This allows quick navigation to different pages within the space, such as project roadmaps, meeting notes, and important files.

- **Create a project space for complex projects**: If a project requires more documentation, consider creating a separate project space. This space should include key components, such as the project's vision, stakeholders, goals, and progress-tracking metrics.

- **Document product requirements**: Use Confluence's product requirements blueprint to document the product's requirements. This should include high-level details, goals, business objectives, user stories, design reviews, and traceability to Jira issues.

- **Update regularly**: An SSOT is only as good as its data. Ensure that the information in Confluence is regularly updated and reflects the current state of a product.

- **Encourage usage**: Make sure all team members are trained to use Confluence and understand its role as an SSOT. The more it is used, the more valuable it will become as a central repository of information.

Following these steps, you can leverage Confluence to create a powerful SSOT for your product management activities while facilitating collaboration, improving efficiency, and driving informed decision-making.

Using Confluence in conjunction with product management tools

In the digital age, collaboration tools have become essential for teams to manage their work efficiently. They facilitate communication, streamline workflows, and help manage and organize various tasks, driving productivity and efficiency. Among these tools, Atlassian's Confluence stands out, thanks to its comprehensive features designed for content collaboration.

Confluence serves as an efficient platform to create an SSOT, where teams can collaborate in real time to create, share, and update documents. Its seamless integration with other Atlassian tools (Jira, Trello, etc.) makes it a powerful platform for project management. When combined with these tools, Confluence can significantly enhance team collaboration, enabling teams to maintain project transparency, improve the visibility of tasks, and ensure everyone is aligned toward the same goals.

Now, we are ready to take a brief look at how Confluence can be effectively used alongside cloud-based tools used by product managers worldwide. The objective is to help you understand the potential of these integrations and how they can contribute to maximizing your team's productivity.

Figure 7.11 – Using Confluence in conjunction with product management tools

Project management tools (e.g., Jira and Trello)

Confluence can be tightly integrated with project management tools to enhance the visibility and traceability of work items. For instance, you can link Jira issues and Confluence pages with Jira, allowing your team to directly see the background, discussion, and design related to a particular issue from the Jira ticket. You can also create Jira issues instantly from Confluence. This integration helps ensure that all team members have access to the same information and understand the context behind each task.

We will discuss the integration of Jira and Confluence in detail in *Chapter 13*. However, we want to give you an idea now of how well these two products integrate with each other. In the following screenshot, you can see the first step to easily convert a selected paragraph on a Confluence page into a task in Jira.

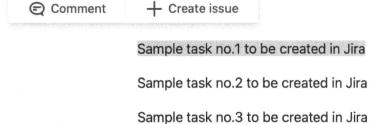

Figure 7.12 – Creating a Jira issue from Confluence (step 1)

As shown in the previous screenshot, the steps you need to follow are:

1. Select the relevant text.
2. Right-click.
3. Click on the **Create issue** button.

Now, you need to select in which Jira project and of what type the issue will be created. You can see this user interface in the following screenshot.

Figure 7.13 – Creating a Jira issue from Confluence (step 2)

You can see the fields that need to be filled in to create the issue in Jira in the previous screenshot. At this stage, you should first select in which project and of what type the issue will be created. Then, you can update the summary of this issue, and finally, you should enter a description. In this example, an issue of type `Task` will be created in the Jira project named `Sample Jira Project`.

Communication tools (e.g., Slack and Microsoft Teams)

While Confluence is a powerful tool for asynchronous communication and documentation, tools such as Slack and Microsoft Teams are often used for more immediate, synchronous communication. You can integrate Confluence with these tools to get notifications in your chat when updates are made to Confluence pages. This helps keep the team informed in real time about important updates, even if they're working remotely and asynchronously.

File storage and sharing tools (e.g., Google Drive and Dropbox):

Confluence allows you to embed files directly from file storage tools such as Google Drive and Dropbox. This means you can have an SSOT where all relevant documentation and resources are located. For instance, you might have a Confluence page that includes the project plan, links to relevant Jira issues, and an embedded Google document with the project proposal. Centralizing all these resources ensures everyone can easily find and access the necessary information.

Design tools (e.g., Figma and Adobe XD)

Using tools such as Figma or Adobe XD, you can embed designs and prototypes directly into your Confluence pages. This allows you to discuss the designs in the context of the project documentation, making it easier to reference decisions and feedback. It also means that anyone looking at the project can quickly see and understand the latest designs without searching through different platforms.

Code repositories (e.g., GitHub and Bitbucket)

Confluence can be integrated with code repositories such as GitHub or Bitbucket to provide more context about the code base. For example, you could have a Confluence page that documents a particular feature, with embedded links to the relevant code in GitHub and related Jira issues. This can be particularly useful for onboarding new team members, as they can see the code and the discussion and decision-making process that led to that code.

In summary, integrating Confluence with these other tools can help create a more efficient, transparent, and collaborative workflow for remote and asynchronous product management teams. By centralizing information and providing context across different platforms, Confluence can help ensure everyone stays on the same page, reducing the time spent searching for information.

Leveraging Confluence and Jira for effective product management in remote and asynchronous teams

Today, effective product management is considered critical to the success of any organization. It involves orchestrating numerous interconnected tasks, from conceptualization and design to development and final deployment. This complex process is often further complicated by the rise of remote and asynchronous work models, which can introduce unique challenges such as communication gaps and coordination issues. However, tools such as Jira and Confluence can significantly streamline the product management process by offering comprehensive solutions tailored for remote and asynchronous work environments.

Jira, a leading project management tool, excels at task tracking and workflow management. Meanwhile, Confluence is perfect for documentation and collaboration, providing a robust knowledge management system for teams. When used together, these platforms can address the key challenges faced by remote and asynchronous product management teams, fostering a culture of transparency, alignment, and efficiency. In this section, you'll discover the synergy between Jira and Confluence in product management, with real-world scenarios demonstrating their combined potential.

Scenario 1 – project planning and tracking

The planning phase is crucial for any project. This stage involves defining the scope, objectives, and deliverables. With Confluence, product managers can create a project space where all this information can be documented and easily accessed by a team. This space can also provide a snapshot of the project's goals, stakeholders, and progress metrics. Once the project is underway, tasks and deliverables can be tracked using Jira. This integration allows for a seamless transition from project planning in Confluence to execution in Jira. It gives teams a clear view of what needs to be done, who is responsible, and how progress is tracked against the project plan.

Scenario 2 – managing product requirements

When developing a new product or feature, capturing and managing requirements is key. Confluence offers a collaborative space where requirements can be documented in detail, including goals, business objectives, strategic fit, and user stories. Requirements can then be linked directly to Jira, broken into actionable tasks, and assigned to the respective team members. This integration ensures that all team members understand what needs to be developed and why, providing a direct line of sight from the high-level requirement to the individual tasks needed to implement it.

Scenario 3 – collaborative decision-making

In a remote and asynchronous environment, fostering collaboration can be a challenge. However, Confluence and Jira make collaborative decision-making easier. Confluence can create a dedicated space for decision-making where team members can share their thoughts, ideas, and feedback. This space can also serve as a repository for all decisions made, providing a historical record that can be referred to in the future. Additionally, Jira can track decision-making tasks, ensuring that all necessary decisions are made promptly.

Scenario 4 – team and project spaces

Having centralized spaces for teams and projects can enhance collaboration and communication in a remote and asynchronous setting. Confluence provides a platform to create spaces where all relevant information can be shared, discussed, and updated in real time. Team members can quickly see who is working on what, the status of different tasks, and upcoming deliverables. This visibility is especially crucial in an asynchronous work setting where real-time communication is not an option.

Scenario 5 – documenting and sharing knowledge

Confluence and Jira can facilitate knowledge sharing across an organization. For example, after a project is completed, a post-project review can be documented in Confluence, capturing key learnings, challenges encountered, and how they were addressed. Other teams can then easily access this knowledge, helping them avoid similar project challenges. Similarly, Jira can be used to record and track bugs, issues, and their resolutions, creating a knowledge base that can be referred to in the future.

In conclusion, using Jira and Confluence in harmony can revolutionize product management in remote and asynchronous work settings. These tools can mitigate the common challenges associated with distributed work models by bridging communication gaps, fostering collaboration, and keeping all stakeholders in the loop. From creating a unified space for team collaboration to documenting product requirements, tracking project progress, and conducting efficient retrospectives, they can seamlessly handle the full spectrum of product management tasks. As each organization is unique, the key is to adapt and tailor these tools according to specific needs and workflows, thereby harnessing their full potential.

Remember, the journey toward effective product management is iterative and continuous. As teams evolve and grow, so should the tools and processes they employ. Embrace the combined power of Jira and Confluence, and embark on a journey toward enhanced productivity, collaboration, and success in your product management endeavors.

Summary

Although the world of product management is dynamic and rewarding, it comes with specific challenges. With teams often spread across different time zones, working remotely and asynchronously, maintaining a cohesive and well-aligned group can be tricky. This is where Confluence can become a powerful, professional ally.

Confluence offers a centralized platform where your team can create, share, and discuss all its projects, acting as a lynchpin to keep everyone on the same page. The space home page is a team dashboard, allowing anyone to quickly understand important upcoming deliverables and see what their teammates are working on. It's crucial to highlight the most important information, such as team identity and quarterly goals, making it immediately noticeable. Space shortcuts and a well-structured page tree enhance the accessibility of information and make it easy for anyone to find relevant work or see what a team is currently focused on. The overview page, shortcuts, and page tree are all highly customizable, as shown in the following screenshot, and they can be designed to form a powerful team dashboard.

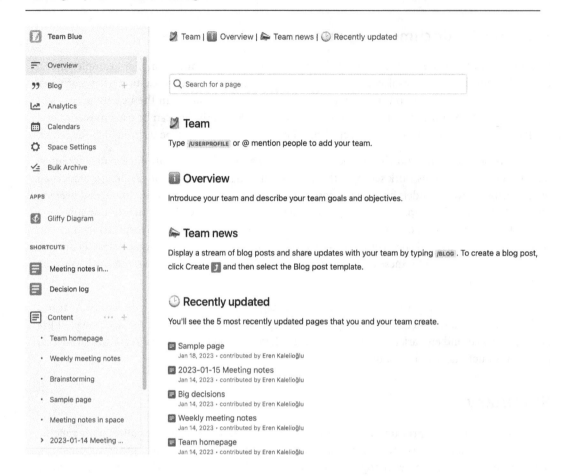

Figure 7.14 – The Overview page as a team dashboard

Similarly, project spaces in Confluence can be utilized effectively for larger, more complex initiatives. The home page of a project space should act as a dashboard, presenting key details such as the project's vision, stakeholders, goals, and metrics used to track them. Including a project schedule using a roadmap planner or a team calendar can help track important deliverables and milestones. This visibility keeps team members in the loop, allowing stakeholders and other teams to get a snapshot of the project's progress at any time.

When it comes to documenting product requirements, Confluence, once again, proves its worth. The platform offers a collaborative environment to define product requirements, outline goals, create user stories, review user experience and design, address questions and clarifications, and trace requirements to Jira issues. With the power to bring all this information together, Confluence helps to build a shared understanding among a team, making the whole process more efficient and visible.

In conclusion, by integrating Confluence into your product management process, you're not only adopting a tool but also embracing a framework that can transform your team's operations. It's a platform that promotes transparency, enhances collaboration, and helps create an SSOT in a remote and asynchronous work environment. Regardless of where your team members are located, Confluence can help drive your team toward its goals and ensure that everyone moves in the same direction.

Questions

1. How can you document product requirements in Confluence?

2. What is the benefit of using the Product requirements blueprint in Confluence?

3. How can Confluence integrate with other Atlassian products?

4. How can Confluence help remote and asynchronous product management teams?

5. How can Confluence be used to track product requirements and progress?

6. Can you share design files and other documents on Confluence?

Answers

1. Confluence provides a Product requirements blueprint for use as a starting point. It should include key details, goals, user stories, design files, and questions or clarifications. You can also link it to Jira issues for easy tracking and organization.

2. The Product requirements blueprint provides a structured way to document all the details about a product feature or release. It helps ensure that all necessary information is included and that the document is easy to read and understand for all team members.

3. Confluence integrates seamlessly with other Atlassian products such as Jira, enabling teams to trace requirements to Jira issues, embed Jira boards, and turn user stories written in Confluence into Jira issues. This ensures a unified workflow across different platforms.

4. Confluence helps remote and asynchronous teams by providing a single, centralized platform where all team members can access and update information. It enables transparent communication, making it easier to keep everyone informed, irrespective of location or working hours.

5. Teams can use Confluence to document product requirements, create user stories, track questions and clarifications, and even trace requirements to Jira issues. This allows for a comprehensive and traceable record of product development.

6. Yes, Confluence allows you to upload and share various files, including design files. Teams can collaborate on these files directly within Confluence, providing feedback and making real-time changes.

8

Setting Up a Knowledge Base

A knowledge base serves as the heart of an organization's informational ecosystem. It is a digital library filled with all the essential details of a company's operations, procedures, policies, and expertise. This centralized informational repository is even more critical in a remote and asynchronous work environment. Employees operating across different time zones and geographical locations should rely on a knowledge base for accurate and timely information.

Take the HR department as an example. A new member joining the HR team can leverage the knowledge base to familiarize themselves with the internal HR policies and procedures, thus reducing the time spent in direct communication and increasing efficiency. An established knowledge base can effectively bridge the information gap, fostering self-reliance and promoting a culture of learning and development in the organization.

A knowledge base also democratizes knowledge, ensuring everyone in an organization has access to the same information. It fosters transparency and a shared understanding, particularly beneficial in a remote work setup. A shared knowledge base can be a powerful tool in aligning diverse teams toward common organizational goals.

Exploring the fundamentals of a knowledge base

A knowledge base isn't just a collection of articles; it is an organized repository of pages, spaces, and labels. Pages form the fundamental unit of a knowledge base and are individual articles or documents on a specific topic. Each page contains a separate piece of knowledge, presented in an easy-to-understand format. A marketing team, for instance, might have a page dedicated to outlining the steps to conduct effective market research.

Spaces are the larger categories or sections under which these pages are organized. A space can represent a department, a project, or a significant organizational function. For example, in a software development team's knowledge base, spaces might be dedicated to frontend development, backend development, and quality assurance. Each of these spaces would house numerous pages relevant to the respective topic.

Labels, conversely, are tags used for further categorization. They are flexible and can be used to group pages with similar characteristics or topics. Labels enhance the searchability and navigability of the knowledge base, making it easy for users to locate the information they seek. The combined use of pages, spaces, and labels can create a structured and efficient knowledge base that caters to various informational needs.

Distinguishing different types of knowledge bases

Knowledge bases are not one-type-fits-all; they can be tailored to the target audience. Knowledge bases can be internal or external. An internal knowledge base is designed for the employees within an organization. It can house information on various topics, from company policies, standard operating procedures, and product details to project documentation and meeting minutes.

Conversely, an external knowledge base is designed for the customers or end users of a company's products or services. It typically includes user guides, tutorials, FAQs, and other resources that help users understand and make the most of a product. For instance, a technical support team might maintain an external knowledge base that provides solutions to common technical issues, enabling customer self-service and reducing the burden on the support staff.

Note that each knowledge base type serves distinct purposes while complementing each other. While an internal knowledge base drives operational efficiency, an external one enhances customer satisfaction and engagement.

Identifying the audience for a knowledge base

A knowledge base is a tool of empowerment for internal team members and external stakeholders. The primary audience for an internal knowledge base is the employees and management, and the information housed in such a knowledge base can span across all departments and functions of an organization. For example, a purchasing team might use the knowledge base to check suppliers' selection criteria and processes, or an IT team might use it to maintain consistent technology standards across the organization.

An external knowledge base can also serve other external stakeholders, such as partners, investors, and the media. They can use the knowledge base to understand a company's product portfolio, track its latest releases, or learn about its operational milestones. In this context, a well-maintained knowledge base can contribute to the company's public image and relations.

Acknowledging the importance of a knowledge base

Having a knowledge base shouldn't be considered a luxury; it is necessary for the digital age we live in. It serves several purposes – a self-service portal for employees and customers, an internal communication hub, and an institutional knowledge repository. Consider a scenario where a customer encounters a problem while using your product. If you have a well-structured external knowledge base, then a customer can search for a solution independently without waiting for customer support. It will consequently enhance customer satisfaction and reduce the load on your support team.

Similarly, an internal knowledge base is beneficial for remote and asynchronous teams. It enables employees to find answers to their queries independently, eliminating constant back-and-forth communication. It also reduces the risk of knowledge loss when employees leave the company, as their knowledge and expertise get documented in the knowledge base.

Recognizing the risks and disadvantages of not having a knowledge base

Not having a knowledge base can cause problems in an organization. The most obvious risk is the loss of knowledge and information. When employees leave, their knowledge and expertise can be lost if not properly documented. A knowledge base ensures that this invaluable information is preserved and accessible to all, even after an employee's departure.

Also, the lack of a knowledge base can cause significant communication hurdles in a remote and asynchronous work environment. Employees might struggle to find critical information, consequently facing delays and inefficiencies. This problem can be exacerbated across different time zones, as employees may have to wait hours to receive answers to their queries.

Another risk of not having a knowledge base could be the difficulty in maintaining consistency and standardization of operations. A knowledge base acts as a single source of truth, guiding employees through approved protocols and standards, and ensuring everyone stays on the same page.

Establishing a knowledge base with Confluence

Follow the following path to create a robust knowledge base using Confluence. First, set up your Confluence account. Once this is done, you can build your knowledge base by creating a dedicated space. Think of this space as a digital room where all related information and resources are housed, such as frontend development standards and a code review checklist. Each page should be detailed, clear, and easily understandable. Don't forget to add relevant images, videos, or diagrams to make the content more engaging and comprehensible.

Finally, use labels to categorize these pages. They are keywords or tags that you can attach to the pages, and they will significantly improve navigability. Labels form an informal way to categorize or group pages and help users quickly find the necessary information. For example, under the software development guidelines space, pages related to backend development can be tagged with a "backend" label. This way, when a team member wants to find all the resources related to backend development, they can search for the "backend" label. Note that the labels in Confluence are space-specific, meaning the same label can refer to different things in different spaces. This flexibility allows you to customize your labeling system based on the unique needs of each space.

Exploring the benefits of a cloud-based and mobile-friendly knowledge base

A cloud-based and mobile-friendly knowledge base offers several benefits. Cloud-based means your knowledge base is accessible from anywhere at any time, which is particularly beneficial for remote and asynchronous teams, as employees can access the information they need outside the office or during standard working hours.

Confluence's mobile-friendly interface adds another layer of convenience. Employees can access a knowledge base from their smartphones or tablets, making the knowledge base more accessible and user-friendly. This is particularly beneficial when employees need to access information on the go. Meanwhile, a cloud-based knowledge base eliminates the need for in-house servers, reducing the need for IT resources to maintain the knowledge base. It also offers scalability – as your organization grows and the volume of information increases, your knowledge base can easily grow with it, thanks to the virtually limitless storage capacity of the cloud.

Understanding the role of a knowledge base in problem-solving for remote teams

As mentioned earlier, the primary challenge in remote and asynchronous work is communication. Without face-to-face interaction, conveying and receiving information can easily become an issue. A knowledge base mitigates this issue by providing a centralized, readily available source of information. In this sense, the knowledge base works as a problem-solver for remote teams. As an example, consider the case of a remote developer encountering a bug in code. Instead of waiting for the team lead in a different time zone to respond, they can refer to the bug-fixing guide in the knowledge base and try to resolve the issue independently.

Also, in a remote setting, new employees might feel isolated and struggle to adapt to a company's culture and protocols. In this case, a knowledge base can be highly beneficial. With resources such as the company culture guide, team introduction, or onboarding checklist, new hires can understand their role in the company culture at their own pace, consequently having a smoother and more efficient onboarding experience.

Realizing the value that a knowledge base adds to remote teams

A knowledge base is not just a tool but also a strategic asset that adds value to remote teams in multiple ways. It fosters self-reliance and a continuous learning culture, as team members can independently find the information they need and stay updated on the latest company news. In a sales department, for example, representatives can leverage the knowledge base to stay updated on the latest product features, pricing strategies, and competitor analysis. Consequently, they are constantly equipped with the most recent information when interacting with potential customers.

A knowledge base also preserves the institutional knowledge of an organization, minimizing the impact of employee turnover. With each piece of documented knowledge, new employees can get up to speed quickly, contributing to the efficiency and productivity of their team. A knowledge base also provides transparency within the organization. With all the available information, there are fewer risks of miscommunication or misunderstanding, enhancing trust and cooperation among team members. As a result, the company will have a more positive and collaborative work environment.

Understanding the role of governance in a knowledge base

Governance is a crucial aspect of maintaining a knowledge base. Without proper governance, a knowledge base can quickly become disorganized and difficult to navigate. Governance encompasses several elements – determining who can create and edit content in the knowledge base, establishing guidelines for content creation and categorization, and periodically reviewing and updating the content.

It is possible to distribute the responsibilities for managing a knowledge base across team members. For instance, each department can have a designated knowledge manager responsible for maintaining their department's knowledge base. This responsibility can include adding new pages, updating existing ones, and ensuring content is up to date and accurate.

Additionally, guidelines should be in place to standardize the content creation process, including instructions on formatting, labels, categories, and guidelines for writing style and tone. Regular audits and reviews of the knowledge base content can help identify gaps, outdated information, and areas for improvement, ensuring that the knowledge base remains reliable and useful for an entire organization.

Summary

In this chapter, we discussed a knowledge base's integral role in organizations, particularly those employing remote and asynchronous work models. We acknowledged that, whether internally or externally, a knowledge base serves as a central repository of information, facilitating self-service and promoting a culture of continuous learning. We learned that organizations risk knowledge loss, communication gaps, and a lack of process standardization without a knowledge base.

We also acknowledged that Confluence serves as an ideal platform to set up a cloud-based, mobile-friendly knowledge base while providing a dedicated space with categorized pages, ensuring that the knowledge base is accessible anywhere, anytime, making it a vital tool for remote teams. We saw that governance plays a crucial role in effective knowledge base management, which involves determining content creation and editing privileges, standardizing the content creation process, and conducting regular audits to ensure the accuracy and relevancy of the content.

Questions

1. Why is a knowledge base essential for remote and asynchronous teams?

2. What are some examples of content in a knowledge base for different teams?

3. What are the advantages of using Confluence for a knowledge base?

4. How can a knowledge base be maintained effectively?

5. What risks does a company face without a knowledge base?

Answers

1. A knowledge base ensures that information is accessible to all team members, regardless of location or time zone, facilitating self-learning and reducing dependence on synchronous communication.

2. An HR team might include pages on company policies, a marketing team might have guidelines for brand communication, a development team might have coding standards and project documentation, an IT support team might have solutions to common technical issues, and a purchasing team might have supplier selection criteria.

3. Confluence provides an intuitive editor, organized structure, robust search function, and extensive permission settings. Its cloud-based nature and mobile compatibility make it especially suitable for remote teams.

4. It is important to regularly update a knowledge base and prune outdated information. Defining clear roles and responsibilities for its maintenance can also aid in its effective upkeep.

5. Without a knowledge base, companies risk losing crucial information when employees leave, face challenges in maintaining consistent communication across different time zones, and might find it hard to keep everyone on the same page.

Further reading

- https://www.atlassian.com/itsm/knowledge-management/what-is-a-knowledge-base

- https://www.atlassian.com/software/confluence/templates/collections/knowledge-base

- https://www.atlassian.com/software/confluence/resources/guides/extend-functionality/confluence-jsm#add-knowledge-base-articles

9
Setting Up a Personal Space

Welcome, fellow remote workers, to the fascinating world of Confluence personal spaces! Being well versed in digital collaboration tools becomes crucial as our work environment evolves, especially when remote and asynchronous work environments are becoming the norm. Personal spaces in Confluence are instrumental in facilitating this process.

In an ever-changing landscape, tools such as Confluence personal spaces serve as pillars of support for teams navigating through remote and asynchronous work challenges. Personal spaces can significantly build a robust, transparent, and seamless workflow, which we'll explore in this chapter. Let's dive deeper and understand the nuances.

Understanding personal spaces

Understanding the concept and importance of personal spaces in Confluence is crucial before implementing them effectively. Let's take a deeper look into what personal spaces are.

A personal space in Confluence is a space that is created by an individual user for their own use. It is a private space where a user can create, manage, and store their own pages and documents. The personal space is a great way to organize your own work, take notes, and create drafts of documents before sharing them with others. It is also a good place to store documents and information that is not yet ready for public consumption or that you want to keep private.

The benefits of creating a personal space

Creating personal spaces in Confluence has a lot of benefits, such as the following:

- **Organization**: It helps with organizing your work in one place. You can create pages and documents, and store all your work-related information in your personal space.

- **Privacy**: It provides a level of privacy as the content in your personal space is private to you unless you decide to share it with others.

- **Personal dashboard**: It acts as your personal dashboard where you can have an overview of all your work, tasks, and activities.

- **Drafts**: It allows you to create drafts of documents and work on them privately before sharing them with others.

- **Personal knowledge management**: It is a great tool for personal knowledge management. You can create a personal knowledge base with all the information that is important to you.

The role of personal spaces

The primary purpose of the personal space is to give users a place where they can manage their own work, create drafts, and store personal information. It helps in organizing your work and keeping it private until you are ready to share it with others.

Personal spaces act as your private work den within Confluence. You might wonder why one needs such a space while working remotely; the answer is simple: to enhance organization, manage personal projects, and streamline workflows. For example, you're a project manager developing a new product strategy. Your personal space can be the breeding ground for your nascent ideas, drafts, project timelines, and essential files to keep them confidential until they're ready to be shared.

A personal space in Confluence serves multiple roles:

- It is a confidential space to work on projects, a personal journal for thoughts and ideas, and even a portfolio to showcase your work

- It allows you to experiment, providing room to make mistakes and learn, all within a safe environment

A concrete example of using personal spaces

Consider a scenario where you are working on a project and you need to create several documents, take notes from meetings, and keep track of tasks. Instead of keeping all this information scattered across different platforms or documents, you can create a personal space in Confluence and organize all this information in one place. You can create pages for meeting notes, a page for tasks, and pages for different documents. You can work on them privately, and once you are ready, you can share them with your team or move them to a project space in Confluence.

Enriching personal spaces

Personal spaces don't have to be text-heavy or monotonous. They can be an extension of your personality, reflecting your work style. You can enrich your personal spaces with pages, blogs, tasks, and attachments. Suppose you're a graphic designer working on a new logo design. Your personal space can house your rough sketches, color palettes, font choices, and perhaps even a blog about your design journey. It can be your creative hub within Confluence.

Your personal space is yours to mold. It can store work-related content, learning resources, meeting notes, or personal reminders. With the right mix of content, your personal space can transform into a comprehensive work and learning place. Confluence creates a simple home page for you when you create a new personal space. You can use it as a starting point and develop it according to your needs. We recommend you meticulously design your personal space's home page.

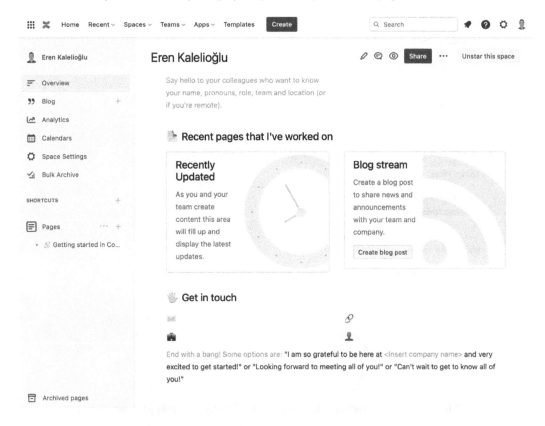

Figure 9.1 – Default home page created for your personal space

Let's take a closer look at the home page. Here, there is a **Recently Updated** macro that operates dynamically. All pages updated on Confluence will appear here. Thus, you can easily follow what's happening in the Confluence environment. On the right, you see a blog section. Here, you can create new blog content. The blog content you create will appear in this section.

There is no limit to the content you can add to your personal space. We encourage you to be creative as much as possible. For example, we find Atlassian's My User Manual template very practical. Filling out the blanks on this page and making it accessible to everyone in your company can ensure that people will understand you better in your own words.

My user manual

Environments I like to work in	• Use bullets to describe your preferences for each category.	Add images in this column whenever relevant, or just to inject some fun!
Preferred working hours		
Communication preferences		
Preferred ways to receive feedback		
Things I need		
How I learn best		
Things I struggle with		
Things I love		
If I were an animated gif/meme/animal/song, I would be…		
My favorite saying		
Other things I want you to know about me		
Add your own categories		

Figure 9.2 – "My user manual," a template by Atlassian, can be stored within your personal space

The My user manual content you see in the previous screenshot is just one of the content types you can place in your personal space. Remember that you can get inspiration from the personal spaces of other team members in your company.

Maintaining personal spaces

Similar to a garden that needs regular weeding, your personal space requires maintenance. Since regular decluttering and organizing are essential practices in Confluence, you must keep your personal space up to date and organized as the owner. Maintenance also extends to the timely archiving of obsolete content and the effective use of labels for easy retrieval. A well-maintained personal space enhances productivity and saves valuable time in searching through disorganized content.

Creating, deleting, and managing personal spaces

Now that we understand the importance of personal spaces, let's dive into how to create, delete, and manage personal spaces.

Creating and deleting personal spaces

Creating a personal space in Confluence is as simple as clicking the **Create Personal Space** button in the profile menu. Now, note that once you create a personal space, it's there to stay; deleting it might mean losing valuable content. It's wise to think twice before hitting delete.

Also, it is necessary to set which user groups will have a personal space on Confluence. This setting is done from the **Global permissions** section, as seen in the following screenshot. Remember that you need to be a Confluence administrator to access these settings. To edit **Global permissions**, click the gear icon in the top nav bar to view your site's settings.

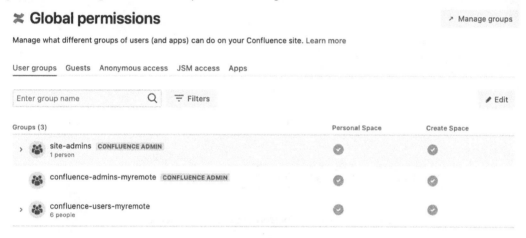

Figure 9.3 – Global permissions on Confluence

As you can see, the user group named **confluence-users-myremote** currently has personal space permission, meaning Confluence will automatically create a personal space for users added to this group. Also, the individuals in this group can create a new personal space if they don't already have one.

Group members are inherently provided with a personal space on your Confluence platform. Disabling this feature won't eliminate current spaces. Instead, it stops new spaces from being generated for users who are added to this group following the adjustment.

When you add a new user to Confluence, a personal space will be automatically created for that user. This feature did not exist in the past; personal spaces had to be created manually. Therefore, if you've been using Confluence for a long time, personal spaces might not have been created for people you added to Confluence a long time ago. In this case, you can create a personal space for these individuals, as seen in the next screenshot.

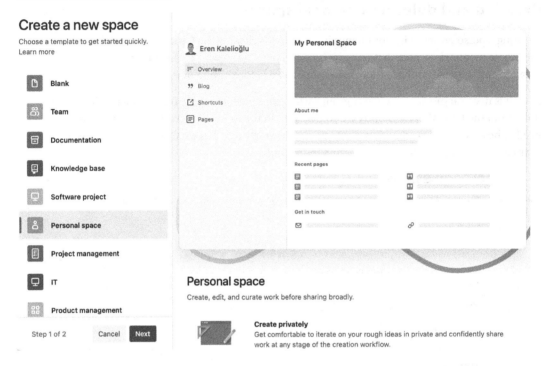

Figure 9.4 – Creating a personal space in Confluence

As shown in the previous screenshot, creating a Personal Space for yourself is a straightforward task if you have the **Create Personal Space** permission. Make sure you follow this path: **All Spaces | Create a new space**. Then, select **Personal Space** as the space type, click on the **Next** button, and enter the name of the space.

We've now learned how to create a new space. If you want to delete one instead, this is the path to follow: **Space Settings | Manage space | Delete space**.

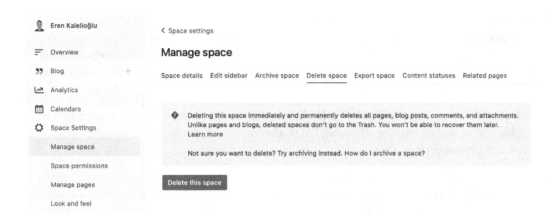

Figure 9.5 – Deleting a personal space

As you can see in the previous screenshot, you will see a warning when you want to delete a space. As the warning reads, deleting a space means all the contents will be permanently deleted. So, if you're unsure about deleting a space, you might prefer to archive it instead. This way, you can clean up your Confluence environment while accessing the space's contents when necessary.

Managing personal spaces

Managing personal spaces involves updating content, modifying permissions, and archiving outdated material. It also means balancing what stays private and what doesn't. In other words, managing permissions in Confluence is about setting the right balance between privacy and collaboration. Choosing appropriate permission levels will help achieve this balance.

Addressing remote team challenges with personal spaces

Personal spaces can be beneficial in addressing the challenges faced by remote teams. Let's discover how.

Tackling asynchronous communication

Communication is often challenging in remote and asynchronous work environments where team members are spread across different time zones. In this case, Confluence personal spaces can help you store and share updates, progress reports, and more, ensuring everyone stays in the loop, no matter when teammates log in. For instance, say you are a content writer based in New York and work with an editor in Sydney. Your personal space can serve as a real-time update system. You can keep drafts, edited copies, final versions, comments, and revisions in one place, accessible to your editor at their convenience.

Another challenge in communication could be delays in feedback or approvals. Personal spaces can help store queries, feedback requests, and more, accessible for team members to see when they are online. Brainstorming in a remote setup can also be challenging, as impromptu meeting-room discussions are off the table. Personal spaces can be a mini brainstorming hub where teammates discuss and iterate ideas asynchronously.

Asynchronous training and learning is another hurdle that remote teams often face. Here, personal spaces, learning materials, training schedules, FAQs, and many more can be stored for team members to access and learn at their own pace.

Finally, building personal connections and understanding team members' work styles can be challenging in a remote setup. However, by sharing and collaborating on personal spaces, team members can learn more about each other's work processes, styles, and even quirks. This will contribute to building a stronger bond among teammates.

Setting guidelines for personal spaces

With all the benefits, it is also essential to establish some rules of engagement for personal spaces. Similar to a physical workspace, maintaining decorum in a digital space is crucial. Here are practical tips to consider:

- **Transparency, not transparency invasion**: Encourage sharing and collaboration and respect privacy
- **Relevance is key**: Encourage relevant content sharing to avoid clutter
- **Archiving over deleting**: Archive obsolete content instead of deleting it as it may have relevance later
- **Permission matters**: Be mindful and intentional when setting and changing permissions
- **Stay organized**: Encourage regular maintenance of personal spaces

Strategizing, implementing, and overcoming challenges with personal spaces

When mastering personal spaces, strategy, implementation, and challenges are the three concepts that go hand in hand. Let's look at each concept and understand how they work to understand personal spaces better.

Strategizing with personal spaces

Strategizing with personal spaces means determining when to use them, how to organize them, and whom to grant access to. Here's a scenario to better understand the concept: assume you're a software developer debugging complex code. Your personal space can be the place where you store all the problematic code, potential solutions, references, and debug logs. You can strategize by planning what to keep in your personal space, how to label and organize them, and when to share them with your team for collaboration.

Implementing personal spaces

The implementation of personal spaces refers to creating, using, and managing the spaces, and the process can vary based on the role, project, or organization. For instance, the implementation for a project manager might mean collaborative content, while for a writer, it might mean private drafts and revisions.

Overcoming challenges with personal spaces

While personal spaces are highly beneficial for your team, they can present challenges. However, with careful planning, you can overcome these challenges. In the next screenshot, you can see the typical challenges you may encounter when using personal spaces.

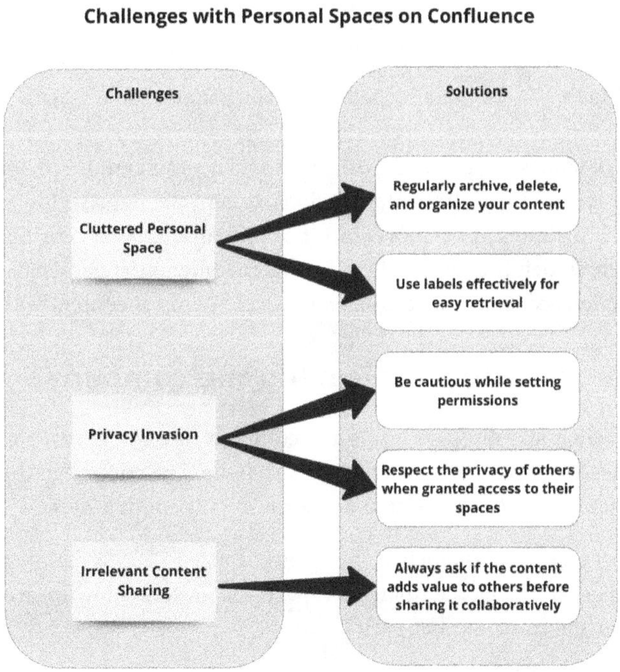

Figure 9.6 – Challenges with personal spaces on Confluence

As you can see, it is possible to overcome each challenge with a specific solution. The more you use personal spaces, the more likely you will be to encounter new challenges other than those listed here. In the following screenshot, you can see how to set restrictions for your personal space. Thanks to this interface, you can set person and group-based authorizations for your personal space.

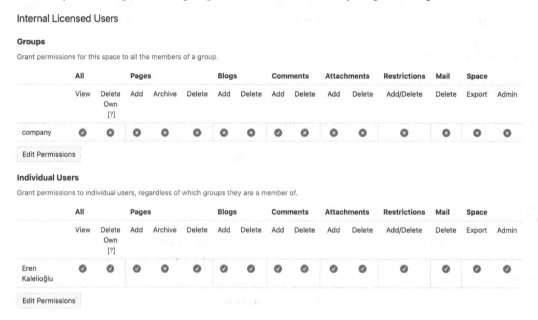

Internal Licensed Users

Groups

Grant permissions for this space to all the members of a group.

	All		Pages			Blogs		Comments		Attachments		Restrictions	Mail	Space	
	View	Delete Own [?]	Add	Archive	Delete	Add	Delete	Add	Delete	Add	Delete	Add/Delete	Delete	Export	Admin
company	✓	✗	✗	✗	✗	✗	✗	✓	✗	✗	✗	✗	✗	✗	✗

Edit Permissions

Individual Users

Grant permissions to individual users, regardless of which groups they are a member of.

	All		Pages			Blogs		Comments		Attachments		Restrictions	Mail	Space	
	View	Delete Own [?]	Add	Archive	Delete	Add	Delete	Add	Delete	Add	Delete	Add/Delete	Delete	Export	Admin
Eren Kalelioğlu	✓	✓	✓	✗	✓	✓	✓	✓	✓	✓	✓	✓	✓	✓	✓

Edit Permissions

Figure 9.7 – Configuring permissions on your personal space

The previous screenshot shows a typical authorization setting you can use in your personal space. As the owner of the space, we have all the permissions, except the page archiving permission. The **Company** group, which includes all employees in the company, only has the right to view content and add comments. Remember, the settings here apply generally to the personal space. It is possible to also apply more detailed access authorizations for specific items of content within the space.

Personal spaces of employees leaving the company

In Confluence Cloud, when an employee leaves the company, their personal space and its content technically still exist, but access to that space becomes an issue. The content in the personal space of a former employee is not automatically deleted or transferred to another user.

When an employee loses access to Confluence, they won't be able to access their personal space or any other space in Confluence. However, their personal space and its content will still exist in Confluence until it is deleted or transferred to another user.

To secure the information in an employee's personal space before they leave the company or lose access to Confluence, you can consider the following options:

- **Transfer ownership**: Before the employee leaves, you can ask them to transfer the ownership of their personal space to another user, such as a team lead or a manager. This way, the new owner will have full control over the content and can decide what to do with it.

- **Move content**: The employee can move important pages or documents from their personal space to a relevant team or project space. This way, the information will be accessible to the team even after the employee leaves.

- **Backup content**: You can also ask the employee to export the content of their personal space. Confluence allows users to export spaces or individual pages in different formats, such as PDF or XML. This exported content can be stored securely and imported back into Confluence if needed.

- **Access control**: If you do not have time to do any of the preceding before the employee leaves, you can temporarily restrict access to the employee's personal space to a small group of trusted users or admins. This way, the content will be secure until you decide what to do with it.

It is important to have a clear policy and process in place for managing the content of personal spaces when an employee leaves the company or loses access to Confluence. This will ensure that important information is not lost and can be accessed by the team when needed.

Summary

As we outlined in this chapter, personal spaces in Confluence are your private havens in the digital workplace. We saw that they help manage your workflow, organize your tasks, and facilitate collaboration with your remote team, having a crucial role in overcoming the challenges that remote and asynchronous work environments often present. A personal space in Confluence is a great tool to manage your work, create drafts, and organize your personal information. It provides a level of privacy and organization that helps in managing your work more efficiently.

In this chapter, we also covered how to set up a personal space and how to use it effectively in different scenarios while discovering important tips to prevent possible challenges and get the most out of personal spaces.

In the next chapter, you'll learn how to connect all your spaces on Confluence and create a company space that will be a hub for all other spaces.

Questions

1. What can be stored in a personal space?
2. Who should have a personal space?
3. Who maintains a personal space?

4. What are the potential risks of personal spaces?

5. How can personal spaces improve remote work?

Answers

1. Pages, blogs, tasks, attachments, and anything relevant to the user's work.

2. Ideally, each team member should have a space to organize their work.

3. The individual who owns the space is primarily responsible for its maintenance.

4. Risks include the development of information silos and data security issues, which can be mitigated using proper access control.

5. They bridge the physical gap by providing a digital space for individual work and creativity. They facilitate asynchronous communication, accommodate different time zones, and help to maintain transparency.

10

Connecting All Teams with Confluence

As we have journeyed through this book, we have seen how Confluence can be used to improve collaboration and communication within distributed teams. We have set up our Confluence site, created and organized our content, and finally set up spaces for software projects, product management, and personal use. Now, it's time to take a step further and bring all these spaces together, creating a unified and collaborative ecosystem within your organization. In this chapter, you will get an idea of how you can interact between the spaces of different teams using Confluence. You'll also learn in detail about two topics that concern almost everyone in a company: creating an effective company handbook and establishing a human resources space.

In this chapter, we will cover the following topics:

- Constructing a comprehensive company space with Confluence for distributed teams
- Confluence for project and program managers, PMOs, and portfolio management in remote teams
- Building a comprehensive company handbook with Confluence for remote teams
- Creating a human resources space in your company that will attract the interest of all teams

Constructing a comprehensive company space with Confluence for distributed teams

In this rapidly digitizing world, creating a central hub for organization-wide information is critical, especially for distributed teams. Confluence is a particularly effective tool for this purpose, fostering not just accessible information, but also collaborative synergy. We will discuss the benefits of Confluence through various real-life examples, detailing how different companies use it to create a comprehensive company space.

Creating a company-wide knowledge repository

Consider our first example, an innovative tech firm aptly named *Pioneers of the Digital Realm*. This organization has fully embraced Confluence, utilizing it as a comprehensive *one-stop shop* for everything from strategic roadmaps and product documentation to company policies and operational procedures. When a team member, for instance, needs to understand the technical specifications of a new product or seeks clarification on the company's leave policy, all they need to do is perform a quick search on Confluence. This efficient access to information, eliminating time-consuming back-and-forth email threads, dramatically enhances their operational efficiency.

Facilitating company culture and community building

The following example is set around *Global Connect*, which is a company with a workforce distributed across multiple continents. Since nurturing a cohesive company culture is a significant challenge for such an organization, they use Confluence as their digital water cooler. In it, they have dedicated communal spaces for project updates, accolades for successful initiatives, "employee of the month" recognitions, and announcements of annual company events. This platform brings employees from different time zones together to feel connected, eventually strengthening the team and company culture while making remote work more engaging and fulfilling.

Enhancing accessibility, organization, and inter-departmental collaboration

Our other example, *Technomancer Corp.*, is an IT-based enterprise. This organization reaps the benefits of Confluence's robust search functionality and well-structured information organization. Each department, from Development to Marketing, has its own categorized spaces with relevant resources and documents. When a project necessitates collaboration between these departments, a shared page within Confluence becomes the collaboration hub, providing real-time updates.

Implementing security measures and access controls

In another scenario, *Fintech Fortress* is a company dealing with financial services where secure handling of sensitive information is crucial. With Confluence's advanced permission settings, they can restrict access to specific spaces and pages, ensuring sensitive resources are only accessible to the relevant personnel. This binding access control is vital for protecting confidential data and maintaining clients' trust.

Maintaining regular updates and active content

As a final example, consider *Health Hub Inc.*, a healthcare firm operating in a dynamic regulatory environment. Due to frequent changes in healthcare laws and internal policies, the firm must keep its resources up to date. The administrative team uses Confluence's page history and version control features to track and implement these changes. They can quickly revert to previous versions if needed, guaranteeing that the most accurate and current information is always accessible to the team.

In summary, a well-constructed company space on Confluence is a valuable asset for remote teams to centralize knowledge, foster collaborative work, uphold company culture, and streamline business operations, empowering distributed teams to operate effectively, making it an essential tool in the remote work toolkit.

Confluence for project and program managers, PMOs, and portfolio management in remote teams

As the world has shifted toward remote work, project and program managers and **Project Management Officers** (**PMOs**) face the challenge of maintaining effective communication and managing project portfolios. Here's where Confluence comes into play to ensure everyone stays on the same page. Now, let's examine how.

Connecting and managing concurrent projects

Confluence offers a powerful way of working for project and program managers tasked with multiple projects simultaneously for effective management and seamless coordination. In Confluence, each project can have its own space, populated with relevant material such as documentation, schedules, responsibilities, and updates. Teams can update these spaces in real time, ensuring everyone stays informed regardless of location. Confluence also allows content creation, specifically tailored for project managers. For instance, spaces can contain rules, tips, and procedures and offer advice on best practices and techniques for managing projects effectively.

Archiving and learning from completed projects

Confluence helps manage ongoing projects and archive completed ones, forming a valuable knowledge repository. It stores records of project objectives, executed actions, challenges faced, and outcomes, offering insights for future reference. This archived data also serves as a resource for PMOs; they can benefit from this stored data to spot trends, identify recurring issues, and develop proactive strategies to mitigate risks in future projects.

Planning future projects

Confluence is also beneficial for planning future projects. Before their official commencement, project plans can be refined by creating initial project spaces in Confluence. These spaces outline crucial elements, such as potential objectives, timelines, resource allocation, and stakeholder involvement, resulting in a comprehensive and well-coordinated approach to project management. PMOs can use these spaces to coordinate across projects, streamline resource allocation, and plan project portfolios effectively.

Confluence for program and portfolio management

In addition to managing individual projects, Confluence can also facilitate program and portfolio management. Using Confluence, organizations can achieve strategic objectives more effectively to oversee a group of related projects within a program or manage an entire portfolio. In other words, Confluence offers a panoramic view of a portfolio, for example, consisting of multiple projects across different teams and departments, providing real-time insights into progress, resource utilization, and performance. This comprehensive overview enables effective monitoring and informed decision-making, helping managers visualize key portfolio metrics, ensure strategic alignment, and make informed resource allocation and prioritization decisions.

PMO content and ideas

PMOs play a critical role in managing project and program risks, standards, practices, and overall performance. With Confluence, they can have dedicated spaces to maintain PMO-specific content, including project documentation templates, risk management guidelines, effective communication practices, and project reporting standards.

Leveraging Confluence as a project knowledge bank

In addition to project management, Confluence doubles its potential as a comprehensive knowledge bank by pulling data from various projects, allowing easy navigation between related projects and resources, boosting cross-functional collaboration, and fostering organizational learning.

Designing a Confluence space as a collective lesson-learned repository

Thanks to Confluence's versatility, project teams can create dedicated spaces that consolidate and integrate valuable lessons learned from various projects. These spaces serve as a centralized knowledge hub, fostering knowledge sharing and enabling continuous organizational improvement. This way, it becomes possible to centralize knowledge and facilitate the transfer of wisdom from one project to a future one, enabling continuous improvement. Meanwhile, PMOs can also lead in driving the adoption and maintenance of this repository, fostering a culture of learning across the organization.

In summary, Confluence offers an unmatched platform for managing, connecting, and learning from various projects for project and program managers, PMOs, and portfolio managers in remote environments. By harnessing Confluence's capabilities, organizations can boost collaboration, transparency, and continuous learning, consequently having efficient and effective project management.

Building a comprehensive company handbook with Confluence for remote teams

In the digital era of remote work, having a robust, easily accessible digital company handbook is necessary for maintaining alignment, culture, and effective communication. As a modern cloud-based platform with a powerful mobile application, Confluence has become an ideal tool for crafting a dynamic, interactive, real-time company handbook. We will discuss now how to create an effective company handbook with Confluence.

Creating an interactive table of contents

Imagine leading *Global Synergy*, a multi-national firm with remote teams distributed worldwide, using Confluence to create an interactive table of contents for your company handbook, which is well organized into sections such as **Our Values**, **Company Policies**, **Employee Benefits**, and **IT Support**. This easy navigation would provide a smooth collaboration experience, regardless of location. You can create an interactive table of contents using the Table of Contents macro.

Detailed document examples

Now, let's dive into the specifics. In the **Our Values** section, you've outlined the company's mission, vision, and core values, but you didn't stop there; you've enriched the content with real-life examples of how these values play out in daily operations and decision-making processes.

Your **Company Policies** section, on the other hand, is comprehensive. For instance, it features a **Remote Work Policy**, detailing expectations for availability, communication norms, data security, and usage of company resources. This clarity sets the stage for professionalism and productivity among your remote employees.

The **IT Support** section has a hands-on, practical style. You've included step-by-step guides to troubleshoot common issues, request help, and effectively use IT resources. It's a significant time-saver that promotes efficiency and reduces downtime.

Tips for an effective handbook

To create an engaging handbook, textual content alone may not suffice. For example, **Innovate Together** is a company that effectively integrates multimedia elements into its handbook. It includes video messages from the CEO, infographics depicting work processes, and even enjoyable GIFs showcasing company events. Thus, it has an interactive and enjoyable handbook for the company.

Creating an effective company handbook is crucial for communicating your company's values, culture, and expectations to your employees. Here are some tips for creating an effective company handbook:

- **Start with a strong introduction**: Begin the handbook by introducing your company, including the mission, vision, and values. This sets the tone for the entire handbook and helps employees understand the company's purpose and what it stands for.

- **Be clear and concise**: Use simple and clear language throughout the handbook. Avoid using jargon and complex legal language that may be difficult for employees to understand.

- **Organize the handbook well**: Use a logical structure with a table of contents, headings, subheadings, and bullet points to make the handbook easy to navigate.

- **Include all relevant policies**: Make sure to include all important company policies such as anti-harassment, equal opportunities, attendance, and leave policies.

- **Highlight employee benefits**: Clearly outline all the benefits that your company offers, including health insurance, retirement plans, and paid time off.

- **Explain workplace procedures**: Provide detailed information on workplace procedures such as how to request time off, report an issue, or request reimbursement for expenses.

- **Use visuals**: Incorporate visuals such as images, infographics, and flowcharts to make the handbook more engaging and easier to understand.

- **Provide contact information**: Include contact information for various departments or individuals that employees may need to reach out to for different issues or questions.

- **Include a disclaimer**: Make sure to include a disclaimer stating that the handbook is a guide, not a contractual document. This protects your company from legal issues.

- **Get a legal review**: Have a legal professional review the handbook to ensure that it complies with all laws and regulations.

- **Make it accessible:** Make the handbook easily accessible to all employees, whether it's in print, digital, or both. Also, consider creating versions in different languages if you have a diverse workforce.

- **Regularly update the handbook**: Keep the handbook up to date by regularly reviewing and updating it to reflect any changes in company policies, procedures, or benefits.

- **Get feedback**: Before finalizing the handbook, get feedback from a diverse group of employees and managers to ensure that it is easy to understand.

- **Welcome questions**: Encourage employees to ask questions if there is anything in the handbook that they do not understand or if they need further clarification on any point.

- **Provide training**: Provide training to all employees on the contents of the handbook and any important policies or procedures that they need to be aware of.

Remember, a well-crafted company handbook is not only a useful tool for employees but also helpful in creating a positive and inclusive work culture.

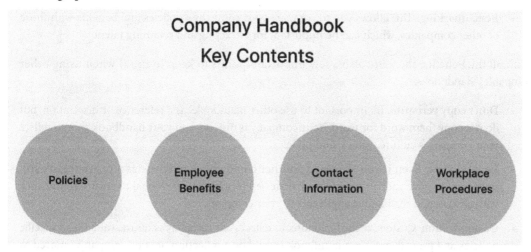

Figure 10.1 – Sample contents to include in your company handbook

A company handbook contains a lot of key content that is relevant to employees, and we have now summarized the most important of this content for you. You are ready to prepare a comprehensive handbook for your company using all the information we've provided.

Learning from other companies' handbooks

Drawing inspiration from other companies' handbooks can be a good option. They are like a gold mine of best practices, letting you learn about effective structure, tone, detail, and design elements. They'll give you a solid image of what makes a handbook engaging and effective.

Utilizing other companies' handbooks when preparing your own can be beneficial for several reasons:

- **Inspiration and best practices**: Other companies' handbooks can serve as a source of inspiration and help you understand the best practices in terms of language, structure, and content. You can identify what works well and what doesn't, then tailor your handbook accordingly.

- **Comprehensive content**: This helps to ensure that you are not missing out on any important policies, procedures, or information that are commonly included in company handbooks.

- **Legal compliance**: Reviewing other handbooks can help you to ensure that your handbook is compliant with all legal requirements and includes all necessary disclaimers and legal language.

- **Benchmarking**: This allows you to compare your company's policies and benefits with those of other companies, which can be important for attracting and retaining talent.

With all the benefits, there are also a few important points to keep in mind when using other companies' handbooks:

- **Don't copy verbatim**: It's important to use other handbooks as a reference or inspiration, but do not copy them word for word. Your company is unique, and your handbook should reflect your company's culture, values, and policies.

- **Legal review**: Even if you are using another company's handbook as a reference, it's still important to have your own handbook reviewed by a legal professional to ensure compliance with all laws and regulations applicable to your company.

- **Customization**: Customize the handbook to reflect your company's culture, values, and specific policies and procedures. Your handbook should be a reflection of your company, tailored to your employees' needs.

- **Confidentiality**: Be mindful of the confidentiality and proprietary nature of the information in other companies' handbooks. Do not share or distribute another company's handbook without its permission.

- **Relevance**: Make sure that the content you are borrowing from another company's handbook is relevant to your company and employees. Not all policies and procedures will be applicable to every company.

By paying attention to these considerations, you can utilize other companies' handbooks to create an effective and comprehensive handbook for your own company.

Company handbook examples

Some companies publish their company handbooks or similar documents publicly on their websites to increase transparency and share their company culture. This approach also provides potential candidates with information about the company's values, principles, and ways of working. Here are a few examples of such companies and links to their handbooks:

- **GitLab**: GitLab has adopted a fully remote work model and comprehensively defines company principles, policies, and ways of working. Here is the link to its handbook: `https://about.gitlab.com/handbook/`.

- **Spotify**: Spotify, a leading music streaming service, also provides insights into its company culture, although it might not be as extensive as a traditional handbook. Here is the link to its handbook: `https://www.lifeatspotify.com/being-here`.

Why Confluence is a good choice for managing your company handbook

Confluence stands out when creating a company handbook. Confluence keeps your handbook content updated and relevant, where you can edit and openly discuss changes, ultimately fostering a culture of collaboration and transparency. Confluence also offers advantages as a cloud-based SaaS with a modern mobile application, letting your team access the handbook from anywhere, anytime, and on any device. This is especially beneficial for remote teams that operate across different time zones.

Confluence allows you to manage the access rights to your company handbook. We recommend providing view access to all employees so they can benefit from the information. However, editing and creating rights should be restricted to relevant stakeholders to maintain the integrity of the content. Additionally, you can get insights about company handbook adoption with the help of Confluence analytics.

In conclusion, you can create a comprehensive, interactive, and up-to-date company handbook using Confluence as a manager of remote teams. It will provide necessary guidelines and resources and help reinforce your company's culture, ensuring everyone feels connected and aligned, even when physically apart. The handbook will be more than a reference tool – it will create a bridge that connects your team.

Creating a human resources space in your company that will attract the interest of all teams

The strategic management of HR resources is crucial for the optimal functioning of any organization. When teams work remotely, they need a robust, easily accessible system for HR-related content. At this point, Confluence emerges as a powerful tool. Confluence's capability to host many content types and robust search functions makes it a go-to platform for managing HR resources. It provides a centralized location where all HR-related information can be stored and accessed. The stored information can include the company's mission and values, organizational structure, employee benefits, compensation policies, onboarding guides, learning and development resources, and various HR forms and protocols.

Why Confluence is an optimal tool for HR resources

Confluence is designed to create, organize, and share information. It provides a digital workspace that is scalable and adaptable to diverse needs, including HR resources. Creating an HR space in Confluence allows the integration of different kinds of content. For instance, it is possible to embed documents, videos, images, links, and more into a Confluence page, making the content more engaging and easier to follow. It is also possible to create a structured hierarchy of pages to organize different types of HR content.

Furthermore, Confluence's powerful search function can be highly beneficial. Employees can easily search for what they want, no matter how vast the content repository is. Confluence centralizes all HR-related information while eliminating the risk of losing critical data, and ensures employees can access information whenever needed.

Benefits of centralizing HR resources for remote teams

Physical boundaries dissolve in a remote working environment, and the digital workspace becomes the nucleus of collaboration and communication. In this case, having a centralized HR resources space provides multiple benefits. Let's look at them:

- **Round-the-clock accessibility**: A well-structured HR space in Confluence is accessible to team members at all times, regardless of their geographical location or time zone. This is a substantial advantage for remote teams spread across different regions.

- **Transparency and clarity**: Having a single source of truth gives all employees clarity on where to find HR-related information, promoting transparency in the organization and reducing potential confusion or misunderstanding.

- **Efficiency and productivity**: With all the necessary information, employees can make quicker decisions without waiting for responses from the HR department or other team members.

Risks of not having a centralized HR resource space

A lack of centralized HR resource space can lead to various challenges. The risks include the following:

- **Information silos**: Vital information might get trapped in personal inboxes, local storage, or chat threads, making it inaccessible to others. This can result in knowledge gaps, duplication of work, and potential loss of essential data.

- **Inconsistency in information**: If HR resources are distributed across different platforms or locations, it can lead to inconsistencies in the information shared with employees, causing confusion and inefficiency.

- **Decreased productivity**: Employees might waste valuable time searching for information across various platforms. In contrast, a centralized system can provide immediate access to the required information, ultimately, improving productivity.

Maintaining updated HR resources

Regular updating and maintenance are crucial for the success of an HR resources space. The HR team should primarily be responsible for this task, keeping the information relevant. Regular audits can be performed to identify and update outdated or irrelevant content. Also, the organization can foster an open culture where employees can provide feedback or suggestions to improve the content. This practice should ensure that the HR resources align with the evolving needs of the employees and the organization.

Access management and stakeholder roles

Confluence allows you to manage the access rights to the HR resources space. We recommend providing view access to all employees so they can benefit from the information. However, editing and creating rights should be restricted to HR personnel and relevant stakeholders to maintain the integrity of the content.

Actively involving stakeholders in managing the HR resources space can also ensure that it stays relevant and beneficial. For instance, team leaders and managers can contribute by sharing insight and feedback from their teams, making the space a genuinely collaborative effort.

The outcome for remote teams and companies

When executed well, an HR resources space in Confluence can revolutionize how a remote team or company operates. Promoting transparency, improving accessibility, and fostering efficiency, a well-managed HR resources space can lead to a more informed and engaged workforce. It can also improve decision-making processes and streamline various HR procedures, increasing productivity and satisfaction among remote workforces. In the long run, it will lead to a robust and resilient organizational culture that thrives in a remote working environment, contributing to the company's overall success.

What can you include within your HR resources space?

Managing HR resources is a cornerstone activity in any organization, more so when teams are working remotely. Confluence, with its decadent array of collaborative tools, is an excellent solution for HR resource management, providing a centralized, easily accessible system for HR-related content. This HR space can include essential company information, organizational structure, HR forms and procedures, and more nuanced content such as diversity and inclusion policies, professional development programs, and employee wellness initiatives. The versatility of Confluence allows you to effectively organize and present these diverse resources, enhancing their utility for your remote team. Now, let's discuss how to create an effective HR resources space.

Company information and organizational structure

A clear presentation of your company's information, including its mission, vision, and values, is crucial for aligning all employees with your organizational goals. Confluence provides a platform where you can vividly communicate your company's ethos and inspire your employees to work toward common objectives. Similarly, a detailed depiction of the organizational structure, including departmental breakdowns and hierarchies, clarifies roles, responsibilities, and reporting lines. It helps avoid overlaps and omissions in tasks, facilitating smoother operations and collaborations.

HR forms and procedures

The HR resources space can also host a variety of HR forms and documents that employees need to access regularly, which include forms for benefits enrollment, expense claims, time-off requests, or performance review forms. Confluence's powerful search feature allows employees to locate and use these forms when needed quickly. Likewise, procedures for standard HR processes – such as requesting vacation time, filing a grievance, or signing up for a training program – can be meticulously documented and shared on this platform. This provides employees with step-by-step guidance for various processes, reducing uncertainties and the burden on HR staff.

Diversity and inclusion policies

Promoting diversity and inclusion stands as a priority for organizations worldwide. Using Confluence, companies can create comprehensive pages dedicated to these policies, fostering an inclusive work culture that resonates with employees. This content also plays a crucial role in driving positive change within the organization. Pages can include the company's stance on diversity, its commitment to equal opportunities, procedures for reporting discrimination or harassment, and resources to help employees understand and embrace diversity. It can also host information about **Employee Resource Groups (ERGs)**, events celebrating diverse cultures, and various organizational initiatives.

Professional development and learning resources

The HR resources space can serve as a repository of learning and development resources, helping employees grow professionally. In it, teams can find internal training modules, links to external courses or webinars, a schedule of upcoming training sessions, or materials from past training sessions. You can also use Confluence to manage and present information about career advancement within the company, including descriptions of different career paths, promotion criteria, and stories from employees who have successfully advanced.

Employee wellness initiatives

Workplace wellness has gained considerable significance recently, particularly in remote work settings. In this sense, your HR resources can include pages on mental health resources, tips for maintaining work-life balance, exercise, nutrition advice, and resources for personal growth.

You can also use Confluence to manage and communicate about employee wellness programs such as fitness challenges, meditation sessions, or employee assistance programs. This not only helps enhance the overall well-being of your employees but also boosts morale and productivity.

In conclusion, Confluence offers a dynamic platform for managing a diverse range of HR resources, helping remote teams stay informed, engaged, and productive. It supports efficient operations, promotes a transparent work culture, and fosters a sense of unity within the remote team by providing a single source of truth for all HR-related content.

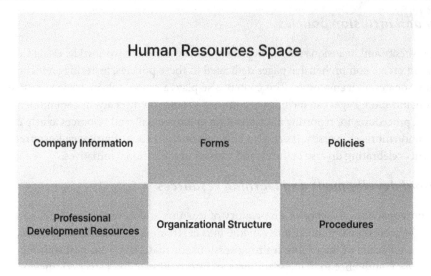

Figure 10.2 – Human resources space

We have summarized the contents that can be found in a human resources space in the previous diagram. You can use them as a starting point when creating your own space.

Summary

So far, we've discussed how Confluence can be a powerful tool for enhancing collaboration and information management in remote work environments. We've seen Confluence's capabilities stretch beyond a typical collaboration platform, making it a versatile tool for managing HR resources, connecting projects, creating company spaces, and building comprehensive company handbooks.

Starting with HR resources, we've highlighted how Confluence can be an HR hub containing essential documents, policies, and information, providing a single source of truth for the entire organization. We've also emphasized Confluence's utility in managing multiple projects concurrently and glanced at building a company space within Confluence, which houses information about company culture, achievements, events, and announcements. Our discussion on creating a company handbook using Confluence underscored its utility as an engaging, accessible, and interactive tool.

As we move forward, we'll explore more use cases, tips, and examples, showing you how to optimize the platform for your unique organizational needs. We'll discover how Confluence can transform your remote work environment into a more collaborative and productive space. In the next chapter, we will learn how to scale Confluence as your organization grows.

Questions

1. Why do we need a company-wide space in Confluence?

2. What are the challenges of creating a master project overview space?

3. What is the role of a company handbook in Confluence?

4. What can be included in the HR space in Confluence?

5. How can Confluence spaces empower distributed teams?

6. What is the significance of the design of a project overview space?

7. Who should manage the company-wide space in Confluence?

Answers

1. A company-wide space breaks down information silos, improves transparency, and enhances team collaboration. It is a central hub for everyone to access company-wide news, updates, and general resources.

2. Challenges include avoiding information overload, maintaining data privacy, and ensuring the updated status of all projects.

3. The company handbook serves as a single source of truth, housing all the rules, regulations, and standard operating procedures that every team member should know.

4. The HR space could contain sections on company policies, benefits, leave procedures, and even wellness resources.

5. Confluence spaces can empower distributed teams by providing shared environments for suggesting ideas, enabling continuous learning, and giving access to all necessary resources regardless of location.

6. The design should facilitate easy navigation and clearly show the status of each project. This increases visibility, enables knowledge sharing, and eases the monitoring of overall project progress.

7. The management of this space should be overseen by a designated admin or team, ensuring that the content remains up to date and relevant.

Part 3: Scaling Business

This part will provide insights on using Confluence in a large-scale enterprise. First, we'll explore the concept of scaling and what it means within Confluence Cloud. We'll then discuss the topic of information security on Confluence. Following that, we'll touch upon integrating Confluence with other systems, as well as enhancing its existing features with additional functionalities. From the perspective of an experienced Atlassian solution partner, we'll shed light on potential challenges you might face when deploying Confluence at a grand scale and share experiences that can help overcome those challenges. As we conclude this part, we'll offer tips on how you can further enhance your proficiency with Confluence.

This part contains the following chapters:

- *Chapter 11, Introduction to Scaling Confluence*
- *Chapter 12, Assuring Security and Compliance*
- *Chapter 13, Integrating and Extending Confluence*
- *Chapter 14, Challenges and Solutions*
- *Chapter 15, What's Next?*

11
Introduction to Scaling Confluence

Scaling Confluence is more than just an expansion; it's an intelligent adaptation to your organization's growing needs and complexities. As teams spread across locations and projects multiply, the collaboration platform must evolve to handle increased data, user loads, and diversified functionalities. Confluence Cloud simplifies this process with its world-standard capabilities, removing the need for concerns over CPU, RAM, or database maintenance. However, a foundational understanding of these concepts is still valuable.

The goal of this chapter is to create a seamless environment where scalability doesn't become a barrier but an enabler for efficient collaboration. This chapter will guide you through the nuances of scaling, help you recognize when its necessary, and offer insights into making this transition smooth and secure. By exploring not just the "what" but the "why" of scaling Confluence, we provide the groundwork for a successful scaling strategy, allowing you to take full advantage of the platform as your operations grow. This approach is the first step toward a more dynamic and responsive collaborative experience fitting perfectly within your organizational context.

In this chapter, we will cover the following main topics:

- Understanding the concept and need for scaling Confluence
- Exploring the challenges and risks in scaling Confluence
- Crafting and implementing an effective scaling strategy
- Optimizing user management in Confluence
- Ensuring security while scaling Confluence

Understanding the concept and need for scaling Confluence

Fundamentally, **scaling** refers to the ability of a system or network to handle growing amounts of work or its potential to be enlarged to accommodate that growth. In the software context, it implies the capacity of a system, network, or process to manage an increasing volume of operations without compromising performance. It's ensuring your digital tools and strategies can grow parallel to your business demands and maintain the same level of efficiency and effectiveness.

When we talk about scaling Confluence, we refer to the ability of your Confluence platform to support the increasing number of users, pages, and spaces without performance degradation. This involves the following:

- **Horizontal scaling**: Adding more machines or instances into the pool of resources
- **Vertical scaling**: Adding more power (CPU, RAM) to an existing machine

However, since this book focuses exclusively on Confluence Cloud, you won't need to deal with managing CPU, RAM, database maintenance, and other technical aspects; Atlassian handles such details with world-class standards. Nevertheless, having a basic understanding of these concepts can still be beneficial.

The relevance of scaling Confluence becomes evident when your organization experiences growth. As your teams expand, you must prepare your Confluence environment to accommodate the increased workload without faltering performance. Without appropriate scaling, your teams can encounter slowdowns or system crashes during peak usage times. On the other hand, a well-scaled Confluence platform can better manage large amounts of data, provide a more responsive user experience, and ultimately contribute to your teams' productivity and efficiency. In other words, scaling Confluence is an indispensable catalyst for achieving seamless growth in dynamic and ambitious organizations, ensuring smooth, uninterrupted workflows as team sizes increase.

Why choose Confluence for scaling your business operations?

Whether you're a startup expecting rapid growth or an established enterprise, Confluence can adapt to your needs with its scalable infrastructure designed to grow with your organization. The ability to scale horizontally by adding more resources as needed and vertically by enhancing the capabilities of existing resources provides the necessary flexibility for evolving businesses. With Confluence Cloud, Atlassian takes care of all the heavy lifting related to scalability, freeing you to concentrate on your core operations.

Confluence's integrative and extensible features make it an ideal tool for scaling. Its seamless integration with other Atlassian products, such as Jira and Trello, and the capacity to incorporate a vast range of add-ons from the Atlassian Marketplace can help streamline your operations as they grow. This interoperability, combined with the extensible nature of Confluence, can significantly simplify the scaling process, making it easier for your teams to collaborate effectively regardless of their size or geographical distribution.

At the heart of Confluence lies the ability to facilitate collaboration at scale. Its comprehensive content creation, management capabilities, and robust search functionality allow teams of any size to share knowledge and collaborate effectively. Also, as your organization scales, maintaining effective communication and collaboration becomes increasingly important. Confluence's tools, such as its dynamic pages, intuitive UI, and powerful search capabilities, support this need by helping teams stay on the same page, streamline decision-making, and boost productivity as the organization grows.

Identifying teams that require Confluence scaling

As an organization evolves, so does its reliance on collaboration and communication tools such as Confluence. The need for scaling Confluence typically begins with recognizing signs of increased demand or strain on your existing setup. Teams experiencing slower load times, encountering storage limits, or finding it difficult to manage and locate content may indicate that your current Confluence setup is starting to fall short. Monitoring these indicators can help you anticipate when a team might require scaling.

An effective way to identify teams that might need scaling is to analyze usage patterns. Teams that consistently create a high volume of pages have a rapidly growing number of members or heavily use collaboration features such as comments and `@mentions` are likely candidates for scaling. Teams operating across different time zones might also benefit from scaling to meet the demand for round-the-clock availability.

Understanding your teams' growth projections can also help to identify who requires Confluence scaling. Teams that are expanding rapidly, taking on large projects, or expected to grow shortly may need scaling sooner rather than later. Being prepared for this growth by scaling can help ensure these teams continue their work seamlessly, fostering productivity and reducing the likelihood of disruption.

We've covered the concept of and need for scaling Confluence so far; let's now disscuss the risks of scaling Confluence.

Exploring the challenges and risks of scaling Confluence

Scaling Confluence comes with challenges and risks. Understanding the potential pitfalls and anti-patterns becomes crucial as you aim to extend the platform's capabilities to fit your organization's growing demands. Mistakes in scaling not only disrupt seamless collaboration but may also pose security risks and operational inefficiencies.

In this section, we will dive into these concerns, elucidating the common pitfalls and the best practices to avoid them. The insight we provide will help empower your team to steer its scaling strategy with confidence and foresight, ensuring that growth and complexity do not compromise the integrity and efficiency of your Confluence environment.

Recognizing potential risks

Scaling Confluence carries several potential risks that must be identified and mitigated for a smooth transition:

- **Data loss or interruption**: The first risk that might come to mind is the potential for data loss or interrupted access during the scaling process. This book focuses exclusively on Confluence Cloud, where Atlassian automatically handles backups, significantly reducing this risk.

- **Decreased performance**: Another risk, especially for growing teams, is overloading the Confluence platform with too many users or pages, resulting in reduced performance. Monitoring usage and proactively scaling resources can help mitigate this risk.

- **User resistance**: With any significant change, there's a risk of resistance from users. To mitigate this risk, clear communication about the benefits of scaling and offering appropriate training can help ensure a smoother transition.

- **Increased costs**: As you scale Confluence, costs will also likely increase. It's crucial to consider these potential costs and budget appropriately to ensure that scaling doesn't negatively impact your organization's financial health.

- **Security risks**: Lastly, as the number of users and the amount of data increase, security risks can also escalate. That's when it becomes important to strengthen security protocols and ensure all users understand and adhere to them.

Acknowledging these potential risks enables you to proactively prepare and implement effective strategies, ensuring a seamless and efficient scaling process.

Avoiding anti-patterns

Anti-patterns refer to standard practices that seem beneficial initially but can result in negative consequences over time. Understanding and avoiding these anti-patterns is essential for a successful scaling process:

- **Scaling too quickly**: One common anti-pattern in Confluence scaling is trying to scale too quickly without adequately planning or understanding your team's needs, which can lead to an over-complicated system that is hard to manage and navigate. It's essential to scale at a pace that aligns with your team's actual growth and needs to prevent unnecessary complexity.

- **Neglecting regular audits**: Another anti-pattern is avoiding regular audits and reviews of your Confluence setup. As your Confluence usage expands, so does the potential for clutter and disorganization. Regularly reviewing your Confluence instance, including user permissions, page layouts, and integrations, can help maintain order and efficiency.

- **Over-reliance on add-ons**: While Confluence's extensive marketplace of add-ons can enhance its functionality, over-reliance on them can become an anti-pattern. Some teams add too many features without considering the potential impact on system performance or user experience. Remember that each new add-on requires resources and can potentially complicate your Confluence environment, so choose and use them wisely.

Being mindful of these prevalent anti-patterns and taking proactive measures to address them will allow you to steer clear of potential pitfalls and guarantees a more streamlined and effective scaling process.

Navigating common pitfalls

When scaling Confluence, there are several common pitfalls that teams should be aware of and strive to avoid for a successful scaling process:

- **Insufficient training**: One common pitfall is failing to adequately train your teams to use Confluence at a larger scale. As your Confluence environment grows, new features and complexities may arise. Without proper training, team members may struggle to use the platform efficiently, decreasing productivity.

- **Outdated governance policies**: Another common pitfall is neglecting to update your governance policies to match your scaled environment. When you scale Confluence, roles and responsibilities might shift and new data management protocols may come into play. If your governance policies aren't updated according to these changes, it can lead to confusion, inconsistent practices, and potential security risks.

- **Ignoring user feedback**: Lastly, ignoring user feedback can be a significant pitfall. The people using Confluence daily are the ones who can provide valuable insights into how the system is performing. If their feedback is ignored, you may miss opportunities to improve the user experience, efficiency, and the platform's overall performance.

In short, recognizing common pitfalls and proactively addressing them can ensure a smoother scaling process and foster continuous improvement in your Confluence environment.

Evaluating potential risks and formulating precautions

The first step in successful scaling is evaluating potential risks, which involves reviewing your current Confluence setup, user roles, data, and integrations to identify potential areas of vulnerability. For instance, you might encounter security risks or performance issues as you increase the number of users and the amount of data in your Confluence instance. Regular audits and performance reviews can help you detect these risks early, allowing you to take proactive measures to manage them.

Once you've identified potential risks, the next step is to formulate precautions. One is to set up clear governance policies, which should outline user roles and permissions, data management protocols, and security measures to ensure your Confluence instance remains secure and well-organized, even as it scales. Regular training sessions can also be vital, ensuring all users understand how to use Confluence effectively and safely in a large-scale environment.

For instance, if you've identified a security risk related to user permissions, the precaution could be implementing a more stringent user access control policy. Or, if you've detected a potential performance issue related to the increased volume of data, the precaution could be to regularly archive older, less relevant data to maintain optimal performance. Lastly, to address the risk of user resistance to the new, larger-scale Confluence environment, the appropriate precaution could be to provide comprehensive training and ongoing support to help users adapt to the changes.

By carefully evaluating potential risks and thoughtfully formulating precautions, you can significantly enhance the success of your Confluence scaling efforts. Remember, staying proactive and addressing potential issues before they escalate is critical.

The importance of risk discovery and mitigation in the scaling process

The first step in effectively scaling Confluence is risk discovery, which entails identifying potential challenges and vulnerabilities that could arise, including data loss, decreased performance, or security threats. Early identification of these risks can empower you to implement preventive measures. Regular audits, performance monitoring, and user feedback can help uncover these risks.

Once risks are identified, it's crucial to implement strategies to mitigate them, which can mean bolstering your security measures, improving user training, or allocating more resources to maintain performance. Each mitigation strategy should be tailored to the specific risk it's designed to address. By tackling these risks in advance, you can ensure a smooth and successful scaling process.

Risk discovery and mitigation play an essential role in the scaling process. Without identifying and addressing risks, you may encounter unexpected challenges that could derail your scaling efforts or, at the very least, cause unnecessary stress and confusion. On the other hand, with proactive risk management, you can confidently navigate the scaling process while boosting the security, performance, and usability of your Confluence environment. These aspects are vital to your team's productivity and ultimate success.

Note that by recognizing the importance of risk discovery and mitigation in the scaling process, you're already taking a significant step toward successful Confluence scaling. Remember, the goal is not to eliminate all risks but to manage them effectively to minimize their impact.

In the previous section, we learned that there are many risks and challenges associated with scaling Confluence. To overcome all of these, it is necessary to have an effective strategy in place. Let's now discuss how to craft and implement an effective scaling strategy.

Crafting and implementing an effective scaling strategy

Creating an effective scaling strategy for Confluence is similar to charting the course for your organization's collaborative journey. It involves striking the perfect balance between functionality, efficiency, security, and user experience. However, formulating the strategy is only the beginning; true success lies in its meticulous and intelligent implementation across various scales and scenarios.

In this section, we will lead you through the essential steps of formulating an adaptive and robust scaling plan. From understanding your organization's unique needs to deploying specific tools and technologies, this guide will be your roadmap, with practical examples and actionable insights. By the end, you will be able to navigate the complexities of scaling with agility and assurance to do the following:

- Craft a scaling strategy
- Implement your scaling strategy
- Monitor and adjust your strategy

Crafting a scaling strategy

Crafting an effective scaling strategy begins with a clear understanding of your current Confluence usage and the goals you aim to achieve through scaling. This process requires a comprehensive review of your team's workflows, the size and complexity of your data, and your projected growth. Once you have a clear picture, you can begin outlining a plan, which can involve deciding on the timing and pace of scaling, the resources needed, and the **key performance indicators (KPIs)** you'll use to gauge your progress.

Apart from comprehending your organization's needs, gaining insight from industry best practices and case studies of successful Confluence-scaling in similar organizations can be valuable. This information can guide you in crafting your strategy effectively. Keep in mind that a sound strategy isn't fixed in stone; rather, it is a dynamic plan that should evolve based on your team's needs and feedback. Regularly revisiting and adjusting your strategy ensures its ongoing relevancy and effectiveness.

Implementing your scaling strategy

Once your strategy is set, the next step is implementation, where you put your crafted plans into action. Clear communication with your team is paramount during this phase, it's essential for your team to comprehend the purpose behind the scaling effort, anticipate the forthcoming changes, and grasp how these changes are beneficial. This approach fosters a sense of ownership and cooperation among team members, facilitating a smoother transition process.

The implementation also involves technical aspects such as adding users, creating new spaces, and perhaps integrating with other tools. Each change should be carried out methodically and following your strategy. Documenting each change is essential to track your progress and revert changes if necessary. As with crafting your strategy, feedback plays an important role in implementation. Regular check-ins with your team can help you gauge how well the changes are received and what adjustments might be needed. Celebrating success can also boost morale and foster a positive attitude toward the scaling process.

Monitoring and adjusting your strategy

Once your scaling strategy is implemented, ongoing monitoring and adjustment are key. Use the KPIs you defined in your strategy to track your progress. Are you meeting your goals? Are there unexpected challenges? How is your team adapting to the changes?

Note that scaling is not a one-time process but an ongoing effort requiring regular attention and adjustment. Regular audits can help detect any issues in advance, allowing you to take corrective action. It is also important to continue gathering and acting on feedback from your team. They use Confluence daily, and their insight can be invaluable in ensuring the platform continues to meet their needs as it scales.

By carefully crafting, implementing, and adjusting your scaling strategy, you can guarantee a seamless and successful transition to a larger Confluence environment. It's important to stay flexible, remain open to feedback, and focus on fulfilling your team's needs throughout the process. This way, you can maximize your chances of achieving the desired outcomes.

Effective user management is essential for scaling Confluence in a healthy manner. Let's now work on how to optimize the user management in Confluence.

Optimizing user management in Confluence

Confluence user management is critical to your system's smooth functioning and security. With clear user roles and permissions, you can ensure that the right people have access to the correct information at the right time. This also helps maintain data integrity and security by restricting access where necessary.

As your team grows and scales, managing user access can become complex. Understanding how to optimize this aspect of your Confluence instance is vital to maintaining efficiency and control as you scale. Let's say a team member inadvertently gains access to confidential information due to improper user management. This could lead to unintentional data breaches, underscoring the importance of meticulous user role definition.

Strategies for centralizing user management

Centralizing user management can provide greater visibility and control over who has access to what within your Confluence instance. This might involve using Confluence's built-in user management tools or integrating with external identity providers.

One strategy might include grouping users based on their organizational roles and assigning permissions accordingly. For instance, an "Editorial Team" group can have edit permissions on specific pages, while a "Viewers" group can only have read permissions.

Regular audits and reviews of user permissions can ensure that access remains appropriate as roles and responsibilities within your organization change. Keeping user management centralized makes these reviews more straightforward and less time-consuming.

Implementing automation and tools

Automation can be a significant asset in user management, especially as your organization grows. By using tools that sync with your HR system or other user databases, you can automate the process of adding, removing, or changing user roles based on changes in job roles or other factors.

This way, you can save time and minimize the risk of human-based error. For instance, imagine a new employee being onboarded. Their access and roles could be automatically defined based on their position within the company without manual input.

Note that there are third-party tools and integrations that can help you implement automation in user management. Researching and choosing the right tools that align with your organization's needs and scaling goals will be crucial.

Regular training and support

Regular training and support are essential as you optimize user management, which includes educating users about their access, the responsibilities that come with it, and the protocols they need to follow.

Regularly updating training materials and supporting queries or issues ensures everyone understands the user management system. This way, you can encourage building a culture of security and responsibility for your team.

Improving user management in Confluence is a complex task that requires careful planning, automation, tools, and ongoing support and training. Focusing on these aspects, you can ensure that your Confluence environment stays secure and efficient as it scales.

If we cannot ensure the security of the Confluence environment, we cannot scale it. Even if we could, it wouldn't be sustainable; scaling and security are closey intertwined. In the next section, we will discuss how to ensure security while scaling Confluence.

Ensuring security while scaling Confluence

Securing Confluence during scaling requires a comprehensive approach that goes beyond technology alone. As your collaborative environment grows, the security landscape becomes more intricate, necessitating a carefully tailored strategy that aligns with your organization's scale and nature of operations.

In this section, we will explore essential security considerations, such as user management and risk evaluation, tailored for large-scale environments. Through real-world examples and practical tips, we'll provide you with a comprehensive understanding of maintaining a secure fortress around your collaborative work as it expands. This understanding lays the groundwork for the next section, where we will dive deeper into assuring security and compliance.

Identifying security requirements in scaling

Identifying security requirements is the cornerstone of scaling Confluence. It involves a comprehensive understanding of data types, access levels, and involved users. Recognizing these elements enables tailored security measures.

Consider a scenario where you are adding external collaborators. They will need access, but how do you grant it without compromising internal security? Understanding the requirements from the beginning will help you create effective security protocols. You should always consider aligning security with your organization's goals and regulatory requirements. It's not a one-size-fits-all approach, but a specific, targeted strategy considering your unique scaling needs.

Implementing robust access control

Setting effective access control is crucial when scaling Confluence. Defined user roles and appropriate permissions help prevent unauthorized access and maintain a seamless workflow. By leveraging automation tools to update these roles and permissions as your organization scales, you can enhance data security while streamlining administrative tasks efficiently.

Regular reviews and updates to these roles are also essential. They ensure that access controls evolve with your organization and adapt to changing needs, keeping your Confluence environment functional and secure.

Auditing and monitoring

Regular auditing and monitoring are critical in identifying and preventing potential security issues. Audits provide detailed insights into access patterns, while real-time monitoring can detect anomalies. Implementing tools that offer real-time alerts and comprehensive reports can ensure that potential risks are identified promptly.

Establishing a culture where security is everyone's responsibility enhances your overall security posture. Regular training and clear communication empower users to identify and report suspicious activities, complementing your technical safeguards effectively.

Data security and backup in Confluence Cloud

Confluence Cloud offers automatic backups to mitigate data loss risks, but this shouldn't replace a comprehensive understanding of data security. Familiarizing yourself with encryption, secure data transmission, and storage practices can allow you to benefit from Confluence Cloud's capabilities. Combining Atlassian's technical expertise with your own tailored security measures, you can set up a robust and reliable security approach. Regular communication with your service provider, understanding their protocols, and aligning them with your security policies can also help create a synergy that ensures robust data security as you scale.

Security checklist essentials for scaling Confluence

A security checklist is a roadmap for implementing and maintaining security as you scale, including encryption standards, multi-factor authentication, and regular vulnerability assessments, which you should revisit and update regularly. As your organization grows, new challenges may emerge, and your security needs will evolve. Keeping the checklist dynamic ensures that it remains relevant and practical.

Real-world examples and practical tips can make this checklist a valuable tool, not just a theoretical guide. Engaging with security experts or utilizing community forums can provide insights to make your checklist robust and applicable.

Strategies for maintaining secure Confluence operations at scale

To uphold security at scale, continuous training, clear strategies, and appropriate tools are essential. Conducting regular security drills and having a well-defined incident response plan can help you prepare for potential challenges. Opting for scalable tools, such as cloud-based security platforms, ensures consistent protection that grows alongside your organization. When selecting tools, it's crucial to consider their adaptability and alignment with your scaling strategy. Also note that collaborating with your IT team and understanding the growing needs of your organization will create a flexible strategy that can adapt and respond to new challenges.

In the next chapter, will delve deeper into the intricacies of security, offering an exhaustive guide to protect your Confluence environment, which will support experienced professionals and those new to these concepts. Incorporating these principles will enable a well-rounded approach to security as you scale Confluence, integrating robust protection with a growing organization's flexibility and adaptability.

Summary

Scaling Confluence is a complex task that requires careful planning and consideration, especially regarding security. In this chapter, we have outlined the integral components that make up a secure scaling strategy. We saw that identifying security requirements involves understanding your organization's specific needs and implementing robust access control to ensure that permissions are well-defined. Also, we have learned that including real-time auditing and monitoring adds another layer of protection. Furthermore, we covered how Confluence Cloud handles data security and backups and how creating and maintaining a security checklist can guide your ongoing efforts. These components form a comprehensive approach to security in the scaling process. In the *Further readings* section of this chapter, we include useful links to give you more information about how Atlassian handles information security.

In the next chapter, we will delve deeper into the intricacies of protecting your Confluence environment. Building on the principles in this chapter, this will provide a detailed guide that both experienced professionals and newcomers can follow as they explore new horizons with Confluence.

Questions

1. What are the main components of identifying security requirements when scaling Confluence?

2. How can robust access control be maintained and adapted as an organization scales?

3. Why is auditing and monitoring essential for security, and how can it be implemented?

4. What is the significance of understanding Confluence Cloud's handling of data security and backups?

5. How can a security checklist be utilized and maintained effectively in scaling Confluence?

Answers

1. The main components include a comprehensive understanding of data types, access levels, involved users, alignment with organizational goals, and regulatory requirements.

2. Effective access control can be maintained through clear user roles and permissions, leveraging automation tools to update them, and conducting regular reviews to ensure they evolve with the organization's needs.

3. Auditing and monitoring provide insights into access patterns and can detect anomalies. Implementing tools that offer real-time alerts and comprehensive reports and fostering a security-conscious culture ensures robust monitoring.

4. Confluence Cloud automatically handles backups and various technical details. Understanding data security, encryption, and secure transmission and aligning them with specific security measures ensures the total utilization of Confluence Cloud's capabilities.

5. A security checklist is a roadmap for implementing security measures and should include encryption standards, authentication methods, and vulnerability assessments. It should be revisited regularly, updated, and made practical with real-world examples and tips.

Further reading

- https://www.atlassian.com/trust
- https://www.atlassian.com/trust/security/data-management
- https://www.atlassian.com/trust/security/ismp-policies
- https://www.atlassian.com/whitepapers/zero-trust-guide
- https://www.atlassian.com/trust/reliability/infrastructure
- https://www.atlassian.com/trust/security/security-practices
- https://www.atlassian.com/trust/reliability/cloud-architecture-and-operational-practices#distributed-services-architecture

12
Assuring Security and Compliance

In this book, we only use Confluence's Cloud version. Therefore, it's important to note that your security-related work here is more accessible compared to the Server and Data Center versions. However, this does not mean that you are 100% secure. You should put in a lot of effort to keep the environment safe. In this chapter, we will give numerous security-related tips and a short yet practical guide to keep your Confluence environment much safer.

In this chapter, we will cover the following topics:

- The basic concepts of information security
- The advantages of the Confluence Cloud edition over the Server and Data Center editions
- Security measures on Confluence
- Atlassian Access

The basic concepts of information security

Being familiar with the basic concepts related to information security will significantly assist you in securing the Confluence environment you manage. Here, we will go over a few of them:

- **Authentication**: Verifying users' identities helps ensure that only authorized individuals gain access
- **Authorization**: Determining what different users and roles can access helps prevent information from falling into the wrong hands
- **Encryption**: Encrypting sensitive information in storage and during transmission makes unauthorized access more difficult
- **Firewalls and network security**: This helps protect a network against internal and external threats

- **Data integrity**: Maintaining the accuracy and consistency of data is critical for secure and accurate decision-making

- **Privacy and compliance**: Personal and sensitive data must be protected, and appropriate legal and regulatory requirements must be met (e.g., GDPR)

- **Monitoring and log management**: Tracking and recording security events can help you detect and respond to abnormal behavior quickly

- **Backup and disaster recovery**: Regular backups and effective disaster recovery plans are necessary for business continuity if there is data loss

- **Risk management**: Identifying, assessing, and managing potential security risks provides proactive protection

- **Training and awareness**: Users should be trained in security best practices and policies

- **Security policies and procedures**: Security policies should clearly articulate an organization's security needs and expectations

- **Third-party plugins and security**: The security of plugins is an integral part of a platform's overall security, so adding plugins exclusively from trusted sources is crucial

- **Human factor**: People can be the weakest link, so it is fundamental to train employees on security protocols

These concepts can form the building blocks of an overall security strategy when using Confluence Cloud. Also, they can be modified according to an organization's specific needs.

Using Confluence Cloud has significant security differences compared to other editions (Server and Data Center). Understanding these differences, and grasping Atlassian's approach to this matter, will help you lay a solid foundation in terms of security. In the next section, we will discuss the advantages of the Cloud edition.

The advantages of the Confluence Cloud edition over the Server and Data Center editions

By using Confluence's Cloud edition, you're delegating numerous routine operations related to information security to Atlassian, which becomes one of the biggest advantages of cloud-based services. In this section, we will briefly summarize the advantages of using Confluence in a cloud-based manner:

- **Updates and patching**: Security updates and patches are applied automatically in the Cloud edition, providing rapid protection against security vulnerabilities and eliminating manual patching

- **Compliance with regulations**: Confluence Cloud often ensures compliance with specific legal and regulatory standards (e.g., GDPR), reducing the need for organizations to manage these requirements independently

- **Network security**: Atlassian manages network security against threats such as DDoS attacks, helping with the in-house security burden
- **Data encryption**: Confluence Cloud ensures data encryption during transit and storage, which is a more effective and efficient route compared to developing in-house encryption solutions
- **Access control**: The Cloud edition offers various access control features such as authentication and authorization, facilitating straightforward management of user capabilities
- **Disaster recovery**: Atlassian offers integrated backup and disaster recovery solutions, ensuring business continuity without organizations having to create their disaster recovery plans
- **Scalability**: The Cloud edition can be scaled if needed, allowing effective distribution of security resources
- **Third-party security audits**: Atlassian receives third-party security audits and has compliance certifications, which can provide additional assurance in evaluating and verifying security
- **Cost-effectiveness**: Atlassian manages the security infrastructure, reducing the costs for organizations to build and maintain their security systems

Despite all these benefits, using the Cloud edition can come with risks and challenges, especially concerning data localization and third-party provider security. However, you can reduce potential threats with a sound risk management strategy and appropriate security protocols.

Atlassian Cloud security shared responsibilities

Atlassian emphasizes security, compliance, and dependability with the Cloud version, which includes the applications, the systems operating them, and the environment they are hosted in. Atlassian ensures that all related standards, such as ISO27001, SOC2, and GDPR, align with Atlassian Trust Center. As Confluence users, you have control over your account data, users, and the choice of Marketplace apps you decide to trust. Your responsibility also includes the compliant utilization of Confluence within your organization.

Your choices in configuring Confluence impact how security gets implemented, so we will underline the important options you can pay attention to:

- You can authenticate one or several domains to affirm ownership by you or your organization. This verification and user claims enable centralized handling of all Atlassian accounts for employees and enforcement of authentication rules (such as password regulations, two-factor authentication, and SAML). After domain confirmation, users within that domain who already have Atlassian accounts get claimed. New sign-ups in that domain will know they are receiving a supervised account.

- Atlassian's offerings are crafted to foster collaboration, necessitating access. You must, however, exercise caution in authorizing access to your information to others and Marketplace apps. Once permissions are set, Atlassian can't prevent users from executing actions allowed by those permissions, even if you don't sanction such actions. Some products permit you to give public anonymous access to your data. If you authorize this access, you may lose control over further distribution or copying of that information.

- We strongly suggest you use Atlassian Access for collective administration and increased security across all Atlassian tools (including mandatory **two-factor authentication** (**2FA**) and single sign-on). Atlassian Access is an Atlassian product that empowers organizations of any size to add enterprise-grade **identity and access management** (**IAM**) features to their central admin console. You can enhance data security and governance for your Atlassian Cloud products with Atlassian Access.

What security risks should remote teams be aware of when using Confluence Cloud?

Remote teams can benefit from Confluence Cloud to facilitate collaboration, but it also comes with certain cybersecurity dangers. Some of them are listed here:

- **Phishing attacks**: Remote workers might be more susceptible to phishing attacks. These attacks are often executed via fake emails or messages and can direct users to counterfeit Confluence login pages.

- **Weak authentication**: Without additional security measures such as 2FA, individuals with bad intentions can access accounts.

- **Insufficient data encryption**: Failing to encrypt data during transit or storage can increase the risk of accessing sensitive information.

- **Insecure connections**: Remote workers often connect via home or public Wi-Fi networks. As these networks are generally not as secure as workplace networks, the risk of data leakage increases.

- **Access control breaches**: Granting access to unauthorized individuals accidentally or deliberately can allow access to significant information.

- **Third-party plugins**: Untrusted third-party plugins may lead to malicious activities or data breaches on the platform.

- **Irregular updates and patch implementation**: Neglecting regular security updates and patches can leave your system vulnerable to exploitation through known vulnerabilities.

- **Backup and disaster recovery deficiencies**: In remote work setups, skipping routine backup and disaster recovery plans can result in data loss.

- **Human errors**: Remote workers may be less exposed to security protocols than in-house employees. Lack of training, distractions, or incorrect configuration can lead to security breaches.
- **Legal and compliance issues**: Teams working in different regions may struggle with compliance with local laws and regulations.

Remote teams should adopt a comprehensive security strategy to overcome these potential threats, including using secure connection protocols, implementing robust authentication, providing regular security training, and reviewing security policies.

In this section, we learned that there are many security-related advantages to using Confluence's Cloud edition. Unfortunately, these alone are not enough to make Confluence secure; there is much work to be done by Confluence users and administrators to ensure safety. In the next section, we will discuss the security measures that can be taken on Confluence.

Security measures on Confluence

Learning what you can do regarding security will help create an effective and sustainable information security policy. It is also beneficial to think about the following layers of security in the Confluence environment:

- Atlassian site and Confluence security settings
- Securing user accounts
- Securing Confluence spaces
- Securing Confluence pages
- Security on Atlassian Marketplace apps
- Securing integrations

Atlassian site and Confluence security settings

When you view Confluence's settings, you will see many options in the **SECURITY** section.

SECURITY

Users

Groups

Security Configuration

Global Permissions **NEW**

Space Permissions

Analytics Permissions

Figure 12.1 – The SECURITY section of the Atlassian site and Confluence security settings

As shown in the previous screenshot, there are six options in the **SECURITY** section:

- **Users**
- **Groups**
- **Security Configuration**
- **Global Permissions**
- **Space Permissions**
- **Analytics Permissions**

Now, let's go through these one by one.

Users

In the previous sections of this book, we saw how to manage users. Now, we will provide security recommendations regarding user accounts.

We suggest making user management as lean and fully automatic as possible. We strongly recommend using another Atlassian product, Access, for the highest security concerning user accounts. We will discuss Access again in the later sections of the book.

Groups

Managing users in groups will make you more resilient against potential changes you may experience in a team. Applying permissions, restrictions, and automation based on groups rather than individuals will make managing the Confluence environment easier. This way, you will have to spend less effort keeping a system secure.

Security Configuration

You can click on the **Edit** button at the top right to change the settings under the **Security** and **Privacy** tab.

Here, we recommend the following settings under **Security Configuration**:

- Activate the **Hide External Links From Search Engines** feature.

- Turn off the **Anonymous Access to Remote API** feature.

- Activate the **CAPTCHA on login** feature and typing 3 in the space provided. You can ensure that CAPTCHA is triggered if more than three mistakes are made on the login screen.

- Enable the **Secure administrator sessions** feature, which allows you to require administrators to re-enter their password before they can access administrative functions.

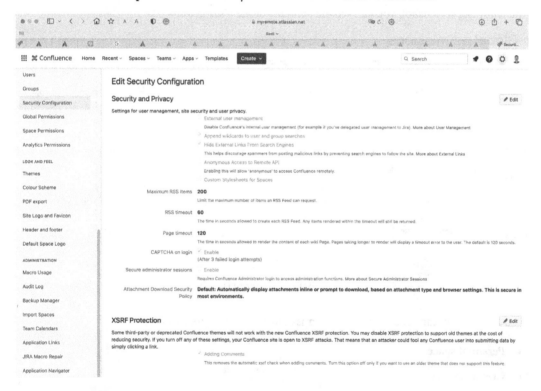

Figure 12.2 – Edit Security Configuration

As you can see in the previous screenshot, this screen has many settings. However, some of them are inactive. When you press the **Edit** button, you'll see that you can't change some of the settings here.

Global permissions

Here, you can set what user groups can do in your Confluence environment.

On the **Global permissions** screen, you will see five tabs:

- **User groups**
- **Guests**
- **Anonymous access**
- **JSM access**
- **Apps**

In the following screenshot, you can see the contents of the **User groups** tab.

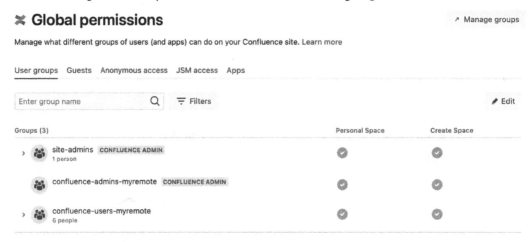

Figure 12.3 – Global permissions | User groups

As you can see, you can set user groups' permissions here. There are two of them:

- **Personal space**
- **Create a space**

Now, let's take a look at the other tabs in turn. In the following screenshot, you can see the **Guests** tab, which is a fairly new feature of Confluence.

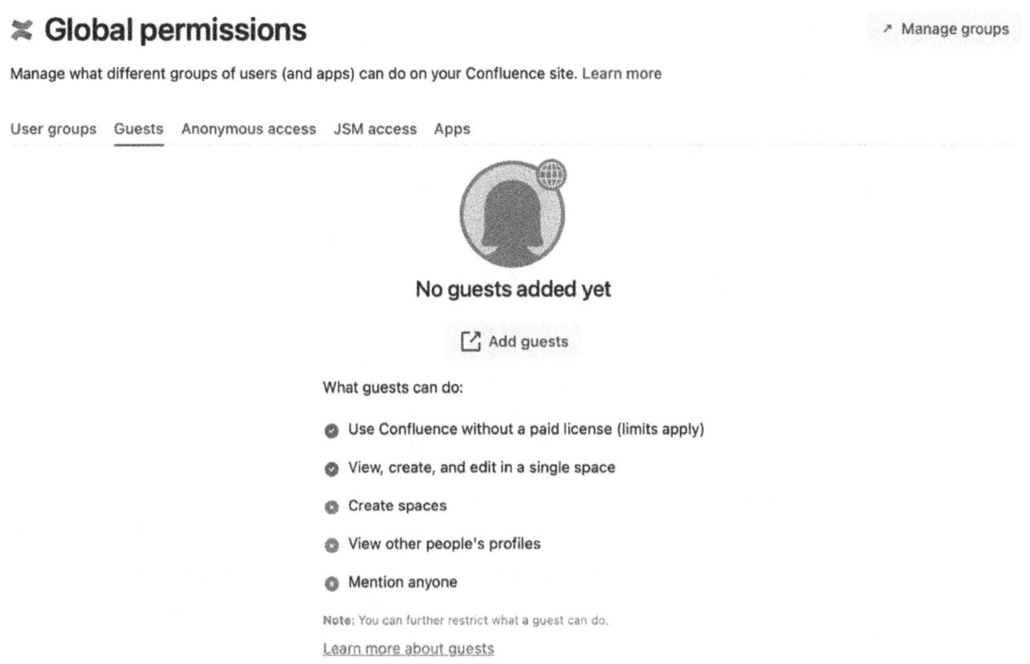

✖ Global permissions

↗ Manage groups

Manage what different groups of users (and apps) can do on your Confluence site. Learn more

User groups   Guests   Anonymous access   JSM access   Apps

No guests added yet

[↗ Add guests

What guests can do:

- ✓ Use Confluence without a paid license (limits apply)
- ✓ View, create, and edit in a single space
- ⊘ Create spaces
- ⊘ View other people's profiles
- ⊘ Mention anyone

Note: You can further restrict what a guest can do.

Learn more about guests

Figure 12.4 – Global permissions | Guests

As seen, what guest accounts do is clearly explained on this screen. By default, guests will have the following space permission settings: View/Add/Edit/ pages, comments, and attachments.

With Atlassian's external user security features, you can manage guests with added security such as two-step verification, periodic re-verification, and API token access.

Note that guests are not counted in the license, but there are some limits – guests are free of charge, at a maximum of five guests per paid user. The total number of users (paid and guests) can't exceed the current Confluence site user limit. More information can be found here: `https://support.atlassian.com/confluence-cloud/docs/invite-guests-for-external-collaboration/`.

We recommend being very careful when granting access to guests.

Now, let's take a look at the **Anonymous access** tab on the **Global permissions** screen.

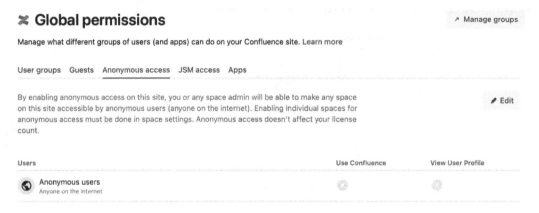

Figure 12.5 – Global permissions | Anonymous access

As shown in the previous screenshot, there are two permissions you can give to anonymous users:

- Permission to use Confluence
- Permission to view Confluence users' profiles

When you grant anonymous users the right to use Confluence, Confluence space administrators can open their managed space to anonymous users, which presents a significant risk. If not handled carefully, your confidential information can be exposed globally. Therefore, we recommend being very cautious when granting access to anonymous users.

You can see the **JSM access** tab on the **Global permissions** screen on the next screen. In the previous sections, we mentioned that **Jira Service Management** (**JSM**) and Confluence can be integrated, so you can serve the content you prepared on Confluence to your customers as a knowledge base through the customer portal on JSM.

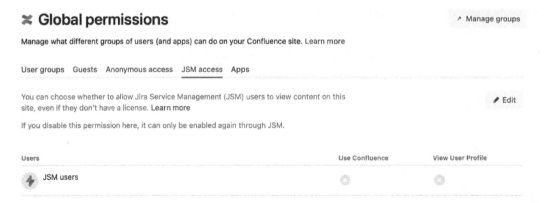

Figure 12.6 – Global permissions | JSM access

As you can see in the previous screenshot, there are two permissions you can give to JSM users:

- **Use Confluence**
- **View User Profile**

This looks similar to the screen that we just saw where we granted permissions to anonymous users. However, here, you give these permissions to customers with access to the customer portal on JSM rather than anyone on the internet. Therefore, you have a bit more control here compared to anonymous accounts. We also want to remind you of the risk here – if you're not careful, you may accidentally make your confidential content accessible to customers on JSM. Therefore, we recommend being very cautious when activating this feature.

In the following screenshot, you can see the **Apps** tab on the **Global permissions** screen. Here, you can grant global permissions to applications. You won't see any records here if no application is installed in your Confluence environment.

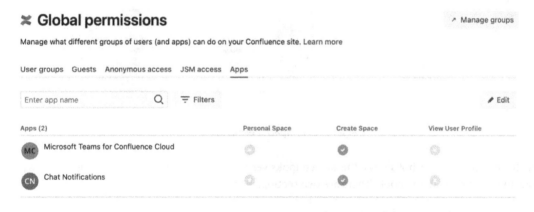

Figure 12.7 – Global permissions | Apps

As shown in the previous screenshot, three global permissions can be granted to applications:

- **Personal Space**
- **Create Space**
- **View User Profile**

We recommend being very cautious when granting global permissions to your Confluence applications.

Default space permissions

In the earlier sections of the book, we learned how to change the permissions on each space. In the following screenshot, you can see the interface where you can set the default permissions of a newly created space.

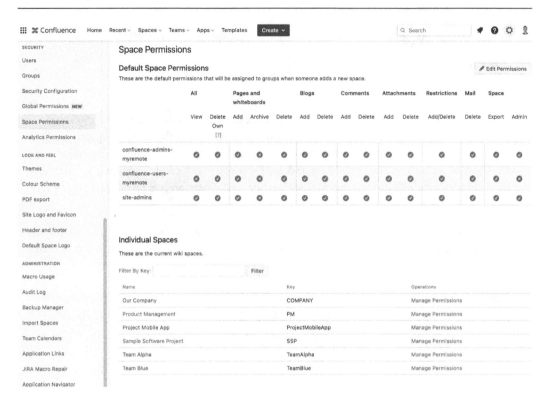

Figure 12.8 – Space Permissions

As the previous screenshot shows, this screen looks very similar to the space permissions screen we saw in earlier parts of the book. There are two sections here:

- **Default Space Permissions**
- **Individual Spaces**

In the **Default Space Permissions** section, you can set the default permissions of the newly created spaces. If you work in a high-privacy environment, you may want to restrict the default permissions entirely. In the **Individual Spaces** section, you can see a list of all the spaces on Confluence and access their permissions screens with a single click.

Analytics permissions

You may remember when we mentioned the Analytics feature on Confluence earlier in the book. You can now set which user groups can use the Analytics feature through the interface shown in the following screenshot.

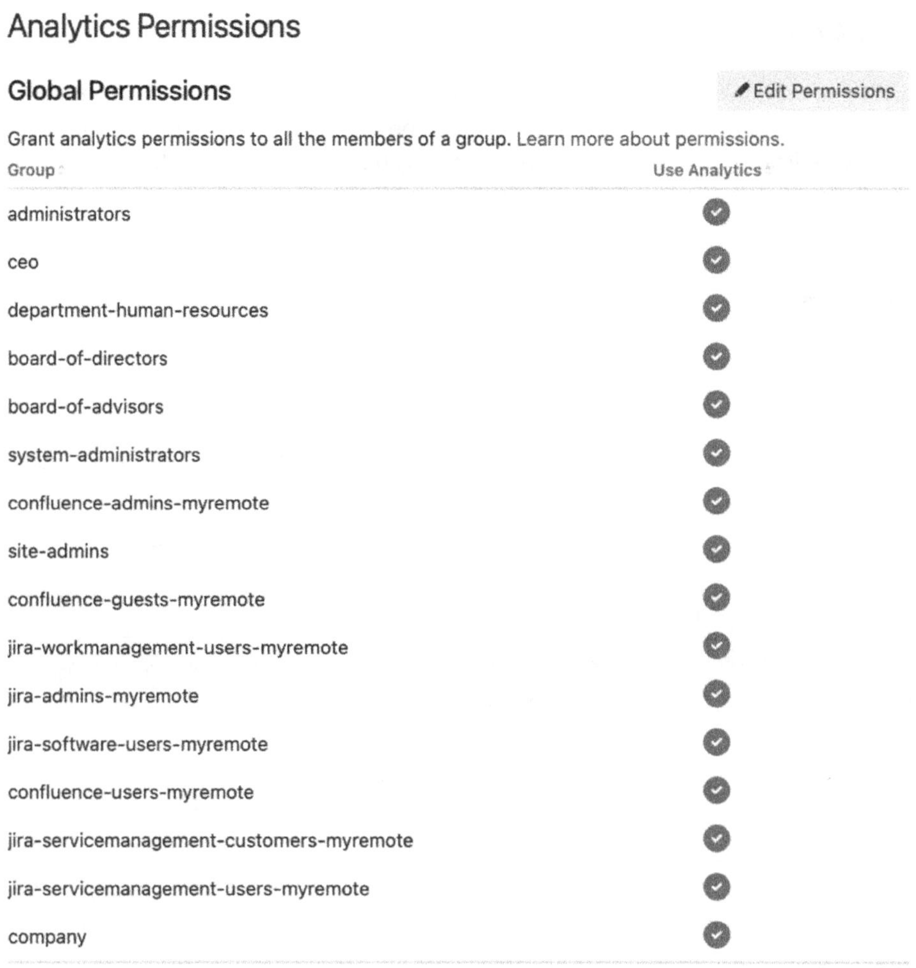

Analytics Permissions

Global Permissions   ✏ Edit Permissions

Grant analytics permissions to all the members of a group. Learn more about permissions.

Group	Use Analytics
administrators	✓
ceo	✓
department-human-resources	✓
board-of-directors	✓
board-of-advisors	✓
system-administrators	✓
confluence-admins-myremote	✓
site-admins	✓
confluence-guests-myremote	✓
jira-workmanagement-users-myremote	✓
jira-admins-myremote	✓
jira-software-users-myremote	✓
confluence-users-myremote	✓
jira-servicemanagement-customers-myremote	✓
jira-servicemanagement-users-myremote	✓
company	✓

Figure 12.9 – Analytics Permissions

The previous screenshot shows all the groups that have permission to use Analytics. You can determine which groups can use the Analytics feature using this interface.

Securing user accounts

For the highest security regarding user accounts, we strongly recommend using another Atlassian product, Access. With it, you will have important capabilities such as two-step verification, password requirements, and idle session duration. Note that you will need an additional subscription for this product, which we will discuss shortly.

Securing Confluence spaces

In earlier parts of the book, we learned that pages, the most essential components of Confluence, are located within spaces. Typically, each space has at least one administrator. The space administrator can determine in detail who will have what permissions on this space through the interface shown in the following screenshot.

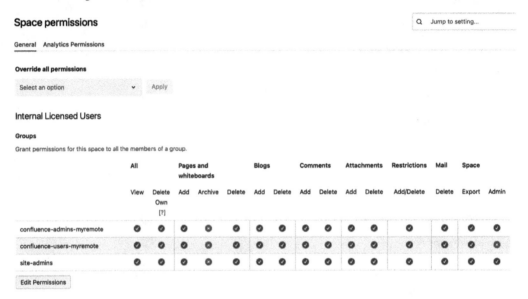

	All		Pages and whiteboards			Blogs		Comments		Attachments		Restrictions	Mail	Space	
	View	Delete Own [?]	Add	Archive	Delete	Add	Delete	Add	Delete	Add	Delete	Add/Delete	Delete	Export	Admin
confluence-admins-myremote	✓	✓	✓	✗	✓	✓	✓	✓	✓	✓	✓	✓	✓	✓	✓
confluence-users-myremote	✓	✓	✓	✗	✓	✓	✓	✓	✓	✓	✓	✓	✓	✓	✗
site-admins	✓	✓	✓	✗	✓	✓	✓	✓	✓	✓	✓	✓	✓	✓	✓

Edit Permissions

Figure 12.10 – Space permissions (part 1)

As you can see, you can assign permissions to user groups through this interface. In the following screenshot, you can see the second part of the same screen.

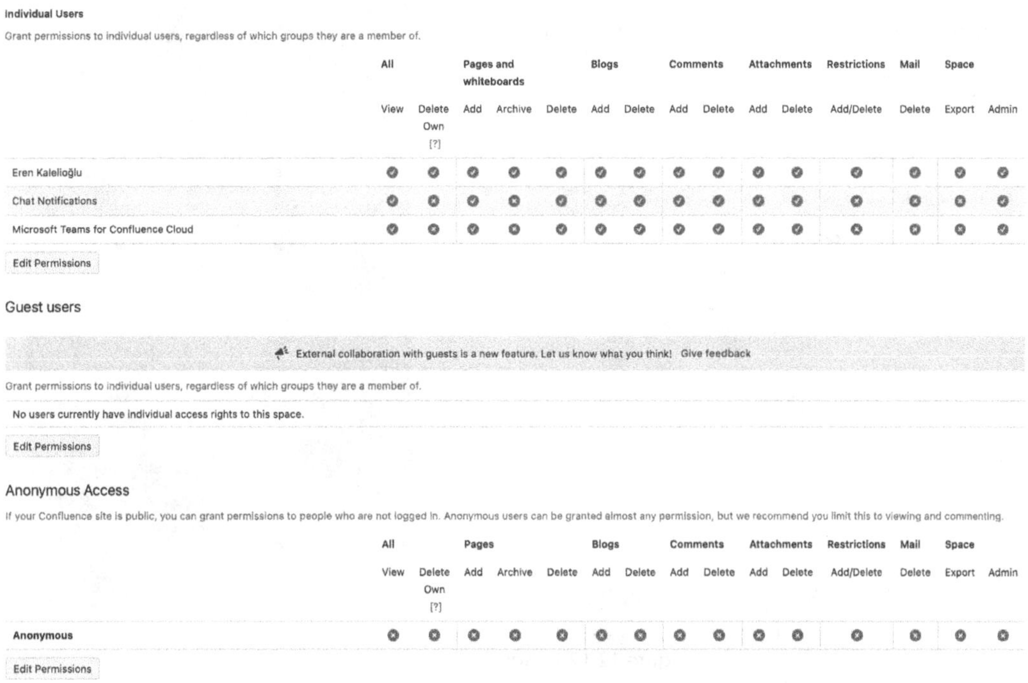

Individual Users

Grant permissions to individual users, regardless of which groups they are a member of.

	All		Pages and whiteboards			Blogs		Comments		Attachments		Restrictions	Mail	Space	
	View	Delete Own [?]	Add	Archive	Delete	Add	Delete	Add	Delete	Add	Delete	Add/Delete	Delete	Export	Admin
Eren Kalelioğlu	✓	✓	✓	✓	✓	✓	✓	✓	✓	✓	✓	✓	✓	✓	✓
Chat Notifications	✓	✗	✓	✗	✓	✓	✓	✓	✓	✓	✓	✓	✗	✗	✓
Microsoft Teams for Confluence Cloud	✓	✗	✓	✗	✓	✓	✓	✓	✓	✓	✓	✗	✗	✓	✓

Edit Permissions

Guest users

🔔 External collaboration with guests is a new feature. Let us know what you think! Give feedback

Grant permissions to individual users, regardless of which groups they are a member of.

No users currently have individual access rights to this space.

Edit Permissions

Anonymous Access

If your Confluence site is public, you can grant permissions to people who are not logged in. Anonymous users can be granted almost any permission, but we recommend you limit this to viewing and commenting.

	All		Pages			Blogs		Comments		Attachments		Restrictions	Mail	Space	
	View	Delete Own [?]	Add	Archive	Delete	Add	Delete	Add	Delete	Add	Delete	Add/Delete	Delete	Export	Admin
Anonymous	✗	✗	✗	✗	✗	✗	✗	✗	✗	✗	✗	✗	✗	✗	✗

Edit Permissions

Figure 12.11 – Space permissions (part 2)

As you can see, this interface allows you to grant permissions to individual users with a Confluence license, guest accounts, and anonymous accounts. Users with space management authority should be aware of fundamental Confluence security practices. Otherwise, they might inadvertently share sensitive content with unintended recipients.

Securing Confluence pages

All the information within Confluence gets collected on pages. This means if we fail to secure the pages, we can't secure the information they contain. The following screenshot illustrates how you can set specific restrictions for each page.

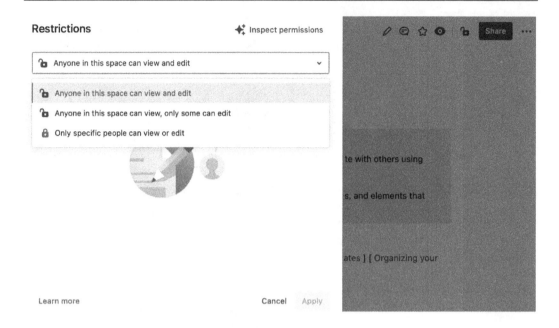

Figure 12.12 – Page restrictions

As shown in the previous screenshot, you can apply three different restrictions:

- **Anyone in this space can view and edit**
- **Anyone in this space can view, only some can edit**
- **Only specific people can view or edit**

We recommend you carefully apply viewing or editing restrictions on your page.

The **Inspect permissions** feature you can see in the following screenshot is very useful. With this feature, you can easily do the following:

- Find the root causes of access problems
- Verify the restrictions you have applied to the pages

Inspect permissions

Find out if someone is allowed or denied permissions for each level of the content, space, and product hierarchy.

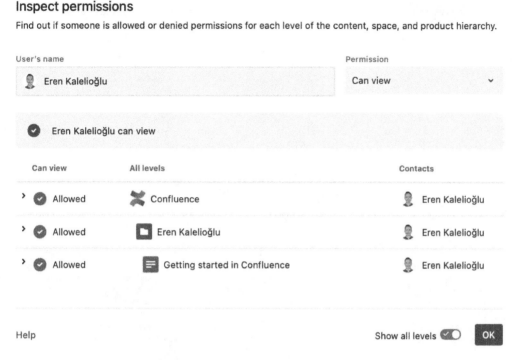

Figure 12.13 – Inspect permissions

In the previous screenshot, the viewing permission for a user has been tested. Confluence indicates this user has access permission to the page; it even describes in detail how the user has obtained this permission. More information can be found here: `https://support.atlassian.com/confluence-cloud/docs/add-or-remove-page-restrictions/`.

Security on Atlassian Marketplace apps

As mentioned in previous chapters of the book, you can install apps in Confluence from the Atlassian Marketplace. In this section, we'll provide security tips that may be helpful when selecting and using these apps.

Atlassian requires apps on the Marketplace to meet specific security standards. However, we still recommend being meticulous when selecting an app to install in Confluence. Here are some tips:

- Investigate the app's developer.
- Read the app's information on the Marketplace in detail. We recommend paying attention to the **Privacy & Security** tab.

In the following two screenshots, you can see information about a popular app on the Atlassian Marketplace.

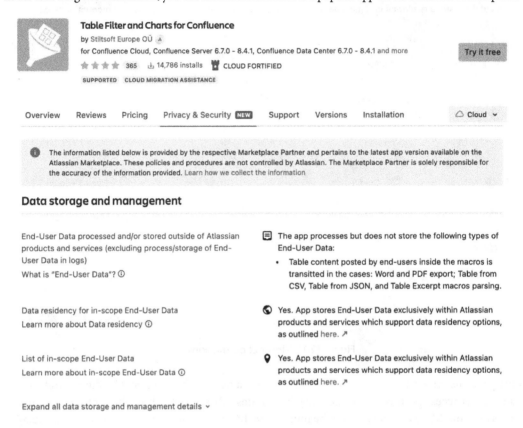

Figure 12.14 – A Marketplace app's Privacy & Security information (part 1)

As you can see, you can find the app's **Data storage and management** details here, such as what data the app processes and what it stores.

The following screenshot shows the rest of the **Privacy & Security** information for the app.

Security and compliance

Integration permissions with Atlassian products

- Act on a user's behalf, even when the user is offline
- Delete data from the host application
- Write data to the host application
- Read data from the host application

Marketplace Security Bug Bounty Program participant
Learn more about this program ↗

✓ Yes. App is a participant in Marketplace Security Bug Bounty Program.

Compliance certifications

None.

Expand all security and compliance details ⌄

Privacy

Privacy policy

Atlassian's privacy policy is not applicable to the use of this app. Please refer to the privacy policy provided by this app's partner.

Partner privacy policy ↗

Company/Organization is a 'data controller' under the General Data Protection Regulation (GDPR) with reference to this app
Learn more about 'data controllers' under the GDPR ↗

✕ No

Company/Organization is a 'data processor' under the General Data Protection Regulation (GDPR) with reference to this app
Learn more about 'data processors' under the GDPR ↗

✓ Yes. Company/Organization is a 'data processor' for the following types of End-User Data:

- Table content posted by end-users inside the macros is transitted in the cases: Word and PDF export; Table from CSV, Table from JSON, and Table Excerpt macros parsing.

Expand all privacy details ⌄

Certification

🏰 CLOUD FORTIFIED

This app offers additional security, reliability, and support through:

🛡 Cloud security participation

🔄 Reliability checks

⏱ 24hr support response time

and more.

View details

Figure 12.15 – A Marketplace app's Privacy & Security information (part 2)

As you can see in the previous screenshot, there are three sections in this tab:

- **Security and compliance**

- **Privacy**

- **Certification**

We recommend reading all three sections in detail.

In the **Certification** section, you can see that this app has the **Cloud Fortified** certification. Take a look at what this certification means:

Figure 12.16 – A Marketplace app's Cloud Fortified certificate

At this point, let's discuss classifying Marketplace applications regarding security. In the following screenshot, you can find a summary of the Atlassian Marketplace's trust programs.

Marketplace trust programs

Marketplace trust signals exist to help you easily identify apps that have gone above and beyond Atlassian's general standards to deliver an exceptionally secure and reliable cloud experience.

		All Cloud apps	Cloud Security Participant	Cloud Fortified
Privacy	App privacy policies	✓	✓	✓
Security	Base cloud app security requirements	✓	✓	✓
	Monitored by Atlassian's app vulnerability scanning platform, Ecoscanner	✓	✓	✓
	Additional app security requirements and fix timeframes defined by Atlassian	✓	✓	✓
	Participates in Marketplace Bug Bounty Program**		✓	✓
	Participates in Security Self-Assessment Program	(optional)	(optional)	✓
Reliability	Additional checks for service reliability and performance at scale			✓
	Incident and review processes integrated with Atlassian's for faster recovery and continuous improvement			✓
Support	Commercially reasonable efforts to provide support	✓	✓	✓
	24 hour response time, 5 days a week SLA for all T1 tickets**			✓

** In addition to these trust programs, the Marketplace Partner Program recognizes partners at three levels: Platinum, Gold, and Silver. Partners with these designations satisfy security and support requirements across a range of their apps.

Figure 12.17 – Marketplace trust programs

The previous screenshot shows a detailed comparison of the three levels within the Atlassian Marketplace trust programs. We recommend comprehensive research of the applications you will use and using Cloud Fortified-featured applications as much as possible. Also, we strongly advise checking the security settings of the applications, carefully adjusting the permissions granted to the applications, and keeping up with developments related to the applications.

Securing the Confluence Cloud mobile application

The Confluence Cloud mobile app supports an organizational mobile app policy to apply additional security settings to a user's Confluence app.

Follow the following steps to configure a mobile app policy:

1. Access admin.atlassian.com.

2. Select your organization (if you have more than one).

3. Click **Security | Mobile policy**.

4. Click **Create mobile policy**.

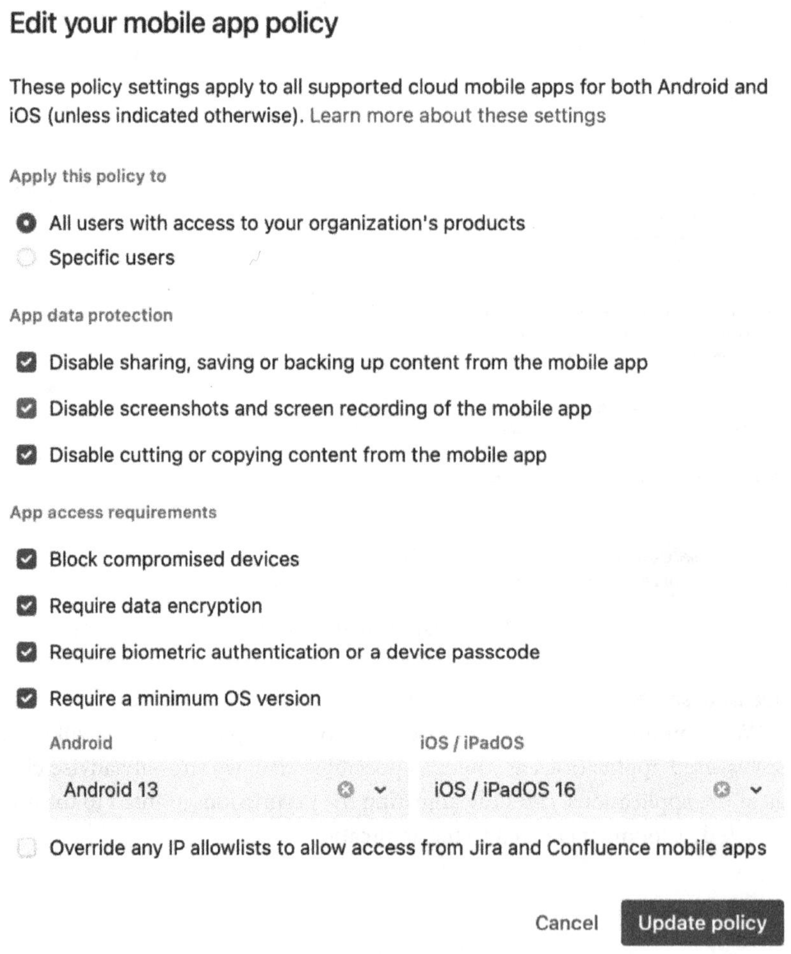

Edit your mobile app policy

These policy settings apply to all supported cloud mobile apps for both Android and iOS (unless indicated otherwise). Learn more about these settings

Apply this policy to

- ● All users with access to your organization's products
- ○ Specific users

App data protection

- ☑ Disable sharing, saving or backing up content from the mobile app
- ☑ Disable screenshots and screen recording of the mobile app
- ☑ Disable cutting or copying content from the mobile app

App access requirements

- ☑ Block compromised devices
- ☑ Require data encryption
- ☑ Require biometric authentication or a device passcode
- ☑ Require a minimum OS version

Android	iOS / iPadOS
Android 13 ✕ ⌄	iOS / iPadOS 16 ✕ ⌄

- ☐ Override any IP allowlists to allow access from Jira and Confluence mobile apps

Cancel   **Update policy**

Figure 12.18 – The mobile app policy

In the previous screenshot, you can see the settings for a typical mobile app policy.

Securing integrations

In the earlier chapters, we learned that Confluence can integrate with many systems, primarily Atlassian applications. We strongly recommend handling the security of these integrations with care.

In this section, we saw numerous techniques that can be used to work securely on Confluence. Now, we'd like to mention that there is another Atlassian product that is not within the scope of Confluence but can enhance its security – Atlassian Access. In the next section, we will talk about this product.

Atlassian Access

Atlassian Access is another Atlassian product. Therefore, it falls outside the scope of this book. However, due to its frequent use with Confluence, we want to provide an overview of Access.

Atlassian Access is in the Enterprise plan and available to buy as a separate product if you are signed up to another plan, such as Premium.

With Access, you can make Confluence much more secure by providing additional authentication options and controls, allowing for a more robust defense against potential risks. Integrating Access with Confluence can form a seamless and safer user experience, reinforcing your organization's security posture.

Your Atlassian Access subscription will apply across an organization, linking Atlassian Cloud services with your identity provider. This connection allows you to implement advanced authentication features and provides further supervision across different domains of your business. The key benefits are as follows:

- Connecting to your SAML SSO provider
- Automating user provisioning (SCIM)
- Enforcing two-step verification
- Revoking unauthorized API tokens
- Reviewing organization-wide audit logs
- Gaining organization-wide insights
- Maintaining visibility with automatic product discovery

It's common knowledge that no application open to the internet is 100 percent secure. Therefore, in the next section, we will discuss a few more security precautions.

Additional recommendations for security

Here are some additional recommendations to improve the security of your Confluence environment:

- **Define security roles and responsibilities**: We advise determining clear roles and responsibilities for security within your organization to ensure accountability and effective management.

- **Create and implement a robust information security policy**: It is essential to craft a comprehensive information security policy and put it into action. This should guide all security-related decisions within an organization.

- **Plan and execute routine security operations**: Regular security operations such as audits, checklists, and development should be planned and carried out consistently. This systematic approach helps maintain a secure environment.

- **Include security in every process**: Integrating security considerations into every process ensures that it is a central focus, reducing vulnerabilities at every workflow stage.

- **Apply change management principles**: Implementing change management principles allows controlled adaptations and minimizes potential risks from sudden changes.

- **Emphasize user training**: Training users on security best practices helps them become a robust defense line against potential threats.

- **Regular monitoring and log review**: Continuous monitoring and examining logs are crucial to detect anomalies on time and respond to security breaches effectively.

- **Continual improvement and maintenance**: Focusing on ongoing improvement and maintenance of security measures ensures your defenses remain practical and up to date.

- **Set your eyes on the technological advancements**: Technological developments allow you to leverage new tools and methodologies to enhance your security posture.

- **Be vigilant against future security trends**: In the ever-evolving cybersecurity landscape, keeping an eye on emerging trends can help you to adapt to new challenges and threats.

Summary

In this chapter, we explored various aspects of security and permissions within Confluence, focusing on creating a robust environment that safeguards data and user access. We delved into the distinctions between default space permissions and individual spaces, detailing how the former allows administrators to set up default authorizations for newly created spaces.

We also examined the Analytics feature, emphasizing the importance of defining user groups with access to this functionality.

We highlighted the importance of utilizing Atlassian's Access product for increased security. Then, we reviewed its various capabilities, including two-step verification and password requirements. We also investigated the detailed controls to secure spaces and pages within Confluence.

We provided guidelines to select and use apps from the Atlassian Marketplace, emphasizing careful consideration of a developer's credentials, the app's **Privacy & Security** tab, and opting for Cloud Fortified-certified applications whenever possible.

We highlighted why we need secure integrations, especially with other Atlassian applications.

Lastly, we took a glimpse at the typical settings for a mobile app policy that could be part of broader efforts to manage security.

Note that we encourage you to follow developments related to Confluence closely. Doing so will keep you promptly informed about security updates and save precious time. We also recommend keeping an eye on new features and changes to Confluence. This way, you can be equipped with the latest methods to protect your systems.

The next chapter will guide you through ways to enhance your Confluence setup further. We will explore various integrations and extensions that can add value to your system and enable a more seamless workflow.

Questions

1. What is the purpose of using Atlassian's Access product for Confluence security?

2. How can an administrator set permissions to use Analytics in Confluence?

3. What should be considered when selecting and using apps from the Atlassian Marketplace?

4. How can a space administrator in Confluence control permissions within a space?

5. What are some of the options to restrict access to a page in Confluence?

6. What does the Cloud Fortified certification mean for an app in the Atlassian Marketplace?

7. Why is it essential to follow updates and changes to Confluence closely?

Answers

1. Atlassian's Access product provides enterprise-grade authentication features for Confluence, allowing for higher security. It enables two-step verification, password requirements, idle session duration, and additional oversight across company domains, thus enhancing the overall security of user accounts.

2. The administrator can define which user groups can access the Analytics feature in Confluence through the interface that controls permissions, ensuring only authorized groups can utilize this functionality.

3. When selecting apps from the Atlassian Marketplace, it is advisable to research the developer, read the app's information on the **Privacy & Security** tab, and preferably choose apps with the Cloud Fortified certification, ensuring compliance with specific security standards.

4. A space administrator can define who has specific permissions within a space through the Confluence interface. This detailed control allows the administrator to manage who can view, edit, or perform other actions within the space.

5. In Confluence, you can restrict access to a page through three different limitations – **Anyone in this space can view and edit**, **Anyone in this space can view, only some can edit**, and **Only specific people can view or edit**. When applying these restrictions, we advise careful consideration.

6. Cloud Fortified certification in the Atlassian Marketplace indicates that an app meets specific security and compliance standards. It is part of the Atlassian Marketplace's trust programs, and using Cloud Fortified apps is recommended for enhanced security.

7. Following updates and changes to Confluence ensures you are promptly informed about security developments and new features, allowing you to apply the latest methods to protect your systems and make the most of new functionalities, keeping your environment up to date and secure.

Further reading

- `https://www.atlassian.com/whitepapers/atlassian-cloud-data-protection`
- `https://www.atlassian.com/whitepapers/cloud-security-shared-responsibilities`
- `https://support.atlassian.com/security-and-access-policies/docs/how-to-keep-my-organization-secure/`
- `https://support.atlassian.com/security-and-access-policies/docs/the-hipaa-implementation-guide/`
- `https://www.atlassian.com/whitepapers/customer-cloud-security-practices`
- `https://www.atlassian.com/trust/security/security-practices`
- `https://www.atlassian.com/trust/data-protection`
- `https://support.atlassian.com/confluence-cloud/docs/invite-guests-for-external-collaboration/`
- `https://support.atlassian.com/confluence-cloud/docs/learn-about-confluence-cloud-plans/`
- `https://support.atlassian.com/security-and-access-policies/docs/create-a-mobile-policy/`

13

Integrating and Extending Confluence

Confluence is a powerful tool, and one of the features that enhances its strength is the ability to expand its capabilities quickly and reliably. You can do this in two ways: either integrate Confluence with other systems you use or add new features to Confluence. In this chapter, we will talk about these integrations and extension possibilities to give you an idea of Confluence's potential in these areas. Some integrations in the following pages can be activated when you start using Confluence, while others may require effort. We can comfortably say that Atlassian has done its part regarding integration. As a result, you will find that Confluence is ready with world-standard infrastructure when you need integration. You may not need integration or expansion, but knowing how to do so will surely broaden your horizons. So, let's examine Confluence's integration and extension capabilities.

In this chapter, we will cover the following topics:

- Integration with Atlassian tools
- Integration with non-Atlassian tools
- Extending Confluence

Integration with Atlassian tools

Confluence's seamless integration with other Atlassian Cloud products is a standout feature that amplifies its capabilities and accessibility. These integrations are ready from the moment you begin using Confluence. In most cases, completing the integration is as simple as clicking a few buttons, eliminating any complex setup or technical hurdles. This way, it's easier to foster a harmonious ecosystem where all Atlassian tools can interact, streamline workflows, and improve collaboration across teams and projects. Here, we will dive deeper into the integrations with Atlassian products and explore how they can provide a cohesive, efficient, and intuitive experience tailored to your organization's specific needs and objectives.

Using Confluence and Jira Software together

You can easily integrate Confluence with Jira Software. Let's look at what you can accomplish by using these two applications together:

- Use embedded Confluence pages in Jira.

- Connect your Jira project to a Confluence space to manage Confluence pages without having to leave the product, eliminating context-switching and creating a more integrated experience. You can even edit within Jira using embedded pages.

- Create Jira issues from Confluence.

- Track Jira issues from Confluence. Many people don't want to spend time constantly switching between applications. Fortunately, the integration between Jira and Confluence simplifies tracking Jira issues directly in Confluence. Whether you spend most of your day in Confluence or Jira, you have the context and traceability you need, which translates to increased efficiency for your team.

- Dynamically list Jira issues on a Confluence page.

- Create Jira Reports in Confluence Cloud.

- Facilitate issue creation by inserting an issue collector on your Confluence page. The Jira issue collector is excellent for gathering customer feedback, allowing your organization to log errors or issues, or perhaps making it faster and simpler for those working in Confluence to create tickets in Jira without disrupting their workflow.

- Embed a real-time roadmap from Jira on your Confluence page. You can find everything in one place without switching between applications or manually copying and pasting content.

After seeing the use of Confluence with Jira Software, it's now time to explore its use with Jira Service Management.

Using Confluence and Jira Service Management together

Integrating Confluence and **Jira Service Management** (**JSM**) combines two powerful platforms, creating a dynamic environment that enhances productivity and collaboration. By connecting Confluence's extensive documentation capabilities with JSM's robust service management, teams can work more efficiently, make informed decisions faster, and provide superior customer service. The following list highlights this integration's key benefits and features, demonstrating how it can be a game-changer for organizations looking to streamline their processes and foster a more cohesive working environment:

- **Better information sharing**: Confluence pages can easily be linked with JSM requests and projects, allowing all team members to have easy access to the needed information.

- **Enhanced collaboration**: Project team members can collaborate on documentation, drafts, and other materials, advancing projects more efficiently.

- **Real-time updates**: Status updates on tasks in JSM can be directly reflected on Confluence pages, giving everyone access to the latest information.

- **Central repository**: Confluence can serve as a central repository where you can gather all documents and information related to projects, providing quicker access to sought-after information.

- **Faster decision-making**: All the necessary information and context can be easily shared between JSM and Confluence, speeding up the decision-making and approval processes.

- **Customer support**: Customer service teams can provide more effective support by leveraging the knowledge base stored in Confluence, increasing customer satisfaction.

- **Advanced reporting**: Data from JSM can be used within Confluence for in-depth analysis and reporting.

- **Reusable content**: Standard templates and pages can be reused across projects and teams to streamline different processes.

- **Knowledge base integration**: The customer portal you've implemented with JSM can perform as a knowledge base when integrated with Confluence, helping your customers find frequently asked questions and resolve their issues more rapidly and independently. This can also reduce your support team's workload and enhance customer experience.

In short, bringing together the strengths of both Confluence and JSM can increase efficiency, collaboration, accessibility, and scalability for your business.

Using Confluence and Trello together

In a dynamic and collaborative work setting, tools that facilitate team communication, planning, and execution are essential. Meanwhile, Confluence and Trello stand out with their distinct yet complementary features. Now, let's explore how these two platforms integrate and uncover their user-friendly nature, security measures, and advantages, along with illustrative examples.

Integrating Confluence with Trello is neither complicated nor time-consuming; it's a matter of copying and pasting Trello card URLs into Confluence, embedding fully interactive Trello boards, or utilizing Confluence Power-Up for Trello. This way, team members can easily switch between envisioning in Confluence and actioning in Trello. Security concerns are also addressed as Trello respects and enforces permissions and access controls.

Now, let's take a look at the benefits of using Confluence and Trello together:

- Both Trello and Confluence are designed for collaboration. Their integration allows teams to visualize more significant stories, plan, and work on detailed tasks.

- Any changes made in either platform are immediately visible in the other, enabling timely communication and responsiveness.

- Confluence provides the blueprint, while Trello helps in organizing and actioning tasks. Together, they systematically ensure that ideas are transformed into reality.

- Content access is carefully controlled. If you don't have permission to view specific content, a note will alert you accordingly, ensuring that sensitive information remains protected.

- Embedding different Trello boards onto a single Confluence page can give an overview of various teams or projects, enhancing management oversight.

Here are some integration examples:

- **Embedding Trello cards or boards in Confluence**: Confluence acts as a repository for your vision and plans, and Trello cards can be integrated to provide actionable tasks

- **Interactive Trello boards in Confluence**: Fully functional Trello boards can be displayed within Confluence, offering all the features available in Trello itself

- **Linking Trello with Confluence pages**: Reverse integration is also possible, allowing Confluence pages to be attached to Trello cards, aiding in smooth navigation between the two platforms

- **Brainstorming and sharing ideas**: You can detail a problem in Confluence and use Trello for brainstorming and innovative problem-solving

Integrating Confluence and Trello is easy and secure; it also offers a comprehensive platform for teams to plan, collaborate, and execute. This integration amplifies the strengths of both tools and enables a smoother workflow that can adapt to various project requirements. Whether used for daily task management or complex project planning, this integration bridges the gap between ideation and execution.

Up to this point, we've seen how Confluence can be integrated with other Atlassian tools, such as Jira and Trello. Now, we want to discuss the integration of Confluence with other systems.

Integration with non-Atlassian tools

Confluence can securely exchange information with many different systems that are not developed by Atlassian. Some have native integration with Confluence, while others can be solved with applications on the Atlassian Marketplace. For some systems, Confluence's Smart Link support is the solution. It is also possible to create your own integrations using the Confluence Cloud API.

At the end of this section, we will suggest questions to guide you on integration. Once you've answered these questions, you will have a solid insight into integrating Confluence with your chosen application. Now, let's take a look at the most popular applications that are used with Confluence.

Using Confluence and Microsoft Teams together

Among many collaboration tools, Confluence and Microsoft Teams have carved out unique spaces. While Confluence is a widely used collaboration platform, Microsoft Teams has been at the forefront of team communication, and their integration can boost efficiency, collaboration, and functionality. Here are some benefits of using Confluence and Microsoft Teams together:

- **Seamless collaboration**: The integration allows users to access Confluence pages within Microsoft Teams, making team collaboration smooth and efficient

- **Real-time updates**: Any changes made in Confluence can be automatically updated in Microsoft Teams, keeping all team members in the loop

- **Single platform convenience**: By bringing Confluence into Teams, you can reduce platform-switching, saving time and enhancing productivity

The integration between Confluence and Microsoft Teams adheres to stringent security protocols. Permissions can be controlled, ensuring that only authorized users share sensitive information. Here are some examples of using Confluence and Microsoft Teams together:

- Share Confluence meeting notes directly in Teams, ensuring all participants have access

- Embed Confluence pages into Teams for project planning and tracking, creating a unified workspace

- Set up notifications in Teams for updates in Confluence to never miss a critical change

- Create and edit Confluence pages from Teams

- Add a Confluence page in a Teams tab

- Preview the Confluence pages you share from Teams

- Search within Teams for previously shared Confluence pages

Integrating Confluence with Microsoft Teams unites two powerful platforms, enhancing team communication and collaboration. Whether your goal is to streamline the workflow process, keep everyone on the same page, or bring the power of Confluence into your Microsoft Teams environment, you can benefit from this integration. With an easy setup process and robust security, it's an option worth considering for any team aiming to elevate their collaborative efforts.

Using Confluence and Slack together

Integrating Confluence and Slack offers an exciting solution for teams to enhance collaboration and streamline communication. Here are some benefits of using Confluence and Slack together:

- **Unified notifications**: You can receive your Confluence notifications in Slack instead of in your email or directly in Confluence itself
- **Real-time updates**: You can configure notifications in Slack channels for updates in specific Confluence spaces, pages, and blog posts
- **Interactive previews**: You can view link previews of pages, blog posts, and comments when they're shared in Slack messages
- **Enhanced engagement**: You can like pages, respond to comments, and do more all without leaving Slack

This is how to integrate Slack and Confluence:

1. **Find the Confluence app in Slack**: Go to Slack's App Directory and search for the Confluence Cloud app.
2. **Install and configure**: Install and configure the Confluence Cloud app for Slack application from Atlassian Marketplace.
3. **Install the app**: Follow the instructions to install the app in your Slack workspace.
4. **Configure notifications**: Set up notifications for specific Confluence spaces, pages, and blog posts according to your preferences.
5. **Authorize and connect**: Connect your Confluence and Slack accounts to ensure seamless interaction.

Also, note that the integration provides robust security protocols, allowing only authorized users to access sensitive Confluence content within Slack.

Let's take a look at some examples of using Confluence and Slack together:

- Set up a Slack channel dedicated to a Confluence project, receiving real-time updates and previews
- Reply to Confluence comments directly within Slack, keeping the conversation flow intact
- Easily like and engage with Confluence pages without switching platforms
- Customize notifications to individual or team channels, ensuring the right people get the information at the right time

The integration of Confluence and Slack brings collaboration to a new level. With straightforward implementation, there is no extra cost for the basic features or powerful security measures. Whether for project management, content creation, or simply keeping everyone on the same page, the Confluence-Slack integration offers tangible benefits so that you can adapt to various needs and preferences.

The following screenshot shows the page of Atlassian's official Confluence Cloud for Slack app:

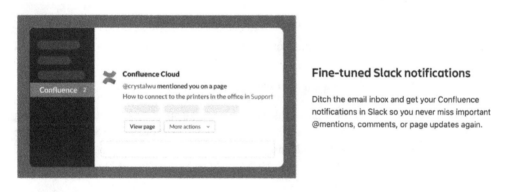

Figure 13.1 – The Confluence Cloud for Slack application

As you can see, the Confluence Cloud for Slack app is free. By installing this app, you can securely facilitate communication between Confluence and Slack.

Smart Links

Confluence's Smart Links offer an intuitive solution that fosters productivity and efficient collaboration. Smart Links are more than just hyperlinks; they provide a more prosperous way to share content across various applications by transforming traditional links into interactive previews or information-rich cards. Whether it's a Google Drive document, a Jira issue, or a Trello card, Smart Links offer a glimpse of the content without you having to leave Confluence. Let's look at what Smart Links offer:

- **Enhance collaboration**: By offering previews, team members can engage with the content more effectively
- **Save time**: There's no need to navigate away from Confluence; the vital information is presented within the platform
- **Create a cohesive experience**: A unified view across different applications makes information handling more intuitive

Using Smart Links is as simple as pasting the URL of the content into a Confluence page. Confluence automatically transforms it into a Smart Link, presenting a preview or detailed information card. Follow these steps to experiment with a Smart Link:

1. **Copy the URL**: Copy the URL of the content you want to share.
2. **Paste in Confluence**: Paste the URL into your Confluence page – it'll be automatically converted into a Smart Link.
3. **Enjoy the preview**: Hover over the link or view the detailed card to see the content preview.

The continuous improvements to the Smart Links feature ensure compatibility with an expanding list of platforms, further enhancing its versatility. Smart Links are supported for various popular applications and platforms, including the following:

- Google Drive
- Microsoft Office
- Jira
- Trello
- YouTube
- Dropbox
- Box
- Asana
- GitHub
- GitLab

- Figma

- Adobe XD

- Miro

- Zeplin

- Invision

As safety is a paramount concern when sharing links across platforms, Confluence's Smart Links are designed with security concerns, ensuring only authorized users can access the linked content and the permissions are respected. Confluence's Smart Links foster an environment where information flows freely, securely, and efficiently across different applications. By transcending the barriers between platforms, they create a unified workspace where teams can interact with content effortlessly.

In a world driven by information, the ability to share, preview, and interact with content across various platforms within a single interface is not a luxury, but a necessity. Confluence's Smart Links fulfill this need, paving the way for a richer, more intelligent, and more productive collaboration experience.

Using Confluence with other tools

As our space here is limited, we have only talked about the most popular applications. After careful research, you will see that Confluence can integrate with many applications other than those mentioned in this book. When investigating whether an application can be used with Confluence, we suggest asking these questions:

- Does Confluence integrate natively with my chosen application?

- Does Confluence provide Smart Link support for my chosen application?

- Is there a Confluence app for my selected application on the Atlassian Marketplace?

- Can I integrate Confluence with my chosen application using the Confluence Cloud API?

Now that we have provided sufficient information on integration, it's time to talk about Extending Confluence.

Extending Confluence

If the fundamental features of Confluence do not meet your needs, don't worry – you still have options. First, you can enhance Confluence by adding extra functionalities by installing apps from the Atlassian Marketplace. Alternatively, you can either develop your applications or commission them to be built by others. Now, let's delve deeper and explore how these strategies work.

Installing applications via the Atlassian Marketplace

The Atlassian Marketplace offers many applications for Confluence that you can review, try, and purchase. Similar to Confluence licenses, you can easily access these applications through a monthly or yearly subscription. In the following screenshot, you can see the welcome screen of the Atlassian Marketplace, which you can access from `https://marketplace.atlassian.com`:

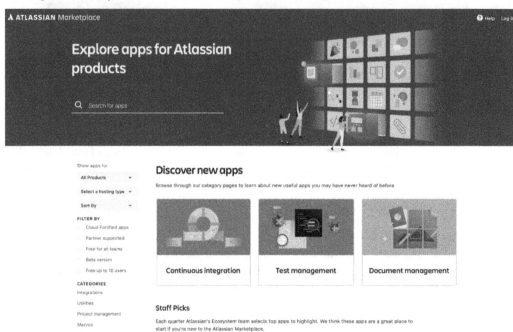

Figure 13.2 – The Atlassian Marketplace

As you can see, there is a search bar at the very top of the screen for you to search for applications. You can browse applications on the Atlassian Marketplace with it.

Regarding the following screenshot, please examine the panel on the left-hand side of the screen:

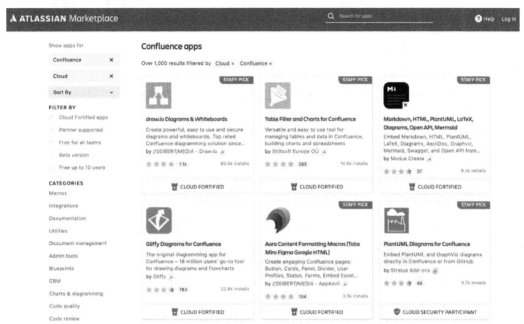

Figure 13.3 – Using filters on the Atlassian Marketplace

In the **Show apps for** section, we want you to change two settings:

1. First, select **Confluence** in the first drop-down list. By doing this, you are specifying to the search engine that you are only looking for Confluence plugins. It's worth noting that there are also applications for other Atlassian products besides Confluence on the marketplace.

2. Then, we want you to select the **Cloud** option in the second drop-down list. By doing this, you are specifying to the search engine that you are only looking for applications that work in the Cloud edition. It's worth mentioning that there are also applications for other editions such as Server and Data Center on the marketplace. Note that Confluence Server is officially decommissioned and will not be supported after February 2024.

If you want to refine your search further, you can use filters. At the time of writing, there are five different filters available on the Atlassian Marketplace:

-   **Cloud Fortified apps**
-   **Partner supported**
-   **Free for all teams**

- **Beta version**
- **Free up to 10 users**

We won't go over all the filters as we think the filter names are highly self-explanatory, but we would like to give you two tips here:

- If you're after the highest possible level of information security, you can use the **Cloud Fortified apps** filter
- If you're looking for applications that are supported by an official Atlassian partner, you can use the **Partner supported** filter

You can also classify applications using application categories.

The following screenshot shows the introduction screen for Gliffy Diagrams for Confluence, one of the most popular Confluence applications on the Atlassian Marketplace. Let's examine this screen:

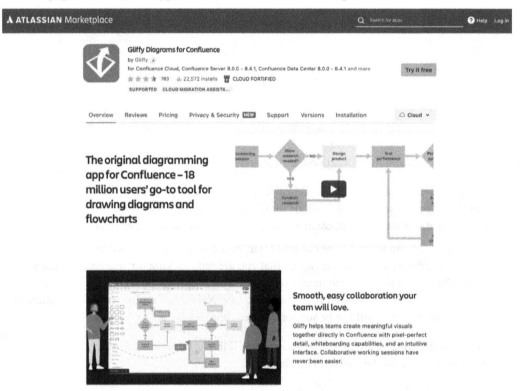

Figure 13.4 – A Confluence app on the Atlassian Marketplace

As you can see, every application on the Atlassian Marketplace has a detailed introduction page. Atlassian expects all companies that develop applications for the Marketplace to fill out this page thoroughly and transparently. With this introduction screen, you can access the basic information about an application. On this page, you can find the following sections:

- **Overview**: The standout features and screenshots related to the application

- **Reviews**: User comments about this application

- **Pricing**: The monthly and annual prices of the application

- **Privacy & Security**: The features related to the privacy and information security of the application

- **Support**: How to reach developer support for the application

- **Versions**: The updated history of the application

- **Installation**: How to install the application in your Confluence environment

Now, let's look at the other essential sections you can see on this screen:

- **22,572 installs**: Customers have installed this app in at least 22,572 active instances. This data can give you an idea about the application's visibility and reliability.

- **By Gliffy**: You can click here for detailed information about the application developer.

- **Cloud Fortified**: You can see that the application has Cloud Fortified, the highest information security accreditation on the Atlassian Marketplace.

- **783**: You can see that 783 people have reviewed the application, and the average rating is 4.5 out of 5. This score can give you an idea about customer satisfaction with the application.

Now that we have enough information about the application, we'd like to mention a fundamental feature of the Atlassian Marketplace. Typically, you can try all applications on the Atlassian Marketplace for a short period (usually 30 days) before purchasing, and not just a restricted version; you can try the full version.

To try the application, click the **Try it free** button in the top right. The following screenshot shows the first screen that appears when you click this button. Let's take a look at this screen:

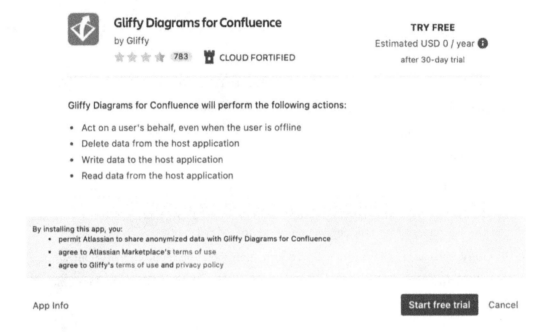

Figure 13.5 – Installing an application on Confluence

As this screenshot shows, you must review essential security and privacy information before initiating the free trial period. According to the given information, when you install the Gliffy Diagrams for Confluence application in your Confluence environment, the application will be able to perform the following actions:

- Take actions on behalf of a user, even if they're offline

- Remove information from your Confluence

- Input information into your Confluence

- Retrieve information from your Confluence

Note that we strongly advise you to evaluate the information carefully and not skip this step. If the information here suits you, press the blue **Start free trial** button. At this stage, you must select the Atlassian site where you will install the application. The screen should now look like this:

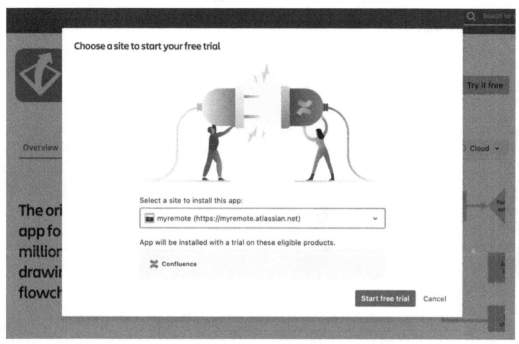

Figure 13.6 – Selecting a site to install a Confluence application

After pressing the **Start free trial** button, the application will be installed.

Here are the steps to manage your installed applications:

1. Go to the **Manage Apps** section by following **Apps | Manage Apps** on the Confluence top menu.

2. From there, you will see a list of all the applications installed on your system. You can see this interface in the following screenshot:

Figure 13.7 – Manage apps

In this interface, you can see all the details about the app Gliffy Diagrams right in your Confluence space, without going to the Atlassian Marketplace. In it, you can access almost all the information on the Atlassian Marketplace and details such as license information. You can also end the trial period or remove the application from the system through this interface. Also, note that you need Confluence Administrator permission to install applications and access the application management screen.

The application you installed is now accessible by users on Confluence. You can access all the installed applications using the **Apps** button in the top menu, as shown in the following screenshot:

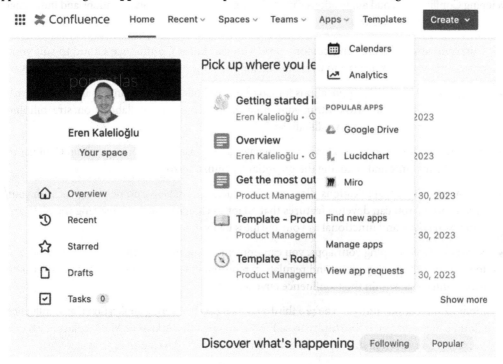

Figure 13.8 – The Confluence Apps menu

Here, you can access all applications installed on Confluence (including apps developed by Atlassian, such as Calendars and Analytics) through this menu. In it, you can find new applications, manage your existing applications, or manage application requests from users. Note that different levels of users will see different options under this menu. For example, the **Find new apps**, **Manage apps**, and **View app requests** options will only be visible to users with Confluence Administrator permissions.

Developing an app

If the features of Confluence and the plugins you have installed are not enough for you, there is another path you can take: developing an app. You can develop an application within your company or seek support from a competent Atlassian Solution Partner such as Ponsatlas. App development is a highly detailed subject and could fill a book on its own. In this section, we'd like to provide a comprehensive summary of the app development needs of your remote working team.

Why develop Confluence Cloud apps?

Developing Confluence Cloud applications can offer several advantages to organizations and individual developers. Here's an overview:

- **Customization**: By creating custom apps, you can tailor Confluence Cloud to suit your organization's unique needs and workflow, making sure the platform aligns with your objectives.

- **Integration**: Developing applications for Confluence Cloud enables seamless integration with other tools and systems used within your organization, enhancing collaboration, streamlining operations, and improving overall efficiency.

- **Automation**: Apps can be developed to automate various tasks and processes within Confluence Cloud, saving time and reducing the potential for human error.

- **Scalability**: Custom applications allow your Confluence Cloud environment to grow with your organization. You can develop features that adapt to changing needs, ensuring the platform remains relevant and functional as your business evolves.

- **Security**: By developing your apps, you can implement specific security measures that adhere to your organization's policies and regulatory requirements, having greater control over data access and usage within the Confluence environment.

- **Monetization opportunity**: If you're a third-party developer, creating applications for Confluence Cloud can present an opportunity to sell those apps on the Atlassian Marketplace. This can become a new revenue stream for individual developers or development firms.

- **Competitive edge**: Adapting and innovating can be challenging in a competitive business environment. Custom apps for Confluence Cloud offer a way to stand out with your business and have specialized services or tools that can give you an edge over competitors.

- **Support and collaboration within the Atlassian ecosystem**: By developing applications for Confluence Cloud, you become part of the Atlassian developer community. This way, you can have access to resources, support, and collaboration opportunities to contribute to the development process and improve the final product.

Overall, it is safe to say that developing applications for Confluence Cloud can enhance productivity, collaboration, and innovation within an organization, offering flexibility and control that off-the-shelf solutions may not provide. The advantages can be significant, whether you're creating a bespoke solution to a specific problem or leveraging the Atlassian ecosystem's opportunities.

In-house development versus outsourcing – a comparative analysis for Confluence Cloud applications

In a competitive business environment, choosing the right approach for software development is a critical decision. Organizations leveraging platforms such as Confluence Cloud often face the dilemma of developing applications in-house or outsourcing them to specialized firms such as Atlassian Solution Partners. Both approaches offer distinct benefits and challenges, and the choice can significantly impact factors such as cost, control, time-to-market, and alignment with business goals.

Here, we'd like to compare in-house development and outsourcing for Confluence Cloud applications so that you can make informed decisions that align with your specific needs, resources, and strategic objectives. Whether you're prioritizing customization, cost efficiency, or expertise, understanding the two development paths can guide you in selecting the option that best fits your business.

Here are the advantages of in-house development:

- **Control**: In-house development provides more control at every stage of the project. Customizations and changes can be made more quickly and directly

- **Privacy**: In-house development can help protect sensitive data and business processes without the need to share them with third-party firms

- **Team alignment**: Your in-house team may already have a strong sense of company culture, which can enhance collaboration and efficiency

Here are the disadvantages of in-house development:

- **Cost**: Developing in-house expertise and providing necessary resources can increase initial costs

- **Time**: The training and development process may take longer if the necessary skills and talent are absent within the company

Let's look at the advantages of outsourcing to an external firm (for example, an Atlassian Solution Partner):

- **Expertise**: A specialist firm, such as an Atlassian Solution Partner, might have specific skills and experience to assist in completing the project more quickly and effectively

- **Cost-effectiveness**: Outsourcing can save on the costs associated with forming and training an in-house team

- **Focus**: You can direct your in-house resources toward your core business, leaving the application development to an external firm

Now, let's look at the disadvantages of outsourcing to an external firm (for example, an Atlassian Solution Partner):

- **Less control**: Working with a third-party firm may provide less control at certain project stages
- **Privacy concerns**: Sharing sensitive information may lead to privacy and security concerns

In sum, the path you'll choose may vary, depending on your company's objectives, budget, timeline, and existing internal resources. In-house development may be better when more control and customization are desired, while outsourcing to an external firm may be suitable when a quicker and perhaps more cost-effective solution is a priority. Understanding that both approaches have unique advantages and disadvantages will help you make the most suitable choice.

Developing a Confluence Cloud application – key considerations

Confluence Cloud is a robust platform for collaborative software solutions, enabling teams to work together more efficiently and creatively. However, developing a new application for Confluence Cloud is a multifaceted job that requires a deep understanding of various aspects. From aligning with Atlassian's familiar user experience to ensuring optimal performance, security, and design, each element plays a vital role in the application's success. Also, considerations such as agility, a comprehensive review of Atlassian's roadmap, mastery of existing plugins, and sustainability further enrich the development process. In this section, we'll concentrate on these critical considerations, providing insight and guidelines to navigate the complex landscape of Confluence Cloud application development.

When developing a Confluence Cloud application, it's essential to stay aligned with the familiar **user experience** (**UX**) that we associate with Atlassian. A consistent UX ensures that users find the new application intuitive and easy to use, maintaining a seamless experience across the platform. It is also important to pay attention to layout, navigation, visual elements, and interactions. By adhering to Atlassian's design guidelines and UX principles, developers can create an application that feels like a natural extension of the existing ecosystem.

Performance optimization is another crucial aspect to consider. An application that takes a long time to load or becomes unresponsive can significantly affect user satisfaction and productivity. That's why it's crucial to prioritize efficient coding practices, optimized queries, and effective resource management. Regular performance testing and monitoring will also help identify bottlenecks and ensure the application runs smoothly, even under heavy loads or large datasets.

Meanwhile, security should be a top priority. Pay attention to the best practices in authentication, authorization, data encryption, and secure communication. Regular vulnerability assessments and adherence to industry security standards will also help protect sensitive data and maintain users' trust. Collaborating with security experts and staying updated on the latest security trends is another option to build a secure application.

An elegant and functional design not only enhances the visual appeal but also contributes to the overall usability of the application. For a refined and engaging user interface, consider employing user-centered design principles, engaging in iterative design processes, and seeking user feedback. Design considerations should also extend to accessibility, ensuring that the application is accessible by as many people as possible, regardless of any disabilities or limitations they may have. The Agile approach to development emphasizes flexibility, collaboration, and responsiveness to change. Regular reviews, iterations, and close collaboration between stakeholders ensure that the development process aligns with the evolving needs of users and the organization.

When developing a new application, another point to focus on is understanding Atlassian's roadmap and strategic direction to stay aligned with Atlassian's long-term goals and upcoming features. By studying the roadmap, developers can avoid duplicating efforts and identify opportunities for integration or enhancement within the broader ecosystem.

Also, being well-versed in existing plugins is essential as another developer may have already created the application you plan to develop. Researching existing solutions, understanding the strengths and weaknesses, and identifying gaps or unmet needs can guide development efforts. Building on existing plugins or collaborating with other developers can also lead to more efficient and innovative solutions.

Sustainability in development is not just about the immediate product – it also considers the application's long-term maintenance, scalability, and extensibility. Ensuring the code is well-documented, following best practices in architecture and development, and planning for ongoing support and updates will contribute to a more sustainable and resilient application.

In conclusion, developing a new Confluence Cloud application is a complex task that requires a thoughtful approach to various aspects, including user experience, performance, security, design, agility, alignment with Atlassian's roadmap, mastery of existing plugins, and sustainability. By adopting a comprehensive approach to these elements, you can create a robust, user-friendly, and valuable addition to the Confluence Cloud ecosystem.

Comparing Connect and Forge

There are two different infrastructures you can use when developing an app for Confluence Cloud:

- **Connect**: The older and more mature infrastructure
- **Forge**: Referred to as Atlassian's new darling, this is a rapidly evolving new infrastructure

If you are starting from scratch to develop an app for Confluence Cloud, we recommend first examining Forge and looking into Connect if it does not meet your needs.

The following screenshot shows the detailed website that Atlassian has prepared for Forge:

Figure 13.9 – Atlassian Developer – Guides – Forge

As you can see, Atlassian offers numerous resources for Forge, including tutorials and example apps.

Resources you can use while developing an app

There are many resources available to you when developing Confluence Cloud apps. You can see the main page of this documentation in the following screenshot:

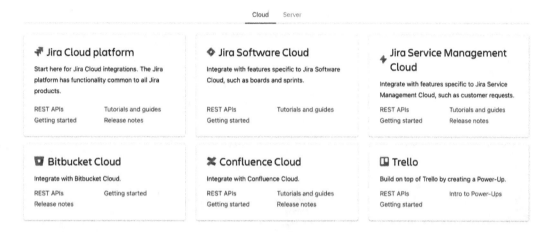

Figure 13.10 – Atlassian Developer – documentation

Atlassian prepares resources for all its products for software developers, and there are essential resources you can use for Confluence as well. As shown in the previous screenshot, the Confluence section includes the following:

- REST APIs
- Getting started
- Tutorials and guides
- Release notes

Of course, the resources aren't limited to what we've covered here. Since Confluence is a highly advanced piece of software, it has had rich and mature documentation developed over the years. You can see the **Reference** section of this documentation in the following screenshot:

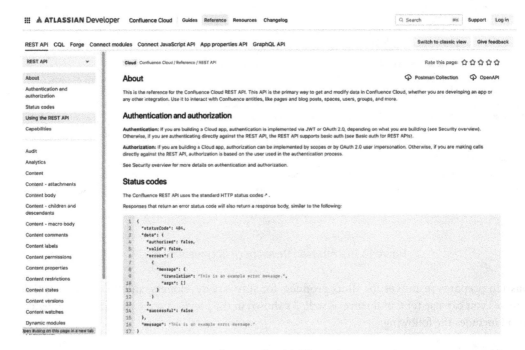

Figure 13.11 – Confluence Cloud REST API documentation

No matter which infrastructure you use (Forge or Connect), you must use Confluence's REST APIs at some point. The previous screenshot shows the reference sources, where you can find all the details related to the REST APIs.

Software development is not just about writing code. Atlassian offers many resources besides code development. The following screenshot shows the content that will support you in learning about building, deploying, and managing Confluence apps:

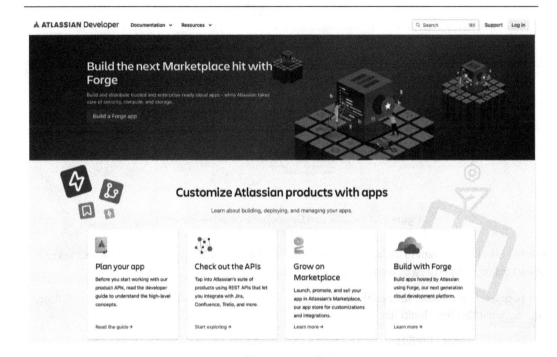

Figure 13.12 – Atlassian Developer – Resources

Other resources you may need while developing an application have also been brought together by Atlassian. As shown in the following screenshot, the **Other resources** section contains the following:

- **Developer community**
- **Success stories**
- **Developer status**
- **Forge platform roadmap**
- **Developer blog**

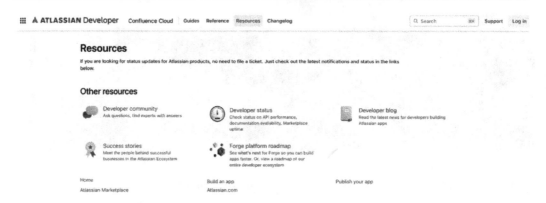

Figure 13.13 – Atlassian Developer – Other resources

Another interface we want to include is the Atlassian **Status** page, which you can access at `https://developer.status.atlassian.com/`.

This page lets you monitor the health status of your software development technologies in real time. Take see what this page looks like:

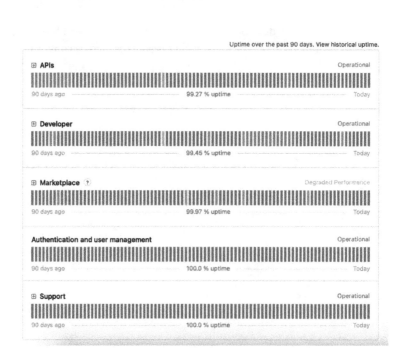

Figure 13.14 – The Atlassian Status page

With this page, you can monitor the health status of the essential tools you will use while developing a new Confluence application instantly and retrospectively. Also, note that issues related to these tools are shared transparently and in detail with the world.

Now, we want to draw your attention to the **Atlassian platform for developers – roadmap** area, which you can see in the following screenshot:

Figure 13.15 – Atlassian platform for developers – roadmap

Atlassian shares its roadmap related to developers with the whole world. Through this tool, you can follow Atlassian's roadmap and monitor the instant status of each feature. You can reach this board at `https://trello.com/b/8XBuIeIu/atlassian-platform-for-developers-roadmap`.

Atlassian also brings all developers together under a Developer Community, which is accessible at `https://community.developer.atlassian.com/`.

The website looks like this:

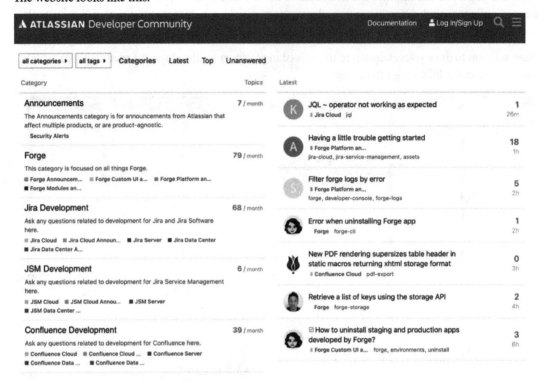

Figure 13.16 – Atlassian Developer Community – part 1

As you can see, you can ask questions and receive support from developers worldwide in the Developer Community. If you have the opportunity, you can support others as well.

Announcements related to Confluence Cloud are also featured in the Developer Community:

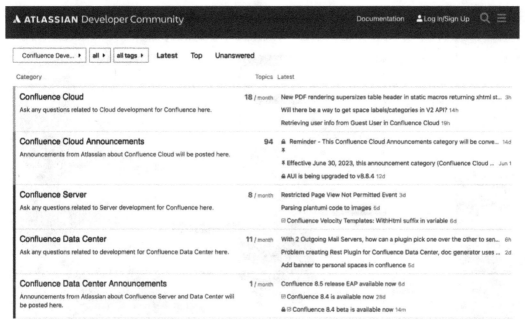

Figure 13.7 – Atlassian Developer Community – part 2

As shown in the previous screenshot, you can easily follow the latest discussions related to Confluence Cloud and announcements made by Atlassian through the Developer Community portal.

Lastly, we want to introduce you to Forge's roadmap:

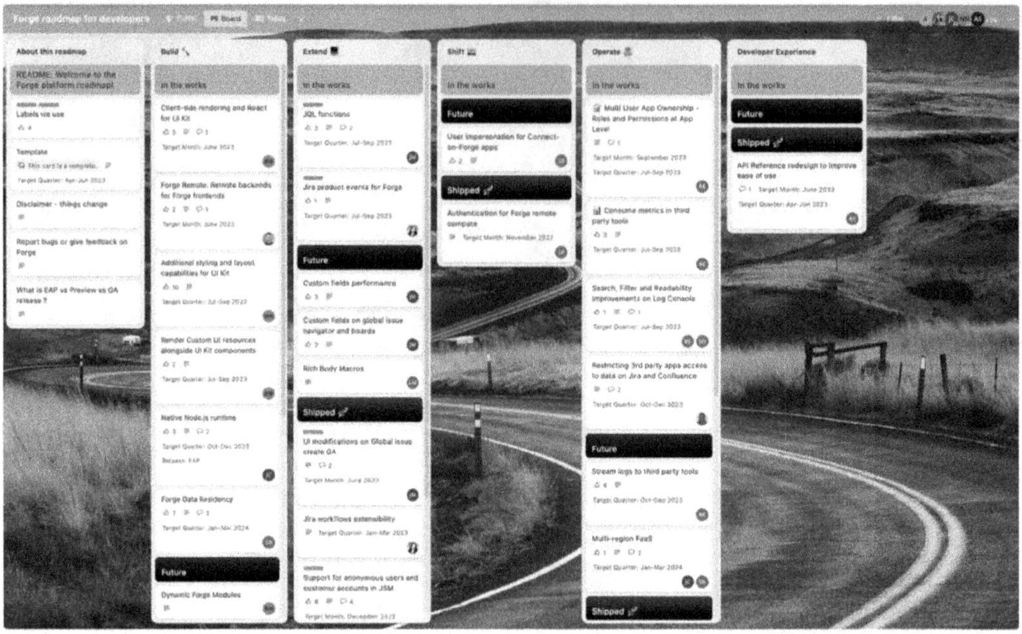

Figure 13.18 – Forge roadmap for developers

With this roadmap, you can instantly follow Atlassian's roadmap related to Forge and get informed about the latest innovations and developments of this rapidly growing platform. You can access this roadmap at `https://trello.com/b/z2GIJ3xD/forge-roadmap-for-developers`

Now that we've introduced the necessary tools, you can be part of the Atlassian Cloud software developers' ecosystem so that you can follow developments and access reliable resources when developing Confluence Cloud applications.

Summary

In this chapter, we explained how to integrate Confluence with other applications and add new features to Confluence. We learned how to rapidly and safely integrate Confluence with other apps, such as Slack and Microsoft Teams.

We also concentrated on adding new features to Confluence. Although developing an application is a deep subject that deserves a whole other book, we provided basic information you may need as an executive summary. Now, it's up to you to do the work regarding details and fill in the blanks as you go. In the next chapter, we will dive deeper into the challenges of remote collaboration, providing insights into the human factors and technical difficulties you will encounter from a management consultant's perspective.

Questions

Answer the following questions to test your knowledge of this chapter:

1. What can you do by integrating Confluence with Jira?

2. What is the fundamental difference between Forge and Connect?

3. What are the differences between having the Confluence application developed in-house and having it developed by an outside company?

4. How do Smart Links work?

Answers

Here are the answers to this chapter's questions:

1. You can connect your Jira project to a Confluence space. This allows you to manage Confluence pages without having to leave the product, eliminating context-switching and creating a more integrated experience. You can even edit within Jira using embedded pages.

2. Forge is Atlassian's brand-new serverless platform. Unlike Connect, you don't need to have your own infrastructure for your Cloud application.

3. The approach can vary, depending on the company's needs, objectives, budget, timeline, and existing internal resources. In-house development means more control and customization, while outsourcing may be suitable when a quicker and perhaps more cost-effective solution is needed.

4. Smart Links are more than just hyperlinks, allowing you to share content across applications by transforming traditional links into interactive previews or information-rich cards. Whether it's a Google Drive document, a Jira issue, or a Trello card, Smart Links offers a glimpse of the content without you having to leave Confluence.

14

Challenges and Solutions

In the previous chapter, we discussed how to integrate Confluence with other applications and how to add features to Confluence. In this chapter, as a consultant who has been working with Atlassian products for a long time, we want to share some of our experiences with you. By the end of this chapter, you will have acquired many tips related to the acceptance of Confluence by your company's employees. It is not possible to convey all experiences, of course, but we think that these experiences will aid your journey while you're working on simplifying collaboration with Confluence.

In this chapter, we will cover the following topics:

- The challenges of remote collaboration
- Solutions for remote collaboration
- Working with consultants
- A sustainable approach to Confluence

The challenges of remote collaboration

In today's globally connected world, remote collaboration has become vital to organizational success. The ability to work together across geographical boundaries, time zones, and cultural differences offers unprecedented opportunities but also brings forth unique challenges. Leveraging tools such as Confluence allows streamlined communication and project management, yet the transition to remote collaboration has its hurdles. The human aspect, technological considerations, and strategic alignment are all factors that must be carefully managed.

In this chapter, we will delve into the challenges of remote collaboration, providing insights into the human factors and technical difficulties encountered. We will emphasize the importance of focusing on people, understanding their needs and preferences, and how the right approach can mitigate potential pitfalls. Here, we will also explore how Confluence can be both a solution and a challenge, depending on the implementation. By examining these challenges, we will better understand the complexities of remote collaboration and how to approach them.

Understanding the importance of focusing on people

In a remote environment, the human connection can easily be lost, leading to feelings of isolation and disengagement. Meanwhile, a people-first mindset can create a supportive and inclusive atmosphere that can increase motivation and productivity. Focusing on people fosters a culture of empathy and understanding. Some common mistakes in remote collaboration include neglecting individual needs, failing to recognize achievements, and allowing a disconnected culture. To avoid these pitfalls, you can do the following:

- Conduct regular one-on-one check-ins
- Encourage open communication
- Recognize and celebrate achievements, big or small
- Use collaboration tools that foster interaction

Managing Confluence adoption

Adopting Confluence for remote collaboration requires thoughtful planning. Here are the key elements to consider:

- **Setting clear objectives**: What do you want to achieve with Confluence?
- **Identifying stakeholders**: Who will be affected, and what are their needs?
- **Defining roles and responsibilities**: Who will lead the adoption, and what are their tasks?
- **Creating a timeline**: What are the milestones, and when should they be reached?

Open work is about nurturing a flexible, transparent work environment. Supporting open work in Confluence means the following:

- Encouraging team members to share ideas freely
- Providing access to necessary resources
- Promoting a culture of trust and autonomy

To ensure that Confluence continues to be a valuable collaboration tool, consider the following:

- Regularly updating to the latest version
- Providing ongoing training and support
- Monitoring usage and collecting feedback for continuous improvement
- Integrating with other tools and platforms if necessary

The challenges of remote collaboration are multifaceted, involving both the human factor and technical considerations. Focusing on people, planning the Confluence adoption with care, supporting open work, and keeping the tool up to date are essential steps in overcoming these challenges. Building a culture of empathy, trust, and flexibility can transform these challenges into opportunities for growth and innovation.

We have now introduced a guide to understanding the challenges of remote collaboration and how to optimize the use of Confluence. Let's dive deeper into tips and solutions to support everything we have learned.

Solutions for remote collaboration

To maintain Confluence as a valuable tool, organizations should adopt a sustainable approach:

- Regularly review user feedback
- Update features as needed
- Train team members on new functionalities
- Monitor integration with other tools

Education is key to the effective use of Confluence. Consider these training strategies:

- Offer varied training formats (e.g., webinars, tutorials, and online courses offered by Atlassian University)
- Provide ongoing support and resources
- Monitor and assess training effectiveness
- Encourage peer-to-peer knowledge sharing

Successful Confluence management also includes financial considerations:

- Establish clear budget guidelines
- Monitor and control costs
- Analyze the **return on investment (ROI)** of Confluence
- Seek opportunities to optimize expenses

An iterative approach

An iterative approach to remote collaboration enables ongoing improvements:

- Encourage regular feedback
- Make incremental changes

- Monitor progress and adapt as needed
- Celebrate success and learn from failures

Implementing an iterative approach involves the following:

- Setting clear and measurable milestones
- Regular review meetings
- Empowering team members to suggest improvements
- Using Confluence to track progress and document changes

Open work and distributed work

Supporting open work fosters a culture of collaboration and creativity:

- Encouraging transparent communication
- Facilitating access to shared resources
- Creating spaces within Confluence for brainstorming and innovation

Distributed work also offers several benefits:

- Access to a broader talent pool
- Flexibility in work arrangements
- Potential cost savings
- Increased diversity and creativity

Although it comes with countless benefits, distributed work can present challenges:

- **Communication barriers**: Overcome them with regular sync-ups and clear documentation
- **Time zone differences**: Manage them with scheduling tools and flexibility
- **Cultural differences**: Bridge them with team-building activities and awareness training

In summary, solutions for remote collaboration require a multilayered approach, focusing on effective management, iterative improvements, and embracing open and distributed work. Confluence can be a powerful ally in this journey when utilized thoughtfully.

So far, we have talked about the challenges related to remote work and proposed solutions. Now, we will share our experiences of working with consultants.

Working with consultants

Consultants can be an invaluable resource, especially in specialized or complex projects. Consider getting help from them in the following circumstances:

- Specific expertise is lacking in-house
- An independent or external perspective is needed
- There are constraints in time or resources

Successful collaboration with consultants requires careful relationship management:

- Define clear expectations and deliverables
- Communicate openly and regularly
- Ensure alignment with the company's culture and values
- Evaluate performance and provide feedback

Here are the advantages of working with consultants:

- Access to specialized skills and knowledge
- Flexibility in scaling efforts up or down
- Fresh perspectives on existing challenges

There are also inconveniences. Here's how to mitigate them:

- **Potential misalignment with company culture**: Overcome this by clear communication and alignment sessions
- **Costs**: Manage them by defining scope and negotiating rates
- **Dependence on external support**: Mitigate this by developing in-house capabilities alongside it

Tips when working with consultants

Choosing the right consultants is crucial for a successful collaboration. Here are some tips to do so:

- Assess experience and credentials
- Consider whether they are a cultural fit
- Evaluate previous work and ask for references
- Discuss expectations and deliverables in detail

To ensure consultants are aligned with your business goals, do the following:

- Share your organization's mission and objectives
- Define clear KPIs and success metrics
- Engage consultants in strategic discussions
- Regularly review progress and realign as needed

Working with consultants can significantly enhance the success of Confluence adoption and other remote collaboration efforts. The key lies in understanding when to engage consultants, selecting the right ones, and managing relationships effectively. Organizations can strategically leverage this external expertise to achieve their collaboration goals by recognizing the advantages and potential inconveniences of working with consultants.

We have now presented an in-depth discussion of the advantages, challenges, and best practices of working with consultants for organizations and teams. Regarding the relationship between Confluence and remote collaboration, this information can help your team understand how to use external expertise effectively.

A sustainable approach to Confluence

Ensuring that Confluence stays up to date and easy to use is vital for ongoing success, since an efficient and user-friendly platform encourages regular use and collaboration among team members.

Here are some strategies for a sustainable Confluence environment:

- Regularly update Confluence to the latest version
- Customize features to match user needs
- Monitor usage patterns and solicit feedback
- Offer ongoing training and support

Supporting open work

Open work, a culture of openness and flexibility, is essential to remote collaboration. With Confluence, you can contribute to open work culture by doing the following:

- Creating shared spaces for collaboration and creativity
- Encouraging transparent communication and feedback
- Establishing clear guidelines and expectations for openness

Training and developing people

Helping team members stay skilled and engaged requires ongoing training and development:

- Provide regular training sessions on Confluence features

- Encourage self-paced learning through resources and tutorials

- Foster a culture of continuous improvement and growth

Managing financial aspects

For Confluence to be a lasting solution, it needs to be financially viable in the long run:

- Monitor and control Confluence-related expenses

- Evaluate the cost-benefit ratio regularly

- Seek opportunities for financial optimization

- Plan for long-term success

A sustainable approach to Confluence involves careful long-term planning:

- Define long-term goals and align them with organizational objectives

- Create a roadmap for continuous improvement and growth

- Engage stakeholders in planning and decision-making

A sustainable approach to Confluence involves multiple aspects, including regular updates, support for collaborative work, ongoing training, careful financial management, and strategic long-term planning. By paying attention to these elements, organizations can ensure that Confluence remains a valuable and effective tool for remote collaboration in the long run, aligning with broad organizational goals while supporting a thriving remote collaborative environment.

Here, we've highlighted different factors contributing to Confluence's sustainability as a remote collaboration tool. Each aspect plays a crucial role in building a successful sustainable approach and, collectively, they enhance the future value and effectiveness of Confluence.

Summary

In this chapter, we mastered the nuances of managing remote collaboration, and we identified the main challenges and proposed solutions. We also concentrated on recognizing the central role of Confluence and how focusing on human interactions can help overcome these challenges. We also highlighted the intricacies of working with consultants, emphasizing their potential advantages and the recurring theme of the symbiosis between technology and people-first strategies, ensuring optimal remote collaboration.

Congratulations on getting this far in the book! In the next and final chapter, you'll find additional advice and resources that will help you improve your Confluence environment.

Questions

1. What are some critical challenges for remote collaboration?

2. How does this chapter suggest managing the relationship with consultants?

3. How does this chapter describe fostering a culture of open work?

4. How is the financial sustainability of Confluence addressed in this chapter?

5. What role does continuous training and development play in a sustainable approach to Confluence?

Answers

1. The critical challenges for remote collaboration include maintaining effective communication, fostering team cohesion, managing technological barriers, and ensuring security and privacy.

2. This chapter emphasizes defining clear expectations, communicating openly, ensuring alignment with company culture, evaluating performance, and managing costs as vital components in working with consultants.

3. The chapter discusses creating shared spaces for collaboration, encouraging transparent communication and feedback, and establishing clear guidelines and expectations to foster a culture of open work.

4. The chapter highlights the importance of monitoring and controlling Confluence-related expenses, evaluating the cost-benefit ratio regularly, and seeking opportunities for financial optimization to ensure its sustainability.

5. Continuous training and development keep team members skilled and engaged, ensuring they can fully utilize Confluence's features, including regular training sessions, encouraging self-paced learning, and fostering a culture of continuous improvement and growth.

Further reading

- https://university.atlassian.com/student/collection/850385/path/1083904

15
What's Next?

In the ever-evolving digital world, the demand for practical collaboration tools and strategies is more significant than ever. The rise of remote work, accelerated by unforeseen global events, has redefined how teams collaborate, communicate, and achieve their goals. Tools like Confluence have become more than just platforms; they're the foundation of new working dynamics, uniting dispersed teams and providing a cohesive and efficient work environment.

But adapting to this new landscape is not without its challenges. The intersection of technology, human interaction, and new working methodologies demands technical know-how and a comprehensive understanding of communication, team dynamics, psychology, and organizational culture. Bridging the gap between traditional office environments and the virtual workspace requires innovative solutions, continuous learning, and the courage to evolve.

In this final chapter, we'll concentrate on the complex ecosystem of remote collaboration while exploring the opportunities, best practices, and potential pitfalls. We'll provide a guide as a comprehensive resource for professionals venturing into this new territory, covering topics ranging from personal growth in Confluence and remote work to broader insights about the future of collaboration and the role of **artificial intelligence** (**AI**). Through real-life examples, expert insights, and a focus on the cutting-edge solutions provided by specialized partners such as Ponsatlas, we'll present a roadmap to thrive in the contemporary world of work.

In this chapter, we will cover the following topics:

- Predictions for remote collaboration
- How to improve in Confluence and remote working
- Artificial intelligence in remote collaboration
- Atlassian Partners and Ponsatlas

Predictions for remote collaboration

The landscape of remote collaboration has been evolving and is shaped by technological advancements, cultural shifts, and global events. As remote work becomes more integrated into our daily lives, there is a growing interest in understanding what the future holds for this dynamic field. From how we interact with colleagues across the globe to how we balance work and personal life, the impact of remote collaboration is far-reaching and transformative.

Predicting the future of remote collaboration is not merely a speculative exercise; it's an essential task for businesses, educators, and leaders who must navigate the changing tides of the digital age. The following short and medium-term predictions offer a glimpse into the near future, highlighting trends and innovations likely to shape how we collaborate and connect. Whether influenced by technology, human needs, or global circumstances, these predictions offer valuable insights to individuals involved in or impacted by remote collaboration.

Also, please note that the predictions mentioned here are our personal estimations. For more comprehensive forecasts on these topics, we recommend reviewing reports from major research firms.

Short-term predictions

In the immediate future, the demand for seamless integration between various collaboration tools and platforms will drive innovation. Expect to see more cohesive ecosystems where tools effortlessly communicate with each other, enhancing the user experience and improving workflow efficiency.

Remote collaboration will increasingly prioritize employee well-being. As organizations recognize the importance of mental health in productivity, tools that enable flexible schedules, mindfulness breaks, and community engagement will become more prominent.

The integration of AR and VR into collaboration platforms, such as Confluence, is set to transform the realm of virtual collaboration. These technologies promise immersive experiences that replicate physical presence, potentially enabling teams to interact within a three-dimensional workspace, thereby making virtual meetings more engaging and interactive. As remote work gains traction, the role of AR and VR becomes pivotal in bridging the gap between virtual and in-person interactions, capturing the essence of physical team dynamics. Furthermore, with the surge in remote work, security concerns have risen to the forefront. It's anticipated that we'll see an uptick in the implementation of robust, AI-driven security protocols, real-time threat detection, and personalized access controls to ensure the safety of these advanced collaborative spaces.

Medium-term predictions

In the medium term, the integration of AI with emotional intelligence will become more refined. Tools will be able to detect users' emotions and adjust communication styles accordingly, creating more empathetic virtual interactions.

Remote collaboration will extend beyond the corporate world. Education and healthcare will embrace these tools, offering remote learning experiences and telemedicine services that are more interactive and patient-centered.

The development of entirely virtual office environments where employees can interact as if they were in a physical office will become more prevalent. These spaces will use VR and AR to simulate real-world experiences, breaking down the barriers of remote work.

Remote collaboration will align with global sustainability goals. Expect collaboration tools that monitor and minimize energy consumption, promote paperless workflows, and adhere to environmentally responsible practices.

Hybrid work models, combining in-office and remote work, will also become the norm. Organizations will invest in technology that supports this blend, ensuring that collaboration is fluid and consistent, regardless of location.

In sum, the short and medium-term predictions for remote collaboration paint a picture of a world where technology, empathy, innovation, and responsibility converge. These trends progressively signal a transformative shift in how we perceive collaboration and work life. Whether it's the integration of cutting-edge technology or the emphasis on human-centric design, remote collaboration is evolving into a multifaceted and exciting landscape. The potential for growth and exploration is immense, and these predictions offer a glimpse into a future that prioritizes connection, creativity, and community.

Now that we've discussed predictions related to remote work, let's move on to the next topic, where we will delve into how you can enhance your team's proficiency in remote work and the use of Confluence.

How to improve in Confluence and remote working

The digital landscape has seen exponential growth in collaboration tools and remote working practices. Meanwhile, among the many platforms out there, Confluence stands out as a crucial tool for team collaboration, sharing information, and managing projects. Where the shift toward remote working has necessitated a new understanding of work dynamics, Confluence and remote working form an essential duo in modern professional life. That's why understanding how to improve in both areas becomes a valuable asset.

In this section, we'll offer insights into enhancing your proficiency in Confluence and polishing your remote working skills. Whether you're a newcomer or an experienced professional, the following guidelines will provide a roadmap to elevate your collaboration capabilities and remote work effectiveness.

Starting with a solid understanding of Confluence's core features is essential. Engage with tutorials, and guides, and seek professional training to fully grasp the capabilities. Leverage Confluence's built-in templates and macros to enhance productivity and familiarize yourself with different tools and plugins to suit your project needs. Join Atlassian Community (https://community.atlassian.com/) and attend Atlassian Community Events (https://ace.atlassian.com/) as engaging with others will provide insights, tips, and practical knowledge from experienced users, and practice using

Confluence in a team setting as a real-world application fosters better understanding and promotes the development of collaboration skills.

Effective communication is also paramount in remote working. It's a good idea to benefit from various communication tools and to work on soft skills that promote clear, concise, and empathetic dialogues. Also, don't forget to designate a space for work that fosters concentration and motivation, invest in ergonomics, and create a routine that aligns with your peak productivity hours.

Remote working can blur the lines between personal and professional life, so setting boundaries and taking regular breaks is essential for mental well-being. Show courage and flexibility in your approach, make adjustments as necessary, and stay receptive to feedback. Remember, continuous learning and flexibility are the key components of remote working success.

Now that we've addressed how you can improve your team's skills in remote work and Confluence, we'd like to briefly touch upon one of today's most discussed topics: AI.

Artificial intelligence in remote collaboration

Integrating AI within remote collaboration tools has become a cornerstone in defining operations and communication. The crossroads of technology and collaboration is a thriving field with implications that go beyond efficiency and convenience. In this section, we will dive into the multiple facets of AI's impact on remote collaboration.

To begin with, it's safe to say that AI has automated many routine tasks in remote collaboration, allowing team members to focus on more complex and creative aspects of their projects. From scheduling meetings to managing workflows, AI's capability to learn patterns and anticipate needs ensures a smoother, more intuitive experience. This optimization extends to resource allocation, where AI's predictive abilities can forecast needs and help decision-making.

AI also offers a personalized experience tailored to individual needs and preferences through **machine learning (ML)** algorithms and data analysis. Whether it's suggesting relevant documents or adapting interfaces based on user behavior, AI enhances the user experience in remote collaboration platforms. It's not solely about user comfort; it's about crafting an environment where tools adjust to the individual, not the other way around.

AI-powered analytics transform how teams understand and evaluate their collaboration. AI can provide actionable insight by analyzing communication patterns, work habits, and project outcomes to help identify improvement areas, potential bottlenecks, and ways to enhance collaboration.

Security is another essential component with the increasing complexity of remote collaboration tools. AI-driven security measures can detect unusual patterns and potential threats, offering a layer of protection that adapts and evolves. Compliance with regulations is another area where AI can be instrumental in ensuring the collaboration meets legal and ethical standards.

The rise of AI in remote collaboration also brings ethical dilemmas. That's why transparency in algorithms, data privacy, and the potential bias in AI-driven decisions must be carefully navigated. Developing guidelines and ethical frameworks around the use of AI in remote collaboration is a growing field of interest, reflecting the societal implications of this technology.

AI's role in remote collaboration is poised to grow. Continuous innovation, alignment with human-centric design principles, and responsible stewardship will guide AI's future in this field. There are exciting frontiers to explore: integrating AI with **virtual reality (VR)** and **augmented reality (AR)** for an immersive collaboration experience, leveraging AI for real-time language translation, and developing emotionally intelligent AI tools.

The fusion of AI with remote collaboration indicates a thrilling advancement and has already started to transform our work landscape. Its multidimensional impact on efficiency, personalization, security, ethics, and future trends illustrates the complexity and richness of this relationship. As we continue to harness the potential of AI, a mindful approach that balances technological advancement with ethical responsibility will define the future of collaboration. The possibilities are vast, and the promise of AI-driven remote collaboration is an invitation to a future filled with innovation, empathy, and intelligence.

Atlassian Intelligence

Atlassian has long championed the power of teamwork. Now, they're integrating the capabilities of AI to enhance collaboration. Atlassian Intelligence, developed with OpenAI, acts as a virtual teammate. It uses two decades of teamwork data to create a *teamwork graph*, helping teams understand their collaborative efforts better.

Atlassian Intelligence accelerates work using OpenAI's generative technology. It can create content, summarize meeting outcomes, and offer insights into team dynamics. The AI tool also provides real-time support in **Jira Service Management (JSM)**, aiding teams through instant responses. Additionally, it helps demystify company terminology, acting as a tailored dictionary for teams.

By interpreting natural language queries, Atlassian Intelligence makes seeking company information straightforward. Whether it's using **Jira Query Language (JQL)** or understanding company policies in Confluence, the tool provides swift answers. It supports multiple languages, covering all those catered to by Atlassian Cloud products.

Soon, Atlassian Intelligence will help you automatically summarize meeting minutes in Confluence, as shown in the following screenshot:

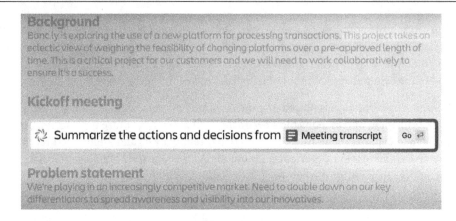

Background

Bancly is exploring the use of a new platform for processing transactions. This project takes on eclectic view of weighing the feasibility of changing platforms over a pre-approved length of time. This is a critical project for our customers and we will need to work collaboratively to ensure it's a success.

Kickoff meeting

✧ Summarize the actions and decisions from 🗐 Meeting transcript   Go ↵

Problem statement

We're playing in an increasingly competitive market. Need to double down on our key differentiators to spread awareness and visibility into our innovatives.

Figure 15.1 – Atlassian Intelligence

In essence, Atlassian Intelligence is shaping the future of teamwork. It offers a range of capabilities, from automating tasks to promoting innovation. By harnessing the power of AI, Atlassian is ensuring that teams can achieve more than ever before.

Remote work combined with AI is indeed a fascinating subject, but it falls outside the scope of this book. This deep and intriguing topic alone could warrant its own book. Having said that, are you ready to move on to our next topic regarding Atlassian Partners?

Atlassian partners and Ponsatlas

Atlassian collaborates with several types of partners to enhance its services and cater to its vast customer base. In understanding the dynamics of these partnerships, it's crucial to delve into the specifics of the distinct types of partners that exist

Here are the three different types of Atlassian partners:

- Atlassian Solution Partners
- Atlassian Training Partners
- Atlassian Marketplace Partners

Let's discuss these partners in detail.

Atlassian Solution Partners

Atlassian Solution Partners are expert organizations that collaborate closely with Atlassian to offer tailored services surrounding its range of products, such as Jira, Confluence, and Bitbucket. Their profound expertise in these tools enables them to assist businesses in adapting and integrating them effectively into their operations.

At the heart of their services lies consulting and strategy. Solution Partners analyze a company's requirements, offering insights into how Atlassian tools can be employed most efficiently. They provide guidance on industry best practices and help formulate strategies, whether it's for scaling existing tools, migrating data, or integrating new Atlassian offerings.

Implementation and customization form another significant aspect of their role. Recognizing that every organization has unique needs, Solution Partners mold Atlassian tools to address specific challenges.

Training is an essential component of the services many Solution Partners offer. While they operate distinctly from Atlassian Training Partners, Solution Partners often equip staff with the knowledge to maximize the benefits of the implemented tools, ensuring a smoother transition and more efficient utilization.

After the initial deployment, the relationship doesn't conclude. Solution Partners typically offer ongoing support, ensuring that Atlassian tools continue to function seamlessly. They also keep businesses abreast with the latest developments, features, and updates, ensuring a consistent and up-to-date experience.

Lastly, the specialized expertise that many Solution Partners possess shouldn't be overlooked. Their in-depth knowledge of specific industries or sectors allows them to provide targeted solutions, making them invaluable allies for businesses in diverse fields.

In summary, Atlassian Solution Partners are pivotal entities that ensure businesses can fully harness the capabilities of Atlassian products. Their blend of consulting, customization, training, and support ensures that companies experience a smooth and beneficial journey with their Atlassian tools.

Atlassian Training Partners

Atlassian Training Partners are specialized entities that assist organizations in maximizing their usage of Atlassian products. They bridge the gap between the technical intricacies of Atlassian tools and the end users, ensuring that teams are well-equipped to utilize the tools effectively.

Training Partners have deep expertise in Atlassian's suite of products, such as Jira, Confluence, and Bitbucket. Their primary goal is to provide education and training, but their value extends far beyond simple instruction.

First and foremost, they offer tailored training sessions based on the specific needs and nuances of an organization. Recognizing that businesses have varied requirements and use cases for Atlassian tools, these partners can customize their training modules to be directly relevant and applicable.

The training isn't just about using the software; it's also about leveraging it in the best possible manner, meaning imparting knowledge on best practices, optimizing workflows, and ensuring that users can navigate and adapt to any updates or changes in the software.

Moreover, for businesses that are new to the Atlassian ecosystem, Training Partners play a crucial role in onboarding. The initial phase of software adoption can often be daunting, and these partners ensure that this transition is smooth. They help reduce the learning curve, enabling teams to quickly integrate Atlassian tools into their daily operations.

Beyond the initial training, many Training Partners also offer continuous learning opportunities. This could be in the form of workshops, refresher courses, or new feature highlights, ensuring that users are always up-to-date with their Atlassian knowledge.

In essence, Atlassian Training Partners are more than just trainers – they are enablers. They empower organizations to get the most out of their Atlassian investments, ensuring that teams are not just using the tools, but are using them efficiently, effectively, and innovatively.

Atlassian Marketplace Partners

The Atlassian Marketplace is a thriving ecosystem where users can discover and acquire plugins, extensions, and integrations for Atlassian products. Behind this marketplace are the Marketplace Partners, who play a crucial role in enriching and customizing the Atlassian experience for countless businesses. These partners develop apps and integrations for Atlassian products, which are then made available in the Atlassian Marketplace. Let's understand their primary purposes:

- **Developing add-ons and integrations**: The central role of a Marketplace Partner is to design, develop, and maintain add-ons, plugins, and integrations for Atlassian products such as Jira, Confluence, and Bitbucket. These extensions can either extend the functionality, automate tasks, or integrate with other third-party tools.

- **Tailored solutions**: Businesses come with varied requirements and sometimes the out-of-the-box features of Atlassian tools might not address specific needs. Marketplace Partners bridge this gap by developing bespoke solutions that cater to these niche requirements.

- **Ensuring quality and compatibility**: Marketplace Partners are tasked with ensuring that their offerings are of high quality, free from bugs, and compatible with the latest versions of Atlassian products. This entails regular updates, patches, and rigorous testing.

- **Providing support**: Once an add-on or integration is live on the Atlassian Marketplace, the partner is responsible for providing support to the users. This includes addressing any queries, resolving issues, and rolling out updates based on user feedback.

- **Enriching the ecosystem**: By introducing new functionalities and integrations, Marketplace Partners enrich the Atlassian ecosystem. They ensure that Atlassian tools remain adaptable, versatile, and equipped to meet diverse business challenges.

- **Staying aligned with Atlassian's vision**: While they operate independently, Marketplace Partners must remain aligned with Atlassian's broader vision and standards. This ensures a level of consistency and quality across the entire marketplace.

- **Feedback loop**: Marketplace Partners, through their direct interactions with users, often gather crucial feedback and insights about Atlassian products. This feedback can lead to the development of new features or enhancements, creating a positive feedback loop and continuous improvement.

In summary, Atlassian Marketplace Partners significantly enhance and expand the capabilities of Atlassian products. They cater to unique requirements, foster innovation, and ensure that businesses have access to a wide array of tools and functionalities to adapt and thrive in their respective domains. By doing so, they play an instrumental role in the success and adaptability of the Atlassian ecosystem.

Ponsatlas

Ponsatlas stands out as an Atlassian Solution Partner with a global reach based in Istanbul. Specializing in team collaboration technologies, Ponsatlas engages in research and development, provides consultancy and training, and creates world-class cloud-based software, primarily focusing on Atlassian plugins.

With proficiency in three languages –Turkish, English, and French – Ponsatlas offers a unique blend of cultural and technological insights. Dedicated to innovation, quality, and customer satisfaction, Ponsatlas goes beyond simple business transactions; instead, the company acts as a guide, assisting organizations in enhancing their collaboration and teamwork capabilities. Whether it's about implementing new tools, training staff, or developing tailored solutions, Ponsatlas ensures that clients achieve their goals and exceed them. Deeply believing in collaboration as an evolving journey, the company is passionate about facilitating each goal with excellence and integrity.

Summary

The transformative power of remote collaboration has redefined the traditional workspace, ushering in a new era of connectivity, creativity, and innovation. By aligning with technological trends and tools such as Confluence, the global community can search for unique ways to collaborate that transcend geographical limitations. The fusion of various cultures and skill sets fosters innovation, which seemed unimaginable a decade ago.

Engaging with communities, understanding cultural nuances, and harnessing the power of continuous learning are not mere buzzwords, but the building blocks of success in this new landscape. Embracing courage and agility, fostering open communication, and aligning with the latest trends in collaboration software can unlock doors to unlimited potential. The road to success in remote collaboration becomes not just a possibility but a fascinating journey filled with growth and opportunities.

In this chapter, we have learned that the essence of remote collaboration lies in the intricate balance between technology and the human touch; as we navigate the complex interplay of tools, communication, psychology, and culture, we can find out that the heart and soul of collaboration lies in our shared goals, understanding, and empathy. The future of remote collaboration is promising, and its ever-evolving nature ensures that it continues to be an inspiring, rewarding adventure for those willing to engage, learn, and grow.

Congratulations, and thank you for staying until the end.

Questions

Answer the following questions to test your knowledge of this chapter:

1. What makes Confluence a valuable tool for team collaboration and information sharing in a remote working environment?

2. How can professionals enhance their skills in Confluence and remote working? What resources are available to support this growth?

3. What role does Ponsatlas play as an Atlassian Solution Partner, and how do they contribute to enhancing collaboration and teamwork capabilities?

4. How does AI shape the future of remote collaboration, and what are some examples of its application?

5. What are some short and medium-term predictions for remote collaboration, and how can individuals and organizations prepare for these trends?

Answers

Here are the answers to this chapter's questions:

1. Confluence is a valuable tool for remote collaboration due to its comprehensive features, which enable real-time collaboration, document sharing, project tracking, and integration with other tools. Confluence's flexibility and customization options allow teams to adapt to various workflows, creating a cohesive virtual workspace that bridges geographical barriers.

2. Professionals can enhance their skills through formal training, engaging with online tutorials, joining Confluence forums and user groups, and actively practicing in a team setting. Following blogs, attending events, and leveraging resources from industry leaders such as Atlassian and GitLab can also foster growth in remote working.

3. Ponsatlas, an Atlassian Solution Partner, specializes in team collaboration technologies. The company engages in research and development, consultancy, training, and cloud-based software development, primarily focusing on Atlassian plugins. Ponsatlas' global reach and expertise in multiple languages facilitate the seamless integration of collaboration tools, providing valuable support for organizations.

4. AI influences remote collaboration by automating routine tasks, enhancing data analysis, and facilitating real-time communication. AI-powered bots, predictive analytics, and ML algorithms are examples of how AI improves efficiency and personalizes the collaboration experience.

5. Short and medium-term predictions include a continuous shift toward remote and hybrid working models, increased AI and ML integration, and a focus on improving mental well-being and work-life balance. Individuals and organizations can prepare by embracing flexibility, investing in technology and training, and building a resilient and adaptable work culture.

Further reading

To learn more about the topics that were covered in this chapter, take a look at the following resources:

- `https://community.atlassian.com/`
- `https://ace.atlassian.com/`
- `https://www.atlassian.com/trust/atlassian-intelligence`
- `https://www.atlassian.com/blog/announcements/unleashing-power-of-ai`
- `https://www.atlassian.com/trust/atlassian-intelligence`
- `https://www.atlassian.com/software/artificial-intelligence`

Index

Packtpub.com

Subscribe to our online digital library for full access to over 7,000 books and videos, as well as industry leading tools to help you plan your personal development and advance your career. For more information, please visit our website.

Why subscribe?

- Spend less time learning and more time coding with practical eBooks and Videos from over 4,000 industry professionals

- Improve your learning with Skill Plans built especially for you

- Get a free eBook or video every month

- Fully searchable for easy access to vital information

- Copy and paste, print, and bookmark content

Did you know that Packt offers eBook versions of every book published, with PDF and ePub files available? You can upgrade to the eBook version at packtpub.com and as a print book customer, you are entitled to a discount on the eBook copy. Get in touch with us at customercare@packtpub.com for more details.

At www.packtpub.com, you can also read a collection of free technical articles, sign up for a range of free newsletters, and receive exclusive discounts and offers on Packt books and eBooks.

Other Books You May Enjoy

If you enjoyed this book, you may be interested in these other books by Packt:

Supercharging Productivity with Trello

Brittany Joiner

ISBN: 978-1-80181-387-7

- Explore Trello's structure and the important features
- Customize Trello cards and fields to fit your use case
- Create Trello views to get a mile-high view of your projects
- Discover Trello's automation features to save time and automate tasks
- Use Power-Ups for documentation, reporting, contacts, and more
- Get the most out of Trello with real-world examples and practical tips

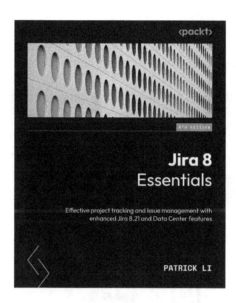

Jira 8 Essentials - Sixth Edition

Patrick Li

ISBN: 978-1-80323-265-2

- Examine various deployment options and system requirements for hosting Jira Data Center
- Understand Jira's data hierarchy and learn how to design and work with projects in Jira
- Use Jira for agile software projects, business process management, customer service support, and more
- Explore field configuration schemes and find out how to apply them to projects
- Develop and design customized screens and apply them to different projects
- Create configurable reports on projects and share information through dashboards for reporting and analysis

Packt is searching for authors like you

If you're interested in becoming an author for Packt, please visit `authors.packtpub.com` and apply today. We have worked with thousands of developers and tech professionals, just like you, to help them share their insight with the global tech community. You can make a general application, apply for a specific hot topic that we are recruiting an author for, or submit your own idea.

Share Your Thoughts

Now you've finished *Implementing Atlassian Confluence*, we'd love to hear your thoughts! Scan the QR code below to go straight to the Amazon review page for this book and share your feedback or leave a review on the site that you purchased it from.

https://packt.link/r/1800560427

Your review is important to us and the tech community and will help us make sure we're delivering excellent quality content.

Download a free PDF copy of this book

Thanks for purchasing this book!

Do you like to read on the go but are unable to carry your print books everywhere?

Is your eBook purchase not compatible with the device of your choice?

Don't worry, now with every Packt book you get a DRM-free PDF version of that book at no cost.

Read anywhere, any place, on any device. Search, copy, and paste code from your favorite technical books directly into your application.

The perks don't stop there, you can get exclusive access to discounts, newsletters, and great free content in your inbox daily

Follow these simple steps to get the benefits:

1. Scan the QR code or visit the link below

https://packt.link/free-ebook/9781800560420

2. Submit your proof of purchase
3. That's it! We'll send your free PDF and other benefits to your email directly

www.ingramcontent.com/pod-product-compliance
Lightning Source LLC
Chambersburg PA
CBHW060651060326
40690CB00020B/4602